Bird Dog Days, Wingshooting Ways

Bird Dog Days, Wingshooting Ways

ARCHIBALD RUTLEDGE'S TALES OF UPLAND HUNTING

Edited by

JIM CASADA

THE UNIVERSITY OF
SOUTH CAROLINA PRESS

Introduction © 2016 Jim Casada

Hardcover and ebook editions published 2016
Paperback edition published 2026
by the University of South Carolina Press
Columbia, South Carolina 29208

uscpress.com

Printed and bound by CPI Group (UK) Ltd, Croydon, CR0 4YY

Library of Congress Cataloging-in-Publication Data
can be found at http://catalog.loc.gov/.

ISBN 978-1-61117-654-4 (hardcover)
ISBN 978-1-64336-675-3 (paperback)
ISBN 978-1-61117-655-1 (ebook)

The manufacturer's authorized representative in the EU for product safety is
Mare Nostrum Group B.V, Doelen 72, 4831 GR Breda, The Netherlands.
Email: gpsr@mare-nostrum.co.uk

CONTENTS

Contents

ACKNOWLEDGMENTS

This is one of five collections of Archibald Rutledge stories I have edited and compiled, and as was the case with the first three, I owe a deep debt of gratitude to the late Judge Irvine Rutledge. Prior to his death, he was consistently supportive and complimentary of my efforts, as have been other members of the Rutledge clan.

In a wider sense, every sportsman owes the University of South Carolina Press, along with a relative handful of other publishers, a tip of the sporting cap. They are offering us fine books on sport even as the "big boys" of the publishing world turn their backs on works dealing with the quest in a misguided belief that there is something fundamentally wrong with the ethos of the hunt or that the joys of being afield and astream no longer have currency.

The staff of Dacus Library at Winthrop University, where I taught for many years, was helpful in answering research questions and obtaining copies of obscure articles through interlibrary loan. I have acknowledged the role of my parents, Anna Lou and Commodore Casada, in every book with which I have ever been involved, and with good reason. They actively nurtured my love of the wild world, scraped and scrimped financially to see to it that a mountain lad had ample exposure to education, and shared my pleasures connected with hunting and fishing adventures. Similarly, it was my good fortune to establish a meaningful relationship, one which otherwise almost certainly would not have existed, with my late father-in-law, Earnest Fox, through shared bird-hunting adventures. I am grateful to the memories he thereby gave me. As ever, my wife, Ann; my daughter, Natasha; her husband, Eric; and their daughter, Ashlyn, are sources of support and inspiration. They tolerate my constant ventures afield in good spirit, encourage my literary efforts, and give me their love. Every sporting scribe should be so lucky.

A NOTE ON SELECTION

It is a testament to Archibald Rutledge's enduring popularity among those who cherish fine writing on the wild world that publication of this collection is possible. Previous volumes in what I presume it is now safe to say is a series have focused on his deer- and turkey-hunting tales, along with a selection of his writings on Christmas and an anthology of *The Best of Archibald Rutledge.* There remains work on a full-length biography of the sage of the Santee to complete my long-running labor of love connected with his life.

Here, as the title suggests, the focus is on dogs and bird hunting. Both were near and dear to Rutledge as a man and a sportsman, and when he wrote of them he wrote from the heart. The place (or places) where each selection has previously appeared in print is given at the appropriate point in this book, although it should be noted there are in all likelihood other printings of the stories which have escaped my eye. For example, with a number of the selections, only a previous appearance in a book is noted, yet I feel confident that in virtually every case the material also was published in a magazine. Rutledge was not only a prolific writer; he was exceptionally adept at selling second (or third, or fourth) rights to his material. All of his major books on hunting and the outdoors comprise pieces that, for the most part, first appeared in magazines. Indeed, his stories appeared in so many forms and places (magazines, books, anthologies of the writings of multiple authors, school readers, and the like) that compiling a comprehensive bibliography of his work would be a project well worthy of a doctoral thesis. Still, I feel serious students of Rutledge would like to know where these selections have previously seen the published light of day.

Today, most of Rutledge's books are out of print or else available only in shoddy print-on-demand form. Indeed, original editions of many of them have become valuable collector's items, and copies of many of his outdoor-related books bring prices in the three-figure or even low four-figure range. As a result, many modern readers are not conversant with or else are unable to afford works by a writer who was a household name among sportsmen in the 1930s, 1940s, and 1950s. Even those who do remember Old Flintlock probably recall him primarily as someone who wrote on deer and turkey hunting.

The present collection makes it abundantly manifest that he was a serious bird hunter as well, and few indeed are those writers who have understood the ways and wiles of dogs the way Rutledge did. His writing on the outdoors belongs to the sporting ages, and everyone who thrills to a whopping covey rise or a dog going "birdy" in a grouse covert, every sportsman who has been privileged to own a "dog of a lifetime" or who has marveled at a miraculous retrieve, will find a kindred soul in the pages that follow.

INTRODUCTION

Archibald Rutledge was a sportsman and naturalist for all seasons. A staunch son of the Southland, he was a hunter from his earliest days. From the time when he took his first tentative footsteps toward becoming a nimrod until he was a bedridden octogenarian, hunting was an integral and vitally important part of his life. In many ways he was blessed in his early exposure to sport. For a mentor he had his father, to whom he paid loving and richly deserved tribute in *My Colonel and His Lady*. He had a brother close to him in age, and their boyhood partnership is immortalized in *Tom and I on the Old Planta-tion*. Then there were the dozens of black "huntermen" who served as tutors, guides, and field companions. One of these, Prince Alston, whom he styled a "companion to my heart," was probably the dearest friend Rutledge ever had. They grew up together and hunted constantly in season while pursuing other adventures, as boys and then men, with unflagging avidity. Even in the long years of exile when Rutledge was away from Hampton Plantation teaching at Mercersburg Academy in Pennsylvania, the pair remained close. Indeed, the real "running" of Hampton during those three-plus decades in Pennsylvania rested squarely on Prince's broad, capable shoulders.

Along with the joys of a sporting adolescence and being in close contact with adult companions who let him accompany them afield, the youthful Rutledge was always surrounded by dogs. There were deer hounds, bird dogs, yard dogs, and as those of us resident in the South are wont to describe ca-nines of questionable lineage, "just dogs." Along with this panoply of friends, human and canine, there were the wild, expansive environs of Hampton Plantation on which to wander and wonder. It was, quite simply, a wildlife paradise. Vast acreage along the Santee River, much of it too swampy or prone to flooding for cultivation, formed fine habitat and a refuge for all sorts of game. This was nicely balanced by the farm and rice fields of the plantation, which fed not only those who cultivated them but wildlife as well. Rutledge came to know every part of this wondrous world intimately, and he sang the praises of his homeland in books such as *Home by the River, Santee Paradise*, and *The World around Hampton*. From an early stage he knew a oneness with the land that few, even those who hunt, are privileged to experience. Indeed, so deep were his love for Hampton Plantation and his connection to the land that he would devote most of the prime years of his manhood to unstinted labor, as a teacher and a writer, rescuing the home and surrounding lands from the shabbiness, genteel neglect, and pressing financial problems which threatened ruination. Once he retired from teaching and returned to Hampton (he was only in his fifties at the time), he added intense physical labor to this noble effort. That he succeeded, ultimately deeding Hampton Plantation to the state of South Carolina so its citizens could enjoy it in perpetuity, was a singular achievement and one of the highlights of a life marked by many notable achievements.

Obviously, Rutledge was a man born into a world in which nature and sport loomed large, and posterity is fortunate that he sang the praises of life in the outdoors so long, so wisely, and so well. The story of his life is in many ways one of ongoing evolution as a writer and student of those things he knew best: nature's creatures and myriad wonders, various types of hunting, and his fellow man. To delve into his writing deeply is to realize how well he knew these subjects, and in time one feels almost at Rutledge's side in the field. Certainly, to join him vicariously in that sporting world which we have largely lost is to tread trails of literary wonder.

Rutledge's entry into that world comes on October 24, 1883, at the family's "Summer Place" in McClellanville, South Carolina. This was the beginning of a childhood that can only be described as idyllic. For eight or nine months of the year, the Rutledge family, which traced its roots back to one of the signers of the Declaration of Independence, lived at their ancestral home, Hampton Plantation. Each year, though, when the oppressive heat of a lowcountry summer bred mosquitoes in droves and made life miserable, they would retreat to the nearby Summer Place or even to the high country of the Great Smokies and Blue Ridge in neighboring North Carolina.

His father, Henry Middleton Rutledge, was one of the youngest Confederate soldiers to attain the rank of colonel during the Civil War, while his mother, née Margaret Hamilton, epitomized the grace and gentility of southern womanhood. Theirs was a good life, although it was lived with appreciably less sumptuousness and splendor than that to which previous generations of Rutledges had been accustomed. The economic ravages of war had left Hampton, like most of the South, in rather desperate straits. By the time "the Colonel" died, there had been a family diaspora of sorts, and for years afterward Rutledge and his siblings were at distant removes from Hampton Plantation. Not until he was in his mid-fifties was Archibald able to return and begin the arduous work of restoring Hampton to something of its former glory.

Still, during those long, languishing years of necessary exile, Hampton and its sport were always in his thoughts. Each year at Christmas, Rutledge made the glorious pilgrimage southward from Pennsylvania back to the plantation, and the bittersweet parting at New Year's merely reinforced his determination to return Hampton to its one-time grandeur. All that, of course, lay years ahead when Rutledge's halcyon days of youth ended with his departure from Hampton Plantation. Local educational opportunities were severely limited, and in 1896 he enrolled at Charleston's Porter Military Academy. A precocious youngster, he excelled in his studies despite the agonies of homesickness which were his constant companion. Four years later, though a year junior to most of his fellow students, Rutledge graduated as the academy's salutatorian in the class of 1900. He earned a number of academic medals, and his prowess was sufficient to procure a Lorillard Scholarship to attend Union College in Schenectady, New York.

As someone who was saddened to the depths of his soul when he went off to college—and I stayed in the South—I can imagine just how difficult this stage of Rutledge's life must have been. He hints at this in some of his writing, although he did say that he "met only a single person, from the highest to the lowest, who was not gentle and courteous." Hardy, determined young man that he was, Rutledge weathered those "Yankee years" of college in fine fashion, excelling in the classroom and graduating with honors in 1904.

He led a full, active life in college. He was a stellar member of the Union track team, displaying the same spirit and endurance that stood him so well during long days in the hunting field. He also made numerous friends outside the somewhat narrow confines of the college, and one of these, noted naturalist and writer John Burroughs, made a particularly deep impression on young Archibald. Several decades later, when Rutledge received the prestigious John Burroughs Medal for his writings on natural history, he must have looked back on his links to the man with warm reflection.

Rutledge was still a few months shy of his twenty-first birthday when he received his bachelor's degree from Union, and he must have appeared terribly young when, a few months hence, he interviewed for an interim teaching position in English at Mercersburg Academy in Pennsylvania. Certainly that was the impression he made on the wife of William Mann Irvine, the headmaster. When she met the young man, her unthinking reaction was: "He will never do—he's too young." She could scarcely have been wider of the mark.

What had been offered as an interim post would mark the beginning of a remarkably close association with Mercersburg Academy. Rutledge taught there, raised a family, wrote, and all the while dreamed of restoring Hampton

Plantation for the next thirty-three years. It was also at Mercersburg that he met and wooed his first wife, Florence Louise Hart, whom he married in 1907. She was the younger sister of Mrs. Irvine. A fetching southern belle who was a published poet in her own right, Florence shared her husband's literary interests and proved an ideal mate for the twenty-seven years they had together.

Those years at Mercersburg were busy, bustling, and joyful ones. The young couple had three sons, and from all accounts their father was a popular, highly successful teacher. The present writer has received correspondence from a number of Rutledge's former pupils; to a man, they revere his memory. Another souvenir of how well liked he was among the students is the cherished Parker double-barrel shotgun they gave him. Most of the bird hunts described in the pages that follow were taken with this gun in hand, and it proved equally suitable for bobwhites, big bucks at Hampton Plantation, or lordly gobblers.

Rutledge enjoyed hunting in the Appalachian hills and hollows around Mercersburg, although he confined his activities in Pennsylvania to bird hunting. He wanted no part of the vast horde of deer hunters—today known as the "pumpkin army"—who annually went afield with rifles. It was a strikingly different approach to deer hunting from that pursued in the Carolina lowcountry. For him, a shotgun was weapon enough, and the grouse and quail hunting of the area provided enjoyable sport. For all his delight in teaching at Mercersburg, for all the pleasures provided by ventures with his sons in the fields and streams near where he lived, Hampton Plantation remained constantly in his thoughts. His roots drew him homeward every Christmas and summer vacation, and particularly after the deaths of his parents in the 1920s, he harbored a cherished vision of the day when he could once more truly call Hampton home.

Indeed, every story in this book can be viewed as a part of his tireless quest to return to Hampton, for with the publication of each piece he was a few dollars closer to realizing his dream. He wrote in virtually all of his idle hours that were not devoted to sport or his family. By the time World War I drew to an end, Rutledge, while still a young man, was already well on his way to becoming a nationally recognized writer on nature, field sports, dogs, and the southern hunting ethos. His writings garnered awards; poems and essays soon began to be pulled together as books; and from the appearance of *Under the Pines* (his first collection of poems) and, even more notably, the 1918 publication of *Tom and I on the Old Plantation,* full-length works emerged from his prolific pen in a steady stream.

Although he would, over the years, earn numerous medals, several honorary doctoral degrees, and various other recognitions, the career distinction which was most meaningful to Rutledge was being named South Carolina's first poet laureate, in 1934. Today a new figure is named to the post on a fairly frequent basis, but such was not the case when Rutledge was accorded the honor. He would be the Palmetto State's poet laureate from 1934 until his death in 1973.

As much as he cherished this particular distinction, for Rutledge 1934 was a bittersweet year. The death of his beloved Florence in that year deeply saddened him, and his thoughts turned ever more longingly toward Hampton. He knew that once in the comforting bosom of the plantation he could find surcease from sorrow as well as inspiration for the future. The draw of his boyhood home became even stronger with his second marriage, in 1936, to Alice Lucas. She had been a childhood sweetheart, and they both belonged to the lovely lowcountry and its easygoing yet elegant way of life.

Rutledge's three sons had all reached manhood, thereby relieving him of the burdens associated with their upbringing and education, and this, too, constantly directed his thoughts southward toward Hampton. Thus it was in 1937 that Old Flintlock decided the time had finally come for his exile to end. The decision was a daring one. The Great Depression still held much of the country tightly in its grip, and Rutledge was anything but an affluent man. The post of poet laureate carried with it a modest stipend, and in an unprecedented action, the trustees of Mercersburg Academy awarded him retirement benefits. He could also count on royalties from a baker's dozen books, and the year of his return to Hampton saw the appearance of what many consider his magnum opus, *An American Hunter.*

Any way it is viewed, that final pilgrimage back to Hampton must have been as fraught with economic trepidation as it was filled with all the glories of homecoming. The return was in many ways the high point of Rutledge's life, and he plunged into restoring Hampton and its grounds to their former glory with energy and enthusiasm worthy of a much younger man.

Rutledge, who was in his mid-fifties at the time of the move, would spend much of the remainder of his life at Hampton. The sole exceptions were brief periods of failing health when he moved upstate to Spartanburg and lived with family members for a time and his final weeks of life in the Summer Place in McClellanville where he was born. Once back at his beloved home by the river in the Santee delta, Rutledge wrote, labored long and hard at a myriad of tasks ranging from planting camellias to refurbishing the plantation home, hunted, played the genial host to countless visitors, and in general lived the life of a southern squire (albeit one of limited financial resources) to the hilt.

Anyone who visits Hampton Plantation today, and it is a pilgrimage every lover of Rutledge and his legacy should make, is sure to be touched by the evidence of his devotion to his ancestral home. There are the lordly live oaks which he so prized framing the entrance road leading to the home, vestiges of the old plantation way of life in dikes for rice paddies, but most striking of all are the camellias. As devoted a horticulturist as he was a hunter, Rutledge grafted, grew, and transplanted literally hundreds of these lovely flowering shrubs on the plantation grounds. To visit Hampton on the cusp between winter and spring, when camellias bloom, is to be enchanted by their breathtaking beauty.

For all the gladness associated with his return, there was also sadness. Prince Alston, his beloved black friend who had been a constant companion in childhood, a caretaker at Hampton during the long years of Rutledge's economically enforced exile, and the first to greet him at each return, had died. Similarly, many of the other black people, whom he warmly described as his "black huntermen" or "black henchmen," were likewise gone. Indeed, as one can clearly see in retrospect, they were part of a fast vanishing breed, for the black people and folkways Rutledge described in *God's Children* are no more. Their loss is in some ways America's loss, and while one can speculate that the blacks of the world of Hampton were, as a group, happier than their present-day lowcountry descendants, much the same can be said of any modern-day folks who carry on traditions such as deer hunting with dogs and cling uncertainly to old plantation lifestyles.

Rutledge sensed some of the radical racial changes that were in progress, although he did not full approve of them or, for that matter, countless other changes. He was in that regard a true conservative—a man who despised change for the sake of change and clung tenaciously to what he considered good and glorious in the past. He viewed blacks as part of an extended plantation family, and anyone who is offended by some of the language in this book which describes his interaction with them is, in effect, trying to impose the perspective of the present on the realities of the past. Plantation workers played a vital role in restoring Hampton, and as Rutledge wrote, the wizened "huntermen" residing there were marvelous mentors who opened before his eager eyes "the pages of nature's gigantic green book."

The loss of Prince was but the first in a series of stark tragedies to beset Rutledge in his middle and later years, and the stoicism and strength of character shown in dealing with them speak eloquently of the man's character.

The lean, howling wolf of poverty was never all that far from the door, though Rutledge continued to keep it at bay through his productivity and popularity as a writer. Still, there is a discernible degree of encroaching impoverishment, not far beneath the facade of a genteel life, in Rutledge's later years. This is visible in his worn though impeccable attire and in his fractious dealings on a pair of books. One was to have been a biography of a president of Winthrop College, the South Carolina college for women; the second a book on turkey hunting scheduled to be published by Thomas G. Samworth of Small-Arms Technical Publishing Company. The latter never saw the printed light of day, which can only be lamented by today's turkey hunter, but it seems likely the fault lay primarily with Rutledge. He wanted to recycle previously published turkey pieces to create a sort of anthology (the approach employed in most of his outdoor-related books) while Samworth had in mind an original work of a "how to" nature.

Another sad change was in the diminished glories of the "Hampton Hunt," an annual occasion at Christmastime which Irvine Rutledge, Old Flintlock's youngest son, poignantly described as "twenty shining years." In its original form, at least, it came to an abrupt end when one of Rutledge's sons, Middleton, died in 1943 as the result of a traffic accident. During the same period, the troubled times of World War II took the surviving sons, Irvine and Arch, to duties overseas. Coming on top of other concerns, this was a heavy burden for a man well into his sixties to carry, but Rutledge did so manfully. He continued to write, pouring his energy, money, and very soul into Hampton, and all the while found escape in sport. That is why, in virtually all of his work, there are precious few hints of the worries that weighed heavy on him. That he could weather the storms of his life in such fashion, remaining ever ebullient, speaks wonderfully well of the man who was Archibald Rutledge.

He was a man who seized the sponge of life, wringing from it every drop of moisture, as he lived each day to its fullest. In his final two decades at Hampton, there were bright moments, sometimes almost daily, to offset the unfilled void left by the departure of Middleton, Prince, and various others. His oldest son, Archibald Jr., joined the ranks of departed companions well before Old Flintlock's death. Countering this burden of sorrow were the countless admiring readers who made their way to Hampton, and always the squire of the Santee was there to greet them graciously, invite them to tour the grounds, sign copies of his books, or give school children small cards on which one of his poems had been printed. Similarly, each day's mail brought letters from admirers, and each of these he answered faithfully and courteously. Several times each year he spoke to schoolchildren, and he seemed to have a special knack of bonding with them. The signed poem cards they carried home with them became, for many, treasured mementos, and on a personal note I cherish the dozens of these in my personal collection of Rutledge material.

Rutledge exercised conscientiously, hunting quail, dove, deer, and turkey in their respective seasons; occasionally enjoying sojourns in the North Carolina high country where he hunted grouse; or merely walking about the spacious grounds of Hampton with a canine companion or two at his heels. There were still members of the Alston clan with whom to share a hearty laugh or who would join him at a moment's notice for a day of hunting, and as is ever the case as age begins to make its inexorable inroads, memories of the past provided comfort in the present.

Carefully, consciously, and courageously, Rutledge eased into his final years. While he declined physically, his mind lost none of its considerable power, and his prose continued to cut with a razor's edge of literary sharpness. As late as 1970, only three years before his death, one of his finer books, the appropriately titled *The Woods and Wild Things I Remember,* was published. He even invoked the privilege of advanced years to publish a penetrating, forthright look at some of the inhabitants of the nearby little town of Mc-Clellanville. Apparently this book of poetry was too frank, its veneer of fiction overlaying fact too thin, for *How Wild Was My Village* was suppressed soon after publication. Copies are exceedingly rare, and even today, some four decades later, the book is a subject best avoided in certain company in the environs of Hampton and McClellanville.

In 1970, already well into octogenarian status, Rutledge took an action which must have been both painful and a source of considerable pride. Working closely with his sole surviving son, Irvine, who provided his father invaluable legal advice as well as an admirable degree of fidelity and love, he sold his beloved Hampton Plantation to the state of South Carolina. With the sale came a number of stipulations. The grounds of Hampton Plantation, along with the home itself, were to be maintained and open to the general public. Some of the adjacent land remained in family hunts, and to this day descendants hunt deer on it. Moreover, in a touching act of devotion, Rutledge specified that members of the Alston family were to be allowed to live and work at Hampton as long as they wished.

Three years later, on September 15, 1973, just five weeks shy of his ninetieth birthday, Rutledge died. Fittingly for a man with such a deep sense of history and family tradition, the end came at the Summer Place in

McClellanville where he had been born. Thus was closed the full circle of life for a southern scribe who sang his homeland's song in sweet, sure fashion. The music and magic of his words remain, though, and to join him through this enduring legacy is to know staunch points, whopping coveys of bobwhites, grouse-filled covers, and splendid shooting. His words evoke all that is joyful and rejuvenating about being afield, and in the pages that follow we join Old Flintlock in sampling the bird-dog days and wingshooting ways he knew and described so well.

Part One

THE FRIEND OF MAN

When the reader who is well versed in sporting literature thinks of enduring writing on hunting dogs, names such as Corey Ford, John Taintor Foote, or Rutledge's fellow South Carolinian, Havilah Babcock, most likely come to mind. Yet no one who reads deeply in the vast corpus of Rutledge's work can doubt the depth of his knowledge in this field. On topics associated with dogs, as in so many areas related to hunting, he excelled. As is true of most of his work, there is no clear dividing line between fact and fancy in his tales of canine companions, and for my taste they are more appealing because of this characteristic. It should also be noted at the outset that the perceptive reader will likely notice occasional contradictions in Rutledge's writings. He was, quite simply, a staunch believer in the old adage that holds, "'tis a poor piece of cloth which cannot use some embroidery."

Hunting dogs were an integral part of life at Hampton, as characteristic of the plantation scene as freshly plowed fields in spring, a bustling household at Thanksgiving and Christmas, or rustic tenant cabins and the cheerful African Americans who called them home. There was always a household pet or two that had the run of the place, but the dogs that really mattered earned their keep.

The nature of the labors of these "working dogs" was as varied as their lineage. "Yard dogs" did guard duty, occasionally dealt with a rogue boar, might be called on to help in a deer hunt in a pinch, and were common companions on rabbit or squirrel hunts. They were also playmates for and protectors of youngsters, self-ordained guardians of hearth and home, and as common at Hampton as cornbread and crowder peas. That much being duly recognized, they ranked far down the totem pole of canine importance.

True hunting dogs did not run free. They were confined to kennels except when taken afield, for a free-ranging hunting dog soon developed bad habits that were virtually irreversible. Nobody wanted a back tracker, an egg sucker, or a canine that thought the epitome of hunting was to raid a chicken roost. Along with good manners and good breeding, careful control of the habits of hunting dogs was considered vital. Similarly, the diet of such dogs was carefully controlled to keep them lean and fit, especially in the fall and winter months. After all, they had vital roles to fill. For breeds such as the fice and mountain cur, there was squirrel hunting. Rangy hounds ran deer or the occasional wild hog. Bandy-legged packs of beagles chased swamp rabbits and cottontails. Elegant pointers and sprightly setters devoted themselves to the pursuit of partridges. At Hampton, as at most lowcountry plantations of the era, there were likely to be several representatives of each of these breeds in residence at any given time.

Rutledge knew them all, and knew them well. Take, for example, his thoughts on the trials and tribulations connected with the education of a puppy. "Every puppy begins by conceiving his master to be a god; it is that master's business never to do anything to make that dog change his mind." That is advice anyone involved in training a dog would do well to heed.

Rutledge had an uncanny feel for the special relationship that can exist between a hunter and his loyal friend, but what really sets him apart is the fact that he was able to describe this bond with the sort of insight few have matched. He loved dogs and writing about them, and canine companions loomed large in his life as they do in his literary legacy. The stories in this section, most of which deal with hunting dogs, offer ample indication of his ability as a dog writer.

The Friend of Man

Originally published in *Forest & Stream* (October 1923), and reprinted many years later in *Pointing Dog Journal* (January–February 1995), this story exemplifies Rutledge's great love of and feel for dogs. As the subtitle of the piece, "Little Stories of Bird Dogs in the Field," suggests, it deals with several of the author's fond recollections of glorious days with canine companions. Told with warmth and charm, two of the distinguishing features of Rutledge's writing, this piece is precisely the sort of material certain to warm the cockles of any serious bird hunter's heart. When Rutledge writes of someone qualifying as a "sniper of spirits" or speaks of the difficulties of getting a decent shot "while climbing miniature Matterhorns," the reader knows that here is a man who has, as old-timers are fond of saying, "been there." We have an intriguing tale of a day afield featuring a staunch, long-held point in the South Carolina lowcountry that Rutledge so cherished; a hunt in the laurel and rhododendron thickets of the high country of neighboring North Carolina; and some thoughts on the comparative merits of setters and pointers sure to appeal to anyone who admires fine hunting dogs.

The sun was nearly down; we were tired; and we were ready to call it a day. Through the brown cotton field we went toward the old plantation house where we were staying for our outing. Somewhere in the cotton behind us was Max, our English setter. As the house was now in sight, we gave no further attention to the dog. We took it for granted that he would simply follow us in. An hour later we had finished dinner and, in the afterglow of the mild winter's evening, we had come out on the porch to have cigars and sarsaparilla. Incidentally we called Max. He was not to be found. It then occurred to us that he might be still in the cotton field. To it we repaired.

Near its ten-acre center there was a thicket of wild plums. Toward this I drifted in the twilight. Just as I reached it, I saw a glimmering shape ahead of me. Then I heard the unmistakable sound of the running of quail on dry dead leaves. Then I watched—though the light was almost gone—the kind of scene that makes a man feel like tossing clear overboard all this business of a dog's having instinct but no reasoning power. Max had the birds cornered in the thicket. They would not, of course, roost there; quail, probably from those faroff times when foxes, wildcats, and the like were very much more common than they are now, avoid sleeping in thickets and woods. Even the so-called "wood birds" will emerge toward the end of the day from any dense copse into which they have gone to roost in the comparatively open and grassy woodland, or in the marshes of some swampy margin. Max probably knew that the little birds wanted to leave the thicket. But he considered it wise to keep them there. Hence as they circled, he did likewise; whenever they would come to the edge, they would find him there, serenely alert, always the necessary jump ahead of them. And this thing had been going on, I believe, for the better part of an hour. It illustrates the power of the bird dog, while working alone, to do considerable figuring on his own account. Indeed, the average intelligent setter or pointer in the field is talked to and called at too much. A dog that has breeding and some degree of breaking, hunts best when permitted to "have his head." Many a time a good dog has been whistled off a perfectly good scent in an unpromising piece of cover by a hunter who thought the cover a little farther ahead looked better.

This incident happened down in North Carolina, in a deep mountain pass where through surged a wild little river. There were plenty of quail there; but that had a way of leaving the narrow fields and of heading straight for the laurel-sided hills. Any man who can, while climbing those miniature Matterhorns, shoot quail in the rhododendrons that darken their slopes, can qualify as a sniper of spirits. Our dog had trailed a covey of quail along the edge of one of these hills; had followed it through an acre of brown wet stubble, and had come ahalt at the creek bank. We got ready to shoot, thinking that the pointer whose nose seldom lies had brought the covey to stand. But ere we reached him, he began to edge up, and soon was running back and forth quickly in that distressed way of a good dog which has been badly baffled. We stood there beside a group of huge sycamores to watch Ned work the business out for himself. This he proceeded to do in the following manner: Edging his way gingerly down the steep bank of the broad and deep stream he walked about fifteen feet up one edge, stepping now and then in the clear water that lipped the margin. Then he turned and walked downstream. He looked like a circus horse going through his paces. Then he walked out into the stream (the creek was here about fifteen yards wide) and there stood with his head held high. Once he turned and looked back at us. Then he took the plunge. The current bore him down somewhat, but he soon reached footing. Yet he did not rush out on the bank and shake himself; a bird dog when he is hot after game never acts like a regular dog; he has become for the moment a specialist. Ned waded upstream deliberately, the water being almost to his knees. When he came opposite us, he froze to a stand.

"Well," I said to my companion, "there they are. If we are game, we must follow the dog across. He did a pretty piece of work. The covey is likely in that patch of blackberry canes just off the larboard of Ned's nose. We'll find them." We did.

Mention has been made of the long trail that this pointer brought these birds. It is generally conceded that the pointer, being far back probably of hound strain, is superior in the power of scenting to the setter, likely springs anciently from dogs akin to spaniels. However it may be, these two great breeds have some very clearly marked distinctions: the pointer is all for business, is a slashing, tireless, bold, soldierly sort of a dog; the setter is far gentler, more easily handled, is sensitive, and is so anxious to please as to be positively obliging. It strikes me that, in the field, there is not a great deal of choice; but at home the setter is the better dog to keep. As a matter of fact, the setter appears to be distinguished by having what we call good manners; the pointer is usually a rough-and-ready customer, milling through his work in arrogant style; the setter is deferential, dainty, and I think it is not too much to say that this grand breed of dogs has in it a high artistic strain. Men who know and love setters understand what I mean.

But as of men, so of dogs: there are kinds and kinds. Nor do some dog dealers exercise what we might call a chivalric sense of honor in recommending those bird dogs that they sell. In my experience with dogs, I have bought several that were, if their credentials were to be believed, champions; yet one was gun shy; one had a mighty passion for digging up field mice (of course, had I been compromising and changed my game from quail to field mice, I should have been properly equipped for hunting); one chased the birds and gave tongue while so doing; one seemed to believe that we were out vermin hunting, for every stray field cat, skunk, mole, rat, terrapin, and other wastrel creature that we encountered was assailed with joyous enthusiasm. I've a friend that bought a dog after seeing a dim photograph. He was told that he was purchasing "Champion Leglow." He was after a pointer; but when the creature emerged from the crate he seemed to appear to be a collie, with a strong strain of beagle in him. As a matter of fact, it is a harder thing to buy a first-class bird dog than one would suppose. A man who has a high-grade dog and knows his worth is not commonly willing to part with him. As a general thing, most sport is had over dogs which their owners themselves have broken.

Nor should it take much trouble to break a well-bred pup. Get his trust and affection first; exact implicit obedience from him at home; handle him yourself, and don't encourage him to make up too much with friends and neighbors. In short, make him your dog, and you yourself can break him. Anyhow, most breaking is done at home. A bird dog pup that is trustful and obedient will likely do in the hunting field what you ask him to do. And if he does, why, he's broken.

A friend of mine told me of the behavior of a setter of his in retrieving a quail. He was hunting about fifty yards from an old snag that had caught some trash, and as more collected there, a big pile had accumulated. As the river was affected by tides, the trash heap was deepened as the tide ebbed and flowed, alternately letting it down and lifting it up, though but slightly. The hunter in question shot a quail as it rose out of some bushes on the bank. It was crippled; and in that condition it headed across the river. The setter happened at the moment to have fixed her eyes upon the bird. The dog saw it, as the hunter did, come down on the pile of trash, far out in the stream. Immediately the setter plunged in to retrieve the bird.

Reaching the pile of sedge, after a hard swim, she climbed about on it in an attempt to locate the quail. She got the scent but not the bird. It evidently had crawled deep under the bed of trash. Then the dog did a remarkable thing; apparently she located the bird, but decided that she could not reach it from above. She therefore reentered the water on the leeward side of the trash, swam a few yards, her head far out-thrust as if scenting, and then crawled in under a dense and dripping canopy of the heavy sedge. When she emerged, she had the quail; and when she dropped it in her owner's hand, who had watched and understood the whole performance, the bird was still alive. Even granting that a man has had left out of him the power to scent game, would he have handled the situation so delicately as that, even though he had known exactly where the bird was hiding? Surely it takes more than instinct to do what that setter did.

Whenever we examine the things that bird dogs do, we are reminded of the differences between pointer and setter already mentioned. The behavior of these two strains on the point will illustrate both these distinctions and the main point that I am trying to make—the extraordinary intelligence of these grand creatures of the chase. I used to hunt a good deal with an old Llewellyn; his pedigree was obscure, but it must have been good. This dog was a quail specialist. I never knew him to lie. Field sparrows and meadow larks never fooled him. His actions on winding quail were most extraordinary. Slowly, very slowly he would circle with a strange, waltz-like motion, his head high and on one side, his haunches low, his tail straight up. I believe his circling prevented the birds from running. When he was satisfied that he had the covey in position, he would simply sit down. But at such a time his head would rock slowly and slightly, and there would be in his eye that unmistakably strange light which a bird dog shows when he is sealed to a point. Another setter had the habit of crawling back to find me, and then walking forward again as gingerly as if he were stepping on eggs. Once I had a nervous little English setter that had a peculiar way of whining when she pointed. This, of course, was an eccentricity due to suppressed excitement. All these fashions in points, however, illustrate high intelligence, generous understanding. They are more likely to be found in the setter than in the pointer. When the latter finds birds, he turns statue; and his whole attitude seems to express something like this: "Come on, now; here are your birds. Make your work as businesslike as you can.

Once going through some very heavy brush with my pointer I saw him come to a stand. At the moment both ears were thrown across his head, and his lip at the side had been caught up—his whole dishevelment having been done by the briars and vines. He made a very savage-looking fellow thus pointing. Had he had a heavy coat, he might have been taken for a wolf snarling. This picture illustrates the point that a bird dog, when he does stand, pays no attention to any personal inconvenience. Only this last autumn one of my pointers ran between an oak and a sapling, standing about eight inches apart. There he stopped. I thought he was caught; but as he seemed ready to stay, I approached carefully. A covey of quail was right ahead of him. After the birds had flushed, I had to help the pointer out of his difficulty.

From far-off boyhood comes the memory of a thing that a Gordon setter did for me. Barefooted and hatless, I was shooting ducks on an old rice field bank at twilight. The setter had come along simply because we were inseparable companions. As there was deep water in the morasses on either side of the bank, I could not hope to get the ducks that fell clear of hard ground. My object was to shoot them so that they would fall on the bank. However, as every sportsman knows, it is something to kill an old greenhead mallard, let alone suggesting to him where he shall take his seat. Like a boy, I shot wildly and excitedly. I saw a good many ducks fall. To the dog I paid no attention. One duck I secured. And when the light was over, and darkness suddenly fell, one duck appeared to be all that I would take home. Calling the dog, I turned down the bank. But I stepped on something warm and feathery. Then I made out the Gordon, standing guard over seven mallards that she had retrieved and brought to the bank as fast as I had killed them. And all this had been done without a word from me. Intelligence? The dog showed more than the man on that occasion. Nor is that kind of experience with a good dog exceptional.

A hunter is known to me who sold an English setter that he had had for five years. The purchaser lived in a town in the same state, but seventy-three miles away. The dog went by express. Three days later the seller had word from the buyer that the dog had escaped; four days after the sale, the dog was in his master's yard. I can't tell you how the dog knew the way home. But he got there. And the owner, whose heart had been sore over the selling business, made an arrangement to cancel the sale. His decision was wise. If a hunter may be permitted to moralize, I would say, don't sell your favorite dog any more than you would sell your favorite child.

Dog or No Dog

This interesting little piece appeared in *Hunter's Choice.* Like virtually all of Rutledge's stories published in books, it probably was earlier published as a magazine article. If so, however, I have been unable to locate the source, and the same is true for subsequent stories where no magazine citation is given. The "gamy half-days" (or for that matter full days) to which he refers at the outset of the essay are a realistic prospect for the hunter who understands the habits and habitat of the bird he hunts. Here we are offered some interesting and insightful thoughts on the nature of solitary quail hunting. Indeed, the first half of this piece could well serve as a primer on how to undertake a type of sporting pursuit that too few hunters enjoy today, and the enduring value of Rutledge's advice far transcends the handful of states he mentions.

On the other hand, there is no denying the additional pleasures produced by working and walking with a canine helpmate, and the benefits when it comes to retrieving crippled or lost game are of particular note. Some of those pleasures and benefits are delineated, and Rutledge takes a bold plunge into the turbulent waters of the ages-old controversy on the relative merits of pointers and setters. No matter what one's personal preferences, Rutledge's comments on the matter are provocative and profound. Similarly, the old master's summation of key factors in choosing a puppy speak eloquently to how best to approach this daunting task.

A portion of this story, referring to a dog named Rob Roy holding a covey of birds in a plum thicket for several hours, has been omitted here as it appears in the previous story, "A Friend of Man," in slightly different form with a dog named Max.

————

I do not know how it may be with my fellow sportsmen, but with me there's a lot of genuine sport in finding and following the bonny brown bobwhite without the help of a dog, or with a dog, by using one's knowledge of wild life. Too many hunters are helpless without dogs, or they depend too much on them. A dog should merely supplement the man; and I reason that the hunter should know more about finding game than his dog does. This thing of finding game by knowing its nature can be done; and it is interesting work; and the satisfaction accruing from its successful achievement is about as durable as such satisfactions can well be expected to prove. Many are the gamy half days that I have spent afield without a dog; and the luck, while perhaps not so affluent, was of a rarer sort than when Old Bess or Old Joe was along to do most of the work for me.

To find quail without a dog, or intelligently to direct the movements of a dog in the field or brush, a man should know the inside, home life of the bird "from eggshell to wishbone." It is surely surprising sometimes to find how many an otherwise genuine sportsman takes no pains to discover the habits of a bobwhite and to govern his hunting program accordingly. For example, when I see a quail hunter beating the brush or hunting the thickets and briar patches in the early morning; or I see him ranging the feeding grounds with futile assiduity at midday, I know that he does not understand the strict and unchanging habits of our commonest game bird. Besides, he is killing precious time, of which he probably has little enough.

These habits of which every hunter should have an accurate knowledge are not peculiar to the bobwhite; they apply in some degree to all ground-feeding game birds; and what is true of the quail is also true in a modified sense of the wild turkey, the largest representative of this particular group. Let us, therefore, examine these habits, and then apply our discoveries to the finding and following of the bobwhite.

Quail take two meals a day; one is in the early morning from about sunrise until four or five hours thereafter; the other is in the late afternoon, from two or three hours before sundown to sundown. At sunrise they are beginning to feed; at sundown they are either on the roost or else are moving toward it. According to this schedule, therefore, they are on the feeding grounds early and late, and for a longer period in the morning than in the afternoon. The night is invariably spent in the open: in a field of cover, in a marshy place adjoining the feeding ground, or in high weeds. Quail never roost under trees or in the woods. If scattered in woods late in the evening, they invariably come back to the field before dark. I think that this must be a clear survival of the instinct which, in old days, kept them partly safe from the foxes that then haunted almost every woodland. These marauders had a certain dread of open fields, and the quail must have been quite aware of this; hence they resorted, and still resort, during the perilous night-time to fields rather than to woods. I believe that another reason for this lies in the fact that in the open, the birds, if flushed in the darkness, have an uninterrupted flight, and are thereby afforded a far better chance of escape. And that they are ever ready for a quick getaway is proved by their method of roosting, with their tails together and their heads out, a brown bombshell with the fuse of wild alertness burning, ready at a second's warning to explode in the face of any prowler that might come near.

It is the habit of quail to feed to their roost. How many a sportsman, returning home at twilight, has had his dog strike a hot, dew-damp trail that led to the huddled birds! And how few have succeeded in getting a sight of the brown bullets that whizzed off into the gathering dusk. But if the afterglow happens to be clear, and the birds get up against it, the sport is rare and fine. Occasionally a covey will fly to its roost. This happens when the birds believe themselves to be watched or followed; or when they find themselves at roosting time at some distance from a good place to spend the night. If they are being followed they have in mind throwing the tracker off the scent. Sometimes they will rise high in the air with a great whirring of wings; again, they will rise cheerily, with hardly a sound, and, flying low, will vanish mysteriously in the dusk.

Having now accounted for the night habits and the feeding habits of quail, let us examine the period between the morning and afternoon feeding time. Where are the birds then, and what are they doing? They are doing what practically every wild thing does: they are taking a good rest of several hours. They are doing what Walt Whitman was doing when he wrote, "I loaf at ease and invite my soul." Bobwhite is, during these midday hours, drowsing, dusting himself, sunning himself, or perhaps trooping off to a stream for water. Understanding, therefore, what quail are doing at this time, let us answer the question: Where are they doing it? And the question is most pertinent; for I have not forgotten that my attempt here is to show how to find quail, which presupposes knowledge of where to find them. In short, what are good loafing places for quail?

Such places should be sunny, sheltered, sandy, secluded. Those are the four s's which are almost positive requisites for the bobwhite's siesta. Then, in quail country, what are the likely places? Though depending somewhat on the character of the country, these places nearly always have the same general characteristics. I give the typical siesta places of quail in the five states in which I have hunted them most, and add a note as to the character of the country. (I have actually found a covey in every place here mentioned.) From this list of places it will be possible for the reader to select in his own locality the loafing places of the coveys.

1. SOUTH CAROLINA—Old ditch-banks running through or along the edges of fields; roadside or fieldside thickets, especially those containing greenbriars; stumps on cut-over land, especially when the stumps have tufts of second-growth sheltering them; thickets, edges of marches, rice fields, and swamps; old fields, thickets of wild plum, clumps of blackberry canes, or groups of young oaks; gullies with sandy banks. It must be recalled that the character of this part of the country is generally wild, with woodland and swamp predominating. Also that here there are two distinct types of quail: those feeding in the cultivated areas, and those that spend all their time in the woods. Those latter are shyer, and wilder, are harder to find, and invariably fly farther when flushed than their cousins of the fields.

2. MARYLAND—A swampy gully, with sunny dry retreats in it; a briared fencerow; a tract of woods adjoining a cover field; on the bare bank of a little stream, the covey being partly sheltered by the roots of a huge sycamore tree; a rock break in a grassy field. (Note: Maryland is a state of decidedly varying types of landscapes: the eastern section is not unlike Virginia and the Carolinas; the western is like parts of New York and Pennsylvania, being rocky, gashed by innumerable gullies, having low ranges of hills.)

3. NORTH CAROLINA—Sandy banks of small streams, especially those winding through meadows where there are cover fields; small clumps of laurel bordering a mountain field; a dry warm hillock in a swamp, the little hill being completely surrounded by water; in the dry and sunny shelter afforded by an abandoned mountain cabin, the birds being inside the house, as it were, loafing on the dirt floor; beside a huge rotting stump on a ditch-bank where, as they drowsed they picked at a few terrified ants that came out of the rotting wood; against a stack of hay in a wide dewberry-grown field; beside a pile of dead briars that had been mown from a pasture field.

4. PENNSYLVANIA—On an outcropping of rocks near the middle of a large uncut cornfield (there was some sheltering foxtail grass growing among the rocks); under greenbriars along an old pasture fence; beside a huge pile of peach tree stumps that had been torn out of an orchard; on the sunny side of a pile of wood, racked on the woody end of an upland field; in a rocky "draft" between two stubble fields; under a hedge of Osage orange bushes. (I may add that the birds behaved very cleverly when discovered beside this hedge: they ran out on the far side, rose quietly, and made good their escape across a nearby creek.)

5. VIRGINIA—In many parts of this state there are great tracts of broom-sedge, and in this excellent cover the birds sometimes stay through long periods of

time. But I have found them also in a woodlot near rye stubble; in briars; along watercourses that run through fields or which skirt them; on the steep bank of a river, the bank being weedy and facing south; and on a sandbank among willows beside a stream.

Quail hunters know well enough when any particular stretch of country or even any special field looks birdy. Yet such appearances are only too often deceptive. Where the nature of the range lends itself to a careful examination, the hunter should never take it for granted that quail are in a section, however favorable, until he has concrete evidence of their presence. This evidence consists (not in actual sight of the birds or assurance from someone reliable that they have been seen there) in the signs that their occupancy leaves. These signs are of three kinds: roosts, dusting holes, and droppings. The presence of any one of these is proof positive that the birds are, or have lately been, there; moreover, a skillful examination of such signs will show whether they are old or fresh. I never hunt quail, especially without a dog, without being constantly on the alert for these signs. If I find one sign, and it is fairly fresh, I then am certain that it is worth my while to spend a couple of hours in that locality searching for the birds.

If the birds are present, their signs can readily be found. The dusting places will be along fences, in gullies, in sunny briar patches, or on the borders of woods or thickets; the roosts will be anywhere in the open field, preferably either in the lowest or else in the highest situations; the droppings will be scattered through the field, or can be noticed at their loafing places or where they roost. Belief that quail should be in a field on account of its admirable cover, or stories of their having been seen there are as nothing in assuring value to one of the definite evidences heretofore mentioned. Conversely, many a time a landowner has assured me that there were no quail about—that he had not even seen a young one in harvest time; yet when I discovered a sign, I knew that the birds were there. Where these things are, depend upon it, the birds are; where these things are not, waste no time looking there for a covey of quail.

If the evidence of their presence is clear, it is to be remembered that quail are birds of an exceedingly limited range. Not only are they non-migrating, but when water, food, and shelter are to be had, even though they are hunted hard, a covey will stay on a very small range, not only for one season but for years. As the old birds die, their descendants will be found in approximately the same locality. On this point, Arthur Wayne, the well-known ornithologist, has an interesting comment. He says: "On Oakland Plantation, near Mt. Pleasant, S.C., there are now no less than twenty-six coveys. Mr.

Philip E. Porcher, the present owner, tells me that when he moved to this place in February, 1859, he observed a flock of these birds near the dwelling house—and I may add that the descendants of this particular covey are still to be seen at this date—1910." Of course, much depends on how hard the birds are hunted—not only by man but by predatory creatures as well. Then there is the matter of the changing character of the landscape. The more, for example, a farm is improved for agricultural purposes, by cutting away all thickets and all briared fencerows, the more uncongenial a place it becomes for quail. All they need is a fair chance, and they will adhere to the old range with wonderful tenacity—often, indeed, until the last bird has been killed. When undisturbed through any considerable period, they will not only remain on the same ground, but they will feed, rest, and roost with clocklike precision. Their natural habits are so confirmed that they can often be found, on succeeding days, in exactly the same places where they were found, at that very hour, on the previous day.

As a concrete example of this I will say that on Thanksgiving afternoon, 1917, I found four coveys of birds without a dog; and in no case was any covey more than thirty yards from where I expected to find it. Yet they were coveys that had been hunted a good deal. I may add that a friend of mine, who loves to hunt but who considers the study of bird habits a puerile occupation (and certainly nonessential to a good day's sport), had ranged over practically the same territory that same afternoon without finding a bird; and, meeting me as I was starting out, he assured me with frank discouragement that all the birds had either been killed or else had "moved away" somewhere. When I came home with the day's limit, and told him about it, he called it "wonderful luck." But it wasn't that: I knew about where those birds would be, for I happened to know their habits.

While these habits have about them normally a marked regularity, there are two seasons of the year when the movements of quail are erratic. One is in the spring; but as that is the beginning of the mating season, it does not concern us. The other is in the autumn—at those times when the summer is definitely succeeded by the new season. Quail may then move oddly and suddenly. Perhaps their change of ranges is due to the suggestion to migrate which the autumn inevitably brings. Far more likely it is due to the cutting of corn, the plowing down of cover fields, and to the shedding of the foliage— causes which probably seem to the birds to portend changes of a disastrous nature on the landscape. So they simply pick up and leave. This accounts for the coveys which, at this season, frequently appear, suddenly and unaccountably, in places where before no quail were known to be. Such an erratic flight will often take the birds into towns and villages. During three successive Octobers coveys have come thus strangely into the trees on the street on which I live. They can take good care of themselves, however; and soon, calling regularly, they unite as a covey and "pull out" for parts unknown. Twice I have known coveys to do this tantalizing thing the week before the season opened. Wise birds! But I may have bagged them later for all I know.

And one word more: having found the birds, how can they best be followed? I mean, after they have been flushed and shot at, and after the direction of their flight, and their apparent alighting place have been carefully marked, what is to be done if the birds are not where they surely seemed to go down? My experience has been that quail that have become at all "wise" seldom take the obvious cover. If they fly straight for a dense little thicket, do not feel that some sleight-of-hand trick had been played on you if you do not find them there. Bobwhite learns, I think, especially toward the latter part of the season, that obvious, inviting cover is often dangerous cover; and he is likely to pass an inviting stretch of it to alight in a tree, on bare ground, in green wheat, or beside a clean fencerow. Obviously this habit is seen clearly only among quail of comparatively open farmlands. In most parts of the South, as men who have hunted the bobwhite there know, a bird would have a hard scuffle to find a spot on which to alight that was not grassy.

But, of course, much of the real thrill in quail or grouse hunting comes from watching your dogs work. All my life I have had to do with bird dogs; not all my memories of them, as is the case of any memories of life, are happy and fortunate. I have had my ups and downs, my princely pups and my clowns.

Don't talk to me about a bird dog of the right kind having nothing but instinct. It isn't so. I have known scores of dogs that had reasoning power, and I have owned several that had it. And in choosing a bird dog, above all things else one should get a dog that has sense. One day I was complaining to the best quail shot in North Carolina (and that is saying something, for the Tarheels are quail shooters from away yonder) that my dog was a bit lazy. He asked me abruptly if he had sense. I replied that he undoubtedly had. "Then," said he, "hang on to him for keeps. Most bird dogs of the right sort have every virtue but sense; so if he has that, too, he has them all. And if he doesn't have all the others, and yet has sense, you can teach him all he ought to know."

My friend told me that long ago; but it impressed me so greatly that I never try to get a bird dog without looking for one that is highly intelligent. Such a dog was an Irish setter of mine named Game. He showed what was in him one rainy twilight when the mallards and the widgeons and the teal were pouring into an old rice field in South Carolina. Game was standing beside me on the bank, but I was too busy with the big greenheads and the little bluewings to notice him. I tried in a perfunctory way to mark down the ducks that I shot that fell off in the watery marsh. But the flight was so heavy that this task was nothing but a bewildered attempt and I realized that when the shooting was over the setter and I would have to do some tall swimming to get the dead ducks. When that time came it was almost dark and the setter seemed reluctant to come. He seemed interested in something a few yards down the bank. I went there impatiently and what did I find but that Game had brought in every duck I had shot, and had them all laid out in a row on the bank. He must have gone in after them one after another as I shot; but I was so excited and the rain and duck wings together were making so much racket that I had not realized until the thing had been done what the setter had been doing.

Game was the kind of dog for a man to choose for a companion and an intelligent field dog. He was quiet, patient, well-mannered, and loved to do nothing so much as to please me. And from having worked him and dogs like him many years, I believe I am safe in saying that in selecting the bird dog one should get one that is intelligent, well-bred, affectionate, and has a patient, enduring nature. I never cared much for dogs that are too slashing and stylish in the field they may kill themselves out before half a day is done and at home they may prove to be too high-strung and restless to be happy in confinement or under restraint.

In choosing a bird dog, we have two great breeds to consider and there are several varieties of each breed. But if I were getting a dog I would not get him for his breed so much as for his breeding; not so much for the variety as for those qualities which make that variety excellent. Indeed, many sportsmen will agree with me that there are no substantial grounds for special preference. I have owned and worked all the breeds and I may say that I have shot over pointers and setters in all kinds of cover and have come to the conclusion that a good dog is a good one, whether he is white or black or liver in color, and whether his tail is feathered or smooth. To be sure in parts of the country where the cover is thick, as in the quail sections of the South, a dog with much white coloring is desirable and also a fast staunch dog. In open country a slow-working dog is to be preferred, and this type is better, too, for hill and mountain shooting, but the breed should not make much difference to the practical sportsman.

There are, however, marked differences between the two great breeds of bird dogs that have long been generally recognized; and these differences may influence the choice of other men more than my own. The pointer was the first dog ever used to point game, and he seems to be built strictly for business. His place is in the field. When well broken he is almost unbelievably staunch. One brace of English pointers once stood point for an hour and twenty minutes, while a single English pointer stood game for six hours. A pointer has been known to have been frozen to death while on the point. But for all practical purposes the setter is just as staunch. A setter of mine once found a covey of quail at dusk, gone to roost in tall grass. I suppose I must have searched and called for half an hour before the dog was discovered, statued, with the whole covey just a few inches off his nose. The setter is the better companion; he is more gentle, affectionate, and demonstrative. The pointer always looks stripped for action; he does his work with admirable efficiency, and with a grim determination that is in high contrast to the setter's ease and grace. Of the two, the pointer is the more independent and needs less encouragement. The pointer works as if it were his business to work; the setter as if wanting to please a watching master. The setter seems to work with his master; the pointer works for him. And each can do his work in a way to give eternal joy to the eye and the heart of a sportsman.

When a man has lost a fine bird dog, one that has been his constant companion and his chief sporting reliance for years, or has had a series of disappointments with good-for-nothing dogs, after having once known what a good dog is, he feels as if he can never again get another like Old Sport or Old Don or Old Bess. I know the feeling, for I have been there. Some of the very best dogs I ever had died in their prime; at other times I have tried out long sequences of no-account creatures. But always and invariably I got the right dog in the end; and for every sportsman who wants the right dog, there is the right dog waiting. And be assured the new dog, though he may lack some of the excellent traits of the old one you lost, will have virtues of his own that will delight you with their very newness. I know when I lost my grand English setter, White Star Finder, when he was just coming into his fourth season, I thought that sure enough the end of the dog world had come for me. But by good chance the very next dog I got was Captain Ned, an English pointer, who had a nose keener than Star's and who would work every day in the week, while Star had had no such endurance. So I say that in spite of discouragements and setbacks, and they come with dogs as with everything in the world worth having, there are plenty of splendid dogs for every true sportsman who needs one.

And now the question to be answered is this: How am I to get the right dog? Some suggestions have been made concerning the qualities that should mark the right dog; and some descriptions of the way the right dog can work have been given. The question above will have to be considered as a double one and answered accordingly. In the first place, the securing of a broken dog should be considered; then the buying of a puppy. In choosing a broken dog, be sure that you secure from the owner the privilege of trial. Get the dog and find what he is worth to you in the field. I have always bought and sold dogs on this plan, and it is the only fair one. Then, be sure that the dog you secure has been broken on the kind of game you are going to hunt. Of course, a grouse dog will work on quail or chickens and the reverse; but he will work better on game that he knows. Get a dog whose parents have both been tried and true field dogs—an unnecessary question, of course, if the dog itself is tried and true.

If you have a dog on trial and are judging him, watch especially his ability to locate birds, and then his action when the birds are found. Nor should this trial be limited to covey finding alone, but the singles should be followed. Many dogs are satisfactory on coveys, but are deficient in the more skillful and important art of locating singles. Shoot over the dog; and from the very start act toward him as if you and he had been old familiar friends for years. And don't judge him too harshly if he does not come up to expectations on the first trial; next time he may do better for you. Remember he is a stranger in a strange land and perhaps a long way from home. Give him every chance to make good. If he ranges too far or too close for you, remember that you can, with little trouble, break him to range just to your liking. But—and these are the fatal objections—if he is shy of the gun, if the birds are known to be present and the dog can't find them, or if he flushes badly and chases and will not let you come near him to punish him, re-crate him and send him back home. It never pays to be bothered with a dog that is wild and disobedient, that has "no nose," or that is gun-shy.

There are many trainers and sportsmen who maintain that gun shyness can be overcome. Perhaps it can be in some cases; but the owner of a dog which has once been gun shy can never be sure at what moment the old fault will reassert itself. This is the most trying fault in a dog, and is usually so ingrained in its nature as to be almost ineradicable. When a dog proves definitely gun-shy, the best thing to do (unless a man has an endless supply of time and patience on his hands) is to get a new dog. I have worked with gun-shy dogs, with only halfhearted success. I can't recommend it as a form of recreation.

If one is going to choose a puppy instead of a broken dog, one of the first things to guard against is a gun-shy strain in its blood. This fault is not always transferred to the young, but it frequently is; and there are some men who breed gun-shy males and females and sell the puppies for fancy stock. Naturally, this is a mean thing to do. In buying a pup, the best insurance against gun-shyness is the assurance that both his parents are good field dogs, genuine hunters, and masters of the art. Then, the puppy should be large and bold, with all a well-bred dog's natural fine sensitiveness turned in a positive, objective direction rather than in a negative, subjective one. With the right blood and right treatment, no bird dog should be gun-shy; though occasionally an unaccountable case will occur. After good parentage, the next safeguard against gun shyness is proper treatment of the young dog.

In choosing the puppy, remember that he has the making of a fine sporting companion for you; but that you are chiefly responsible for the right development of those qualities that count in the trained dog. I have known many setters and pointers of the proudest blood and most notable heritage to turn out miserable, cringing creatures on account of negligence on the part of the owners. For a dog not to develop bad faults (of which being gun-shy is the worst) he must get kind and considerate treatment from the very start. The owner must make a friend and companion of him. If he has to punish him he must do so moderately and without anger; and he must be very sure that the dog can understand why he is being whipped. Gain the complete confidence and affection of your growing dog, and then he will not be afraid of anything you do, though you should fire a .42 centimeter off over his head. He will trust you so much that everything you do will seem to be the right thing. But if on the other hand a high-spirited dog is neglected (if, for example, you farm him out for several months, or if you keep him confined alone for long periods, especially in a dark place), you will have ruined him before you get him in the field. I find that, whenever possible, a man should feed his own bird dog. At such a time the growing puppy can be taught the commands that are so vital later in the hunting field, and he and his master are drawn closer than they can be in any other way.

In choosing a puppy, there are some physical characteristics, after his heritage, which should be carefully noted. Markings are a matter of personal preference; though the dogs of double markings are invariably handsomer if the darker coloring prevails over the face. But of whatever breed or color he may be, the puppy should be well formed in body. That may sound too obvious; but I mean several important qualities should be looked for. He should be deep-chested, for on that will depend his staying qualities. He should have straight legs, well-muscled. In the pointer, however, a slight bend in the back legs is a sign of rugged strength. Above all, the puppy's head should be fine. "The child is father of the man" and the puppy is father of the grown dog. The muzzle should be heavy, the eyes should be set low, the head should give promise of noble proportions when matured, and the whole expression should be intelligent and kindly. In the face of the puppy you choose, there should be visible in a latent state good sense, obedience, and affection. If you want to have trouble and disappointment with a bird dog, buy a pup with a shallow head, a sharp face, and small cunning eyes. Large clear eyes often show the true character of a dog; and no mean dog has such eyes.

Some Startling Dogs

This piece originally appeared in *Outdoor Life* (August 1932). Its subtitle, "Describing Very Remarkable Points on Birds," gives a solid indication of the subject matter. A small portion of the story, which recounts the manner in which a dog dubbed Royal held a covey in a plum thicket for several hours, has been omitted because it is included in "The Friend of Man" with the dog named Max. Rutledge was a master storyteller and wrote this particular episode up in differing form, using a variety of dog names. Also, portions of this story concerning specific dog episodes appear later in slightly different form in "My Most Memorable Dog" and have been omitted here. Rutledge enjoyed a long life filled with a great deal of hunting, and over the course of some eight decades of activity afield, he was privileged to observe vagaries and vicissitudes of dog work to a degree granted few outdoorsmen. Better still, he had the mental acuity to recall such experiences in vivid fashion, not to mention the fact that he kept careful notes on his journeys afield. These considerations, when linked with his remarkable gifts of expression, enabled him to share his observations with others in a singularly intriguing fashion. Here we enjoy his rare ability to take us, as vicarious companions, to fond fields and staunch points of memory. The literary journey is one well worth taking, for it involves a variety of game—quail, grouse, pheasants, and woodcock—as well as the sort of unusual but welcome occurrences that are spice in the life of any bird-dog man. As we join Rutledge, though, we can only bemoan the disappearance of the field diaries he mentions in this story. These carefully maintained records, along with his manuscript autobiography and other papers, mysteriously vanished in the aftermath of Old Flintlock's death. How much richer sporting posterity would be had his papers survived, but at least he left us a grand literary legacy in the form of his published work.

The subject of the smartest things that dogs do may seem to be over-worked until we remember that every man who has owned and loved dogs has his own fund of stories concerning the sagacity of his favorites.

I have always taken an unusual interest in this matter, and from my notes about my shooting dogs—notes that have been kept over a period of more than thirty years—I shall select a few in the hope that they may prove entertaining.

But let me confess that I have no stories in a class with one a friend told me. He said that he took an amateur quail shooting with his old dog Prince—a sensitive and high-bred veteran. The tyro missed seven shots straight, at which the old dog disappeared. When at last discovered, he was found lying disconsolately in a ditch, his head ruefully laid on his outstretched paws, with great tears of disgust rolling down his cheeks!

One November day I was hunting with a friend in the mountain wilds of southern Pennsylvania. We had with us Mike, a bold, brash, dependable, but homely pointer. Our game was ruffed grouse, but the dog was too fast for them. A slow, lazy dog is the best for this prince of the woodlands. I have known a very badly crippled dog to be excellent on grouse. Our morning's hunt had yielded us but one bird, which I had in my pocket. When this incident happened we were sitting beside a mountain rill eating our luncheon. There was no cover near us except a tiny clump of mountain laurel immediately behind us, not larger than a dining-room table.

Missing Mike, I said idly, "I wonder where that dog can be?" He was the kind that is always very much in evidence at lunch time.

My friend happened to look around. "Easy," he said; "he's right behind us, on a dead point."

It is hard enough at any time to kill a ruffed grouse. But to do so while munching sandwiches, with our guns laid by while we sprawled on the ground, seemed a feat for some Houdini hunter.

"He must be in that patch of laurel," Jim whispered; "of course, it might be a rabbit."

"Mike doesn't point rabbits," I reminded him; "he runs them." Somehow we got our guns without being too awkward about it, rose to our feet, and gingerly advanced toward the pointing dog. He never moved. That faraway look in his eyes told us that some fascinating and powerful scent had completely charmed him. We walked past him and tramped through the patch of laurel. Nothing stirred.

"Well, doggone!" muttered Jim.

"Maybe he was pointing the lunch," I suggested. "No—I have it! He is pointing me; he's pointing the bird in my pocket."

"Ah, yeah?" asked Jim utterly unconvinced.

But there was a way to prove my theory. I made Jim stay with the dog while I walked away. As soon as I got far enough to cause the scent to be faint, Mike broke his point; but he trailed up to me, when he actually pointed again.

"My chance for a shot," laughed Jim; "but there would not be as much sport in shooting you as in bagging a grouse."

This happening naturally leads one to wonder how in the world a dog with a sensitive nose ever manages to "sort out" the hundreds of alluring scents that he finds wafted to him in damp woodlands and across warm stubble. He will reject scores to follow up the right one. Of course, some scents must be indistinguishable; for example, a land turtle will often fool the best dog; and certain sparrows give off a scent that is as gamey as that from quail. I never blamed old Mike for his singular performance, though it did give Jim a chance to say that the only grouse my dog would ever point was a dead one in my pocket.

While the following story is not of pointing, it seems to belong with this class of tales. When I was a boy I used to shoot ducks on the wild banks of an old plantation rice field. The birds came into this field to feed during the night, and seldom arrived before twilight. The shooting in that half-light was always uncertain and, even after a duck fell, I could never be sure of retrieving it. Not having rubber boots, I just used to wade right in, trying to locate my quarry by dead reckoning. One evening I took along a setter named Redbird, not in the hope of any help from him, but just because he had followed me to the boat.

The flight that evening was remarkably abundant and fast, and I was so busy shooting that I did not stop to retrieve my ducks as they fell in the marsh. I decided to "shoot it out," and then to spend the last half hour of dim daylight in searching. I had forgotten all about Redbird. As a matter of fact, I had not seen him after I began to shoot. When I was ready to hunt for the ducks, I called the dog. He came to me in a moment and as he brushed against me, I noticed that he was wet.

We started down the dark bank together to cross an old log into the field. The dog stopped in front of me and then he turned and looked at me for my approval. And well he deserved it! On the bank, in a neat row, were eleven mallards and two black ducks, all duly retrieved without a word from me. I thought I had shot down about a dozen ducks. Here they were—full measure. And here was the real hero of the exploit.

I have no doubt that Redbird had marked down every bird as I had shot, crossed the old log and retrieved it properly, and then laid it in line with all due dispatch. I felt as anyone would feel who, upon approaching a dreary and difficult task discovers that a comprehending friend has cleaned up the whole mess.

I have spoken of the difficulty that even a good dog must have in unscrambling the scents that he meets on a day which is good for the transmission of odors. To me it has always been rather fascinating to take a good bird dog into deer country just to see what notice he would take of the heavy and intriguing aroma of an old stag. However, it has usually been quite by accident that I have observed the behavior of bird dogs on deer. I have several times seen a bird dog chase a deer, barking at it foolishly, as if it were a cow, but there was nothing interesting in such a performance.

One misty morning my young setter Ben trailed and pointed a fine covey of birds in a little pine thicket just beyond the plantation fields. It was a bad place to shoot. However, I walked in and flushed them, hoping that they would scatter nicely in the open broom sedge beyond the pines. This they did, and I had some good sport following them. Beyond the broom sedge was a watercourse grown to bays and gall berries and sweet myrtles. A head of these bushes jutted out into the sedge. When my setter came to a wary point some 20 yards from this head, I got ready for a bird. What was my surprise when, as I approached cautiously, a fine spike buck rocked out, all sails set. As his bed was directly ahead of the pointing dog, and as there was no bird there, little doubt remains that the setter had stood the buck.

Nor is this fact remarkable. The scent given off by a couched deer is exceedingly heavy and pungent. It is, indeed, possible for a man to detect this penetrant odor when conditions are right. My brother has killed two stags that were pointed for him by an old bird dog. In each case the buck was bedded in low bushes, and the dog worked upwind. The hunter got within 30 feet of each deer before he roused himself. I have not found, however, that a bird dog will trail a deer so well as he will a wild turkey.

I remember seeing a point that was both remarkable and comical, as it involved an acrobatic feature. I was walking down the side of an old stake-and-rider fence looking for a decent place to cross when my English setter Fanny, spying a loose rail with the near end on the ground, walked up it to cross. The rail was broad, and it rested on the top of the fence almost at the balancing point. As a result, when Fan got to the top of the fence, the rail tipped level. She, of course, teetered a little, uncertain what to do.

At that very instant the hot and heavy scent of a covey of quail just over the fence assailed her nostrils. She steadied herself, her feathered tail tipping up a little as it would when she came to a stand. But the rail would not stand. It kept rocking up and down, while Fan balanced herself, pointing. It would be hard to conceive, or to arrange artificially a little woodland tableau of this kind, and I hold it as one of my fondest recollections of my hunting dogs.

Fan knew very well that her holding the covey depended on her holding both her point and her balance. Hers was a piece of spontaneous tight rope walking. She was still in position when I came up and made my shots on the covey's rise.

I remember an old English sporting print showing a slashing pointer with a rabbit in his mouth halting in the act of retrieving to stand a grouse. I have seen the same thing happen, and perhaps, one incident a little superior to it. One day my pointer Prince was bringing a rabbit that I had shot when he suddenly stopped. I did not know just how to account for his procedure, for he warily laid the rabbit down in the grass, then lifted his head, glanced significantly at me, and steadied to a point. His behavior appeared to indicate that he was laying aside inferior game to give the covey under his nose his undivided attention.

While my bird dog notes show me that I have many more remarkable points on record, I shall mention just one more, made on a woodcock by my English setter Star. In our rambles in a mountain thicket, Star and I came at length to a very deep gully down which gushed a brawling stream. Looking for a log on which to cross, I at length spied one a little way above us. This hemlock log was a full 20 feet above the stream, so that crossing was rather ticklish business. Star went ahead. What was my surprise when, only a few feet from the bank, he turned his body so that his head was upwind. More-over, he crouched on the log. Once he turned his fine head to give me an appealing, sagacious, significant look. I thought, of course, that he had the scent of a grouse. But it was a less lordly prize.

Against the bank was a deposit of soft black sand, with some huckleberry bushes giving it shelter. In this tiny nook I made out a woodcock, crouched in his sedate little-gobbler fashion. I threw a piece of bark at him to make him get up, and then had to shoot from the log. It is in the interest of truth to state that, though Star had nobly done his part, I could not maintain my end of the bargain. But I never grieve much over my misses for after all, I love a live thing better than a dead one.

"Start 'Em Early, Arch"

Originally published in *Field & Stream* (October 1919), this short selection makes it abundantly manifest that Rutledge knew a good deal about dogs and their training.

———

I t happened a long time ago; but often we are peculiarly penetrated by the sharpness and strength of an early impression. And in this instance the impression went deep with me, for it was pointed with naked, native truth. I was only a lad of fourteen, to whom the bagging of a half-dozen quail, one ruffed grouse, or a brace of buck rabbits was something of a sportsman's feat; and I was talking to the most famous quail shot in North Carolina. He was advising me concerning the training of a setter pup that had been offered me as a gift. It was to be my first dog. That means a lot to a boy who loves to hunt. I asked my master sportsman how he would go about training dogs for the field. It happened that we were standing at a railway station; and as I put that wide question, his train loomed round a near curve. The roar of the approaching engine drowned some of the precious things he said. But I remember this much: "Don't try to treat all bird dogs alike, 'cause they aren't alike. And the best advice I can give you for training pups is to start 'em early, Arch."

The Odyssey of Bolio

Frequently in Rutledge's work there is no clear dividing line between fact and fiction. He was in many ways a master of the twice-told tale, and any careful perusal of his books will find repeat encounters with majestic bucks or memorable turkeys. There is some of this tendency in his writings on dogs and bird hunting as well, as there are certain stories that are clearly fictional in nature. As I have noted, he contradicts himself from time to time. The present piece, which is the title story in *Bolio and Other Dogs,* first appeared in *Outdoor America,* Part 1, September 1925, and Part 2, October 1925. It is an excellent example of Rutledge's skills in the genre of fiction.

The setting is the North Carolina high country, a region he visited often as a boy and man. Cougars (Rutledge often called them pumas; mountain folks invariably described them as panthers or "painters") are long gone from the region, but romantic remembrances of great dogs such as Bolio remain commonplace in that part of the world. The Great Smokies gave us the Plott hound, and as someone who grew up in the heart of the region, I can assure you that tales of dogs such as Bolio are deeply ingrained in local folklore. Doubtless Rutledge garnered the raw material for this tale while a guest in some humble mountain cabin tucked deep in a lonely cove, but he gives this canine odyssey a power and poignancy few can match. It is a story that must rank as one of Rutledge's finest fictional treatments of dogs.

It was in the cabin on the brink of the hemlock-hung Linville Gorge that Wise was born; incidentally, his father had been born in the same house, and his grandfather, killed in the battle of King's Mountain, had been reared on that very mountain farm, within hearing of the roar of the Linville Falls. When you are in the Linville country, you are neighbor to the highest peaks east of the Rockies—a rugged region of rugged men—a region in which nearly everything in Nature seems appallingly to be standing on end. But, mentally, nothing there is topsy-turvy. Men, dogs, bears, mountain lions— these are as sane as the wilderness can make them—the wilderness, healer of hearts, balm of hurt minds, surgeon to the soul. There are those who may doubt that Bolio had a soul. Let the hearer of this tale judge of that. I believe that had Jefferson Wise, his owner, come upon the title, "The Hound of Heaven," he might have accepted it as a true description of his beloved one.

The business really began that rainy September night. Autumn was palpably corning, and in those high altitudes it arrives urgently. The hemlocks surrounding Jeff's lonely cabin wept in the shower; the gross rhododendron thicket roared under the rain; the falls deepened their thunder; and over them wraiths of spume waved mystic arms as if they were white enchantresses, alluring. It was a night to sleep. But the great hound, Bolio, to whom the rain and the darkness were as challengers to his courage and his watchfulness, was wide awake. Thirty yards in front of the mountain home there was a high shelf of rock jutting over the gorge. The drop was a sheer three hundred feet, to boulders as big as seashore bungalows. It was on this dizzy platform, beetling over nothing and death, that Bolio often slept by day, and watched by night. And on that night, Jeff Wise heard him heave his bulk from the porch-floor, stalk with his nail-clicking walk to the steps, amble down them in stately fashion, heading for the platform, growling the while in a manner to make the roaring falls hang a somewhat diminished head.

"Something's hereabout," Jeff said to his wife; "Bolio says so, and that hound is one dog that don't lie." The mountaineer slipped out of bed, drew on his coat and trousers, and in his bare feet went to the front door. Before he opened it, he picked up his rifle from the deer-horn rack in the tiny hallway.

When Poe opened the shutters, anticipating I know not what, he reports that there was darkness there and nothing more. Jeff encountered darkness, a rainy wind, wild dewy aromas from lashed hemlock and pine—and the sounds of a bitterer strife than those of the elements. The hound Bolio, if he had gone down toward the rocky platform to meet an enemy, had evidently not scouted in vain. In the neighborhood of the black cliff there was a war right now. Even a great war, a world war, cannot, in its essence, be more than an individual encounter. The enemy usually is one man. At any rate, the moment Jeff Wise opened the door, he knew that Bolio and some militant visitor were doing a dance of death on the black shelf that jutted out over eternal night.

"God A'mighty Kingdom," muttered Jeff, meaning no irreverence at all, "but I must have a light." Darting into the kitchen, he fumbled for a moment with match and lantern. He did not go for his shoes. He was again back at the door within a very few moments. But now when he opened it wide, naught could he hear save the tumbling falls, the roaring rhododendrons, the lisping hemlocks. The war was over. Down the steps went Jeff, down the streaming pathway toward the cliff. Darkness and rain and wind held and rocked the world. The earth was like a dying child which a grieving mother cradles closely, over it weeping wildly cold tears.

"Hell," said Jeff, halting near the glimmering black platform. The word seemed to satisfy his desire for expression. All the sounds he now heard he perfectly understood. But the wild tumult of encounter and struggle—this was stilled.

"Damn," said Jeff. "Did they slip off this here rock?"

The wind moaned in the mountain pines. The rain swept like a phantom host across the mighty gorge. The night was filled with voices of autumn, voices of change.

"Damn what done it," Jeff commented with the vigor of elemental bluntness.

He called the hound. His tone rang challengingly above the steady tumult of the storm. But he got no answer. Jeff had never read Hamlet; nevertheless he felt that for Bolio the rest was silence.

"I can't do nothing more tonight," the mountaineer told himself. "Drat my Sunday suit—what will I do without Bolio—now the b'ar season is a-comin' on? I have had dogs what would have give me pleasure to see slip off yon rock; but this one—I'd almost as soon go over myself. Tomorrow I can tell—unless he's dropped into the river and been washed away. And he did it a-guardin' us, too. Damn. What a dog! I don't know what he met, but I'll bet a thousand dollars out of my next week's salary that that stranger thought he'd run plumb into a mangling machine. If Bolio went off that rock, he had company, that's sure. It would be just like him to turn up here tomorrow morning."

But on the following morning, with the rain over and the sky clearing, the great black hound did not appear. Jeff Wise was up by daybreak, and his chief business was to find his dog. He woke to a world washed clean; to delicious fall fragrances; to misty hemlocks and a cloud-filled gorge. Before the sun was up, he had been out on the platform of rock; he had searched the wooded brink of the canyon. But not a sign remained of the desperate struggle that had been waged. What the night had concealed, the day could not divulge. The evidence of that obscure and fatal encounter the storm had completely obliterated. The hemlocks shed their rainy fragrances as before; the falls roared their ancient mountain anthem; the rhododendrons shivered dewily, shedding silver drops into their dusky shadows. Giant red dahlias in Jeff's yard seemed to mock him with the affluence of their gorgeous beauty.

After such a loss as Jeff's triumphant beauty may be repellent. The world for the mountaineer was changed. It would be only a month before the bear season—and Bolio was gone. There was an old bear over on Black Mountain that Jeff Wise coveted with a mighty desire. But he would be helpless without his dog.

After breakfast he made his way down a bright-pebbled path through the kalmias toward the falls. He wanted to search among the boulders directly beneath the rock platform. But his heart was heavy; for his search, if ended successfully, could but confirm his worst fears.

A half hour's painful climbing down through the reeking thicket and over the rocks tumbled in mad fashion near the base of the gorge, brought Jeff almost under the strange shelf-like rock jutting from the tremendous cliff above.

And now Jeff began to search—rather drearily—dreading to find the thing for which he looked. If the strugglers had indeed fallen from that beetling black rock, the plunge had been dreadful, the momentum acquired, appalling; the impact—death. Miserably Jeff searched for Bolio. The waters of the Linville River had been up among these very boulders last night; but now they had subsided somewhat, leaving the rocks glistening, treacherous, satiric. Had they had a silent grim part in a tragedy? Jeff wondered. Their shining peace mocked him.

Suddenly the man was aware of a heavy paw waving helplessly in a frothy eddy behind a black boulder. There was a deep pocket there—a place of fresh backwater in which Jeff had caught many a rainbow-trout. Now the pocket held a strange visitor. The massive paw swayed helplessly, childishly.

"Durn my hide—hit's a painter," said the mountain man—"and drowned as dead as Noah. Now, let your eyes light on this."

Jeff grasped the foreleg of the huge beast and drew it out of the foamy pool. He dragged it over to a rock with a flat top. There it lay—a splendid mountain lion—but now singularly limp and distorted. There seemed to be nothing left of the superb creature's shape. Jeff ran his hand tentatively over it. "It wasn't drowned," he said; "it fell off that rock. There aren't any bones left in it. And my Bolio . . ."

Pathetic was the look that Jeff cast at the ominous rock, far, far above him. Yet in his heart there was something like grim triumph. Bolio had encountered what is, at close quarters, for a dog as formidable an enemy as can be met; and the great hound had thrown his antagonist from the cliff. That much, at least, seemed to Jeff clear. Nor was he beneath appreciating the epic nature of that titanic fight. Bolio the valiant had spent his might against one of the real terrors of the night and of the lonely gorge; and he had at least brought the battle to an equal conclusion.

"If he fell too," said Jeff, "I reckon he was washed away."

Wistfully he looked down the mighty gorge, now serene in bridal mists. No great-hearted lover, I think, "staring into the sunset whence his April love has fled," could with more longing have gazed into those beauteous mocking mists than did this humble mountaineer. But Bolio had not vanished incontinently. He had left his mark, his sign. Here was the dead body of his enemy.

"God, but he died game," Jeff muttered. "I don't b'lieve a man could have died gamer. Damn if I would fight a painter on that rock up yonder." Jeff's feelings toward his hound were precisely Rudyard's toward Gunga Din.

A further search among the wild ruin of rocks yielded nothing more. At the end of an hour the mountaineer abandoned his quest. The pulp-like carcass of the panther, he hauled to the river's brim and hurled it in.

"Damn tom-cat," he muttered, "the fish will eat you."

He watched the tawny-hided beast swirled away by the mad torrent; then he turned and climbed with a heavy heart to his cabin on the cliff.

When Bolio had left his place on the front porch that rainy night, he had expected trouble, and it was like him to stalk grimly to meet it. Some dogs are scared by danger; others are roused and challenged by it. Of this latter class was Bolio. Moreover, he knew pretty definitely the character of his opponent from the moment when the heavy scent of the great cat was wafted to him by the rainy wind. He had met such a fiend before; and he preferred a black bear at bay to one of these lithe and powerful creatures, so ready to slink away, to climb a tree, or to make a desperate stand if cornered. A dog knows the nature of his prey or of his antagonist better than does his master. Witness with what whining reluctance a hound will often follow a bear spoor, when the same dog will create a regular sand-storm after a stag. Witness the savage speed with which a misguided dog will pursue sheep, contrasted with the utter deference he will manifest in the presence of a single goat. A dog that goes into ecstasy over the trail of a wild hog will sagely assume an attitude of conciliatory avoidance when he senses the presence of a rattler. And Bolio, being far wiser than most of his kind, was fully aware of the nature of this night-prowler, the approach of whom it was his duty to challenge. Down the steps the powerful black dog had stalked, his growl warning the intruder. There were stepping stones across the yard to the little gate. Down this pathway the black warder of Jeff Wise's lonely cabin went, slowly, certainly, his head high, his eyes ablaze. What to him were rain and the night, mystery of that vast solitude peril—the lush scent of the enemy? Such a dog has a passion for duty; and Bolio's present duty was to fight.

Loud ramped the white waters of the Linville River down that black tremendous gorge, in affluent rupture storming southward through the lonely mountains. Bolio knew well the meaning of that roar, and of every other sound. But no sound concerned him now; rather it was the sultry, the oriental odor of the panther, close at hand.

Possibly the puma did not hear the dog growl.

The wind was blowing to the warder. At any rate, when Bolio reached the gate, he was face-to-face with the tawny lion. I think the primary instinct in any member of the cat family, when in the presence of peril, is to run. "Discretion is the better part of valor," is a better motto for cats than for men. A cat is too proud to fight. Of course, a feline will make a stand; will even make a charge; but it is very much more of an adept at shrinking. There is something of feminine resourcefulness in such a creature that is intellectually superior to the bold, downright, candid courage of a dog. A cat has a sphinx-like sagacity, a certain ancient sorcery that the dog never possesses.

But vain at this moment were sphinx-like sagacity and ancient sorcery. The puma was on the edge of the platform; Bolio appeared full in the only pathway to escape. Under such circumstances a cat will either jump to safety or will stand at bay to discover what a frightful mien, claws, and teeth can do toward retarding the zeal of an over-impetuous lover. Evidently the panther, familiar with the perilous nature of the ground—able, indeed, even in the darkness and the rain to see his surroundings—knew the risk in a leap. All his life this great male panther had hunted along the edges of the gorge. He did not quite dare to rush upon the grim hound; he could not safely leap. An inch short in such a leap, and he would plunge three hundred feet. Nor was there a bed of roses below to receive his coming. There was nothing now to do but fight. As Bolio was of exactly the same persuasion, the business started instantly. There were no preliminary bouts. It was the impact of these two implacable enemies that Jeff heard the first time he opened the door. While he was in the kitchen, lighting the lantern, the mortal round was being fought! When he returned to the door, we remember, he was met by black darkness, and the rain, and the weird sighing of the reeking hemlocks.

That was a mighty round that Bolio and the puma fought on that black rock hanging above nothing. Johnson used to say that going to sea in a ship was like being in jail with the chance of being drowned. Then fighting on that shelf was like standing off two deaths at once. For either antagonist, a slip meant the end of it all; the odds, therefore, in that respect, were decidedly against Bolio. A cat can cling where a dog has no chance of staying. A cat's feet and claws are made prehensile—like his life.

But Bolio, in his superb courage, showed not a second's hesitancy. He went for the puma's throat. Old hunter that he was, he was well aware of the place where things really live. In any living thing the neck is almost tragically vital; for there all the life-forces converge in narrow compass, in narrow conduits. Into the panther's very bosom Bolio stormed; and he got the beast by the throat.

The puma had struck him savagely, ripping an ear to ribbons. He had reared up at the black hound's demoniac approach; and but for Bolio's momentum, the blow dealt him might well have driven him sheer from the rock. But now they had closed, and in deadliest sort. The puma's game was to claw the dog open with the keen claws on his hind legs. To this end he had gripped the dog's shoulder in his teeth and was trying madly to disembowel the grim and fearless creature that was strangling him. But the dog's grip on the puma's throat was decisive—at least for the moment. Even the superb lithe strength of the puma ebbed under the hound's relentless attack. The puma turned in agony, Bolio thrusting him backward. One of the cat's hind legs slipped off the cliff. He could not draw it up. Bolio continued to crowd his enemy. The puma released his hold of the hound's shoulder. The claws of his forefeet tore hotly into Bolio's back. But the black muzzle of the great hound only sank the more deeply into his victim's tawny throat.

The business could not last. The puma could not loose Bolio's hold. Nor could Bolio free himself from that heavy embrace that now gripped him in smothering cruelty. The puma kept turning—Bolio oncrowding. They were on the brink. The brink was slippery with rain and wet slime of the rock. A second of hot savage panting, a fierce snarl, an answering throat-buried growl—and off they plunged—down, down into the bellowing darkness.

It was just at that time that Jefferson Wise brought the light. The lights of this life not infrequently are brought after there is nothing for them to illumine.

Locked in death's embrace the two great bodies, hurtling frightfully, plunged like an unblazing meteor for the rocks gleaming below coldly in the rain. The wild fall through the darkness in no way abated the fury of their struggle. But of course their plunge could not last. It was of shorter duration than their fight on the rock; and its end was certainly more decisive. Death is, perhaps, the only perfect consummation; and on the gray boulders in the Linville Gorge the puma suddenly achieved this perfection. He yielded with amazing celerity all nine of his lives. He also yielded, with little reluctance, his hold on the hound Bolio. Such a plunge, on such rocks, apparently sacked the puma incontinently of all his sphinx-like sagacity, all his ancient sorcery. And his giving over of them was indubitably final. Moreover, luck, that almost invariably smiles upon a feline as a favorite, was against this one. Of the two fighters, one had to take the brunt of the impact. The puma did. He struck squarely on his back; and the stars that he saw were probably a firmament. After his fall he more resembled a rug than a panther. Bolio had fared a little better. One of his hind legs was broken; he was jarred perfectly senseless; he rolled with the dead puma into the water, with a high-grade chance of being drowned. Otherwise he was unhurt. At least, he was not dead. That is usually a consideration of some moment.

The fur rug to which the panther had been so suddenly reduced was sucked into the backwash pool, whence it was dragged next morning by Jeff Wise. A touch of real current got hold of the black body of the hound, toyed with it gently, purringly, caressingly; then drew it with imperious pride toward the wild ramp of the river. It would be difficult to say whether Bolio there had any more chance of staying alive than the panther had of recapturing his nine fled existences.

Bolio's insensible form, ideal prey for such waters, was now headed full for the epic journey down the mighty Linville Gorge—more than ten miles long, sinking to a depth of eighteen hundred feet—geologists say the oldest gorge in the world, and certainly one of the deepest wooded gorges. It is said that but two human beings have ever traversed its lonely mystery, its solitary peril.

That the fearful impact of Bolio's fall should not have killed him outright was due to his having fallen partly in the water, partly on the puma. The leg that had struck the boulder had been snapped. And now, as his body was swirled swiftly away, that leg drifted at a sick angle. It is putting it rather too strongly to say that Bolio's chance for life was no better than the average woman's chance of winning a silence contest. But it is out of just such desperate plights as Bolio's that the Odysseys of this world are wrought.

The great hound's compulsory itinerary can best be appreciated if you will stand here by Jeff's cabin and look down the first mile of the gorge. You may wonder why men call that brawl of foam a river; yet its volume is considerable. The elevation here from sea-level is nearly four thousand feet; the river drops a full three thousand in the course of ten miles. Such duress of harness put upon rivers is what really makes gorges. Nor is this one finished. Mile after mile the river takes a hop-step-and-jump course. There is a bewildering series of cataracts. That one you see yonder is only sixteen feet high; but below the dead hemlock, far down yonder, the plunge is a sheer ninety feet into a rock-bottomed pool of profound depth. Lower down the gorge there are other waterfalls—many of them—and some of them much higher than this last. And see how perfectly the rhododendron, the mountain birch, the pine, and the hemlock clothe these strange, sheer cliffs, lending a glamour, a soft allurement to the gigantic gulch, hewn through the vitals of these ancient hills. A man, and then a woman, went down that eerie wilderness—only those two. But they were purposeful, in their right mind, wary, forewarned. Bolio's body was being dashed blindly about—now sailing with sick serenity across a smooth stretch of water—now bewilderingly rolled and manhandled by the frantic waters.

Lover seeks not lover with more infallible intent than water seeks its level; and in either case obstacles and obstructions and delayers of such a meeting are sure to suffer. The living body of a helpless creature is, of all such delayers, the most certain to suffer. For that reason Bolio got worse treatment than he had ever had from the paw of panther or of bear. Yet had he been more gently used, more soothingly cradled, he might easily have drowned. He was so far gone that a lullaby might easily have finished him. But when his poor head was unmercifully whacked against a jagged rock, he dimly awoke. He was nearly drowning; he was suffocating, smothering. He tried to get his head above the water. Feebly he paddled with his front legs. He was, indeed, what his appearance declared him to resemble—an accident that had already happened.

It was but a few moments after Bolio regained something like consciousness that he went headlong over the great Linville Falls. There is a story in that country to the effect that a fisherman, by a misstep, took the same plunge, and emerged from the pool below with nothing worse than a broken arm. Bolio, through good chance rather than by design, slithered down over a smooth green cataract, plunged into a smother of foam, arose in a wild maze of effervescence, and was thrust forth into a broad pool dotted with pyramids and obelisks of foam. He drifted against a black rock, ever-shining from the spume of the falls; and here, with his nose above the water, he lay, breathing slowly, faintly conscious. Had he not brought up against this glistening boulder he might have sunk in the pool. Bolio knew that he was alive. All about him was darkness and thunder and a world weeping its ruin. He wondered what had become of the puma. The thought made the hound move his tongue to his lips. He drew himself the least bit higher out of the water. He thought of home and of his master. Of little else a good dog thinks when he is away.

The longing soon got the better of Bolio; Jeff Wise, he knew, could fix his broken leg. He whined uneasily. He felt that he was still in deadly danger. He wanted to get to shore. Using the little strength he had remaining, he pushed himself away from the tiny rock island that had intercepted his drifting with the current. In a moment that current had him again, and against its steady strength Bolio was helpless. The tide took him; to it he yielded. Down the brawling stream he went—over rocks, across pools, slithering along swift, quiet stretches—plunging over low falls, gliding under bridges of fallen trees against which all kinds of debris had been rammed and jammed.

Perhaps it is a full mile from Linville Falls to the glistening white sand bar that rims a deep elbow of the gorge. In this same sand gold has been found; and the woman who went down the gorge here picked up a perfect ruby. Most things that the river brings thus far find harborage here. It is as if the ramping tide, after all its frantic horseplay, had relented—and would here lay gently, even tenderly, whatever it had been pleased to make heartless sport of for so long. And here the river brought the hound Bolio far more dead than alive, some two hours before dawn on that stormy September night.

For a long while the body of the great black hound swayed against the gleaming sands. Little waves lisped against it. Elfin breakers washed into Bolio's face. He was cold. The consciousness of this discomfort made him at last drag himself a few inches up on the bar. The rain was now ceasing. Head on paws the black hound lay—a long way from home now—almost helpless with a broken leg. But he was alive; and in that particular he had an indubitable, if slight, advantage over his late friend, the puma.

The next morning, while Jefferson Wise was discovering the puma in the backwash pool, nearly two miles farther down the gorge Bolio was wondering how in the world he would ever get back home. Despite the fever of his broken leg, he slept from utter weariness; and when he awoke, the sun was steaming off the hemlocks rimming the crests of the gorge. Bolio shivered, blinked sagely, drew himself a little higher on the sand, and then whined pitifully over the pain that was his. His chief danger now would be starving. Already he was very hungry. Sand bearing gold and rubies has no assuaging effect on the appetite. But Bolio was not without resources. Only a dead dog is.

Slowly the sun climbed; the mists left the mighty gorge clean; dazzling blue sky roofed it. Bolio had shifted his position so that he now faced the river. His wounded leg was a little easier. He knew enough not to move it. A strange sound was now filling the gorge. It sounded like another rain. Millions of drops of water, distilled from the contact of the mist with the trees' foliage, were tumbling like myriads of tiny silver bells. The sound of the river was now quieter in its tone—suggestive of a serene joy rather than of robust tumult. But these things interested Bolio little. He was desperately hungry.

Many objects were drifted against the white bar; some of these stranded; others merely touched, and were softly drawn away by the tide. At length came a misshapen, tawny body. Bolio smelt it before he saw it. The puma that Jeff Wise had kicked into the current floated up to where Bolio lay. It stranded. The black hound thrust out his head, seized a fold of the panther's neck-skin, and drew him a little up—high enough to keep him stranded. Bolio's design was clear enough to himself. He felt that this shaggy brute, that had already saved his life once, was destined, by a fortunate chance, to save it again. The dog gave a growl of content and of ownership. Then he slept again.

Balmy autumn sunshine filtering into the profound gorge awakened Bolio. He lifted his massive head, gazed thoughtfully at all his surroundings, as if to make sure that he was not being watched, was not being stalked. It is really extraordinary how soon a tame creature amid wild surroundings reacquires all the ancient traits of his savage kindred. A dog—especially an intelligent one—can go wild very quickly, and become as expert a killer as any fox or wolf. When Bolio was satisfied that he was alone, he dragged the body of the puma nearer to him. Then upon the carcass of his enemy he feasted. So complete a triumph was even more than the big hound expected. As yet he dared not move; but he was now warm, and he had water and food. He felt himself coming back to life.

On that glimmering sand bar, deep in that gloomy gorge, for more than a week the great hound lay—patient, sagacious, silently biding his time. Kept alive by the stranded body of the puma and by several rainbow trout that had been killed by the falls, slowly he recovered his strength. The fever began to leave his leg. It was very stiff; but it had begun to lose its pain. By day and by night his heart turned toward home; and had he known it, by day and night Jeff Wise's heart turned toward him. Three times that week the mountaineer had been down the gorge searching for Bolio. Once he had been within a quarter of a mile of the silvery sandbar. He had called. But his voice had been drowned in the steady roaring of the river. It seemed hopeless to Jeff; yet a man who knows a good dog does not give up until he sees him dead. And as for Bolio giving up Jeff was the last thing in this world that he was thinking of doing.

Another week passed, and the black hound, savage, lean, bright-eyed, began to limp about the shining sands. He had run out of food. He had to move. But whither should he go, and how?

Sheer rock walls, weirdly hung with hemlock and pine, hemmed him in. Clearly he could not climb them. Nor could he go back the way he had come. Bolio dimly remembered the great falls, the many rocks, the swift waters. He would have to go down; there would be an outlet somewhere, he knew. He could hobble downward in some fashion until the line of bee-tling cliffs ended. Then he could limp homeward. He knew the direction. It is almost impossible to fool an old dog on the business of direction. The country into which Bolio now by compulsion ventured has perhaps no rival in its utter lone wildness. Here, man has never come to stay; only to peer into the abysmal gorge, perhaps, to shudder, and to turn away. A thousand feet of sheer rock wall tower above the chasm at the place where the sandbar gleams. From the crests of these majestic cliffs the river can hardly be heard, and its white dashings look ghostly in the far bosom of that gigantic gulch. Wilder ramp the waters through this middle chasm, where the fall is nearly two hundred feet to the mile. Here and there the channel is choked by stayed heaps of debris, by giant boulders, rolled from the cliffs towering above, by dead hemlocks that, for centuries steeped in the rocky wall, at last had paid their final tribute to life and to time. Over the ancient canyon there broods a sense of the infinite—a thoughtful vast spirit of wonder and of immortality. It has the solemn aspect of eternity.

The hound Bolio was less concerned with the mystery and beauty of the great Linville Gorge than he was with searching among the piles of debris for food to sustain life. As he was a sad cripple, his task was not an easy one; but certain refuse he did discover which allayed his pangs. All the while he kept on slowly and steadily down the gorge—avoiding the water, of the treachery of which he was now well aware—dragging himself wearily over rocks—picking his own trail, since, in that blind and black wilderness, trails there were none. By night he crawled under a dry trash heap; and here bedded himself down for all the world like one of his wild ancestors.

For six days Bolio made progress down the gorge. The weather had been mild and sunny. His foraging had prospered. His strength was fast returning. His broken leg, strangely stiff, was healing fast. Because of his exposure and his hardships his coat had grown rough, but it had a sleek look, like that of a wild thing. From his massive intelligent head looked eyes singularly percep-tive, bright, sagacious. Things were going well for him. He had come within two miles of the end of the great gorge. In a few days more he would be out of the chasm—then a bee line would he make for home.

But the elements ruthlessly dispose of many plans, mortal and canine. One night Bolio went to bed in a trash-heap as usual; in an hour he was awakened by a patter on the dead leaves and twigs into which he had snuggled. His cold nose sniffed the air. He smelled rain. With a low growl he slipped out of his lair. Instinct told him that peril was at hand. The voice of the river, responsive to even the slightest rain, seemed already to have deepened. Black night filled the vast canyon; and down through the night and the canyon roared the autumn.

It is said that a mountaineer, when praying for rain, thus petitioned: "O Lord, don't send no gentle sizzle-sozzle. Send us a gulley-washer, O Lord!" Such a rain as now thundered into Linville Gorge might well have been an authentic answer to such an appeal.

Under the steady thrash of the downpour Bolio whined. Not that he minded the drenching, just rather that he previsioned menace. He remembered well that wild night when he had been the plaything of the chasm's waters; he knew he could not climb the sheer walls. On three legs he stood, his noble head lifted high in the rain.

Philosophers say that a woman's pride is the most sensitive thing in the world; and having no knowledge either of philosophy or of woman, I confess that such an opinion, for all I know, may be accurate. But certainly among things most sensitive is the Linville River. No moonshiner on its banks loses control of himself half so quickly over a raw pint as does the river, apparently, over a little shower. And a real rain sets it wild.

This was now a real rain that was soaking the gaunt black hound standing beside the trash heap in the utter maw of the gigantic gulch. When a good dog whines as Bolio was doing, he means to say, "My name may soon be Dennis," or "Wake me when my wings come," or sentiments to some similar effect.

Bolio turned his face southward down the gorge. Painfully he began to pick his way in the savage darkness over the wild debris. He heard, he felt the river rising. In such a canyon the effect of rain is almost instantaneous. Creeping after Bolio the risen water came—calling—shouting—in bursting tumult clamoring, in prisoned frenzy thundering for release. Soaked, limping, haggard with a nameless dread, yet courageous still; the great hound tried to find a way down through the tumbled rocks, over the waste of a thousand destructions and deaths.

But the Linville Gorge belongs to the river. And now the river took its own. Miserably, Bolio, to escape the rising flood, turned to the left and crawled up a slanting rock as high as he could go. To this he clung desperately, while the black roaring gulch filled with the wild thronging voices of the gathered waters. Bolio was assuredly no coward; but his plight made him gulp. He thought of his master. To dogs, men seem supernatural. Jeff, the great hound felt, would have saved him. It is to be doubted if Jeff or any other mortal man could have done aught to lend aid; but Jeff would at least have risked life and limb for Bolio.

Eight miles up the canyon the mountaineer heard the rain roar sullenly on the roof of his cabin. He thought of the night when his matchless dog had vanished. He thought of the bear season, coming in soon with the middle of October. He felt sick at heart.

The storm had come from the north, so that the lower reaches of the gorge received the full benefit of the water that had fallen for miles above; nor had it fallen from the heavens much faster than it now raced down the canyon. The rivulets that meandered purlingly among the rocks had their elfin voices hushed; filmy falls became roaring cataracts; brawling riffles became deep foamy stretches of racing blackness. All the hosts of the rain seemed marshaled in this gorge. The armies of the storm were here mobilized; and now invincible, with many a triumphant shout, with white banners dimly awave, drunk with the wine of might, insolent with power, the hordes swept mightily on. Bolio had no more chance than a hummingbird's egg in a concrete mixer. He heard the tumult onrushing. He clung to his rock. But waves began to lap his legs. Then one took him suddenly. A bit of flotsam in that mad orgy tide of fury and destruction, he was borne afar, fearfully. Grimly he tried to swim. Blindly he fought. But a huge timber rammed him, breaking again his half-healed leg. Almost idly now he rode the foaming thunder out of the tremendous Linville Gorge. He seemed drowned, drifting, a mere black speck in the tumultuous wilderness of waters.

There are some wives who, when their husbands go hunting, know instinctively that they must provide, against their nimrod's return, not only consolation, but meat for dinner as well. It was not so with the wife of Jeff Wise. When he went hunting, she began to get ready to take care of the meat. Yet the night before the dawning of that wine-bright October morning, ushering in the bear season, she had misgivings. Jeff's spirits were low. He had managed to trade five raccoon hides for a half-grown hound; but the appearance of this creature was not reassuring even to Jeff's wife—much less to him.

"He's jumpy," the mountaineer complained. "He seems to be a cross between a scare and a jump. A real b'ar would plumb spile his scenery."

Nevertheless on the first day of the bear season, and nearly six weeks after the disappearance of Bolio, at dawn Jeff set forth toward the south, following the direction of the gorge.

Some three miles from the cabin, and just beyond a thicket which swept backward from the dizzy cliffs, Jeff's dog took a bear trail. It was hot. The young dog yelped eagerly, dashing off under the laurels. Within half a mile the bear came to bay in a shallow cave. When Jeff reached the place, the dog was outside; but from the general dishevelment of his appearance, the mountaineer judged that he had been in. Despite the dog's vociferous ferocity, it was unlikely that he would re-enter the cave.

"Bolio would go in on him—God, if I had him!" Jeff muttered, peering into the glimmer of the rocky den.

It was at that moment that the mountaineer suddenly felt a cold nose thrust into his hand. He looked down quickly. Then he went on his knees.

"Durn my Sunday suit!" he sobbed; "it's Bolio."

Gaunt, huge, marked by suffering, but withal glorified by an utter faithfulness that Jeff fully comprehended, stood Bolio.

"Damn," muttered the mountaineer, gulping—his arms round Bolio's neck, his face against the hound's massive jowl. The joy of this recovery was almost too much for him.

Jeff was really a man great of heart. I think he wept.

"We'll go in on him, old dog," he said; "we'll go—same like we used to." And into the cave they went.

At Jeff's cabin that night, a huge male bear was hung on the hemlock in the yard; and on the porch, after all his adventures, utterly contented, lay Bolio.

My Most Memorable Dog

This piece appears in *The Woods and Wild Things I Remember*. It reminds us, as if any serious dog man needed to be reminded, that every hard hunter should be privileged, at some stage in his outdoor career, to own a "dog of a lifetime." That dog will not necessarily be his most memorable one, though often that is the case. Special dogs inevitably have character, and generally they are characters as well. Such was the case with Mike. Ugly and possessing his fair share of faults, he was also a dog of which you could truly say: "To know him was to love him." As Rutledge wrote, "I shall always remember Mike," and once you share some of the experiences the pair enjoyed, the reasons why will be obvious.

During the years of my young manhood, when I was a teacher in the beautiful Cumberland Valley of Pennsylvania, I hunted quail and grouse a great deal, and I raised and trained a good many bird dogs.

Animals can occasionally be as memorable as human beings; among dogs I give the first place to Mike. Although he was no beauty, he was a joy forever. There was a pathos about him as if he were aware of his unpromising looks.

In those early years I inevitably hunted quail but finally gave it up, for I love the birds too much. One year I went quite overboard in buying a registered pointer with the proud name of Savannah Count. He arrived in a crate that looked like a palace. He was huge, handsome, and supercilious. For some reason, he seemed especially oblivious to me.

On the first day of the season I took His Majesty into the fields. At the first shot he vanished over the rolling countryside. The lordly Count was gunshy. I did not retrieve him for days.

I was reminded of a dog I took to old Galboa to correct the same fault. Galboa was a native African who had a way with animals. Telling the old man my troubles, I left the dog with him for two weeks. When I returned, he gestured with contempt toward the dog lying in the grass. "You must learn," he said, "that nothing can be done about a fool."

There are few plights worse for a quail hunter than to have no bird dog when the season opens. When Count defected, I at once called up a Pennsylvania Game protector, a good friend of mine, to ask him if he could relieve my emergency. He raised bird dogs "on the side," and I had bought several good ones from him. But his report was disappointing. "I did have two dandies," he said, "but I sold both last week. I haven't got a thing now but Mike, and I don't like to sell him to you. You and I have been good friends."

Although this seemed like a sinister introduction, I said, "Ship him to me." As if to sink Mike even lower in my estimation, my friend said, "I could not charge you more than $15.00 for this mutt." (I had paid $100.00 for my airborne Savannah Count.)

When Mike arrived, I found him, in appearance, no "hound of heaven." Undersized, angular, with bristly red and yellow hair, for a bird dog he appeared to be put together wrong. His ears were small and peaked; someone had cut off more than half his tail. No one had lately taken him to a beauty parlor. But, as a judge once said to me, about the possible verdict of a jury, "Brother, you never know."

As if he had everything else against him, Mike's feet were too large, so that he walked as if he had snowshoes on. Despite all these adverse factors, Mike had qualities to admire, and, for me, a human and lovable nature. He had a good head, which should presage wisdom and a keen nose. Mike had, too, like some people, a certain air about him; an ugly air, but unique and unforgettable.

Of course, Mike had not any social background. To gracious living, he was alien. Yet already I could feel his loyalty to me. He was also courageous. As I led him up to my home, which was near the express office, we met a big dog that I knew to be a mean one. The big dog, bristling, made some invidious remarks about Mike's mother. Mike bristled also, took a step forward, growling. He was ready for a fight.

I never learned anything of Mike's ancestry; but somewhere in it a blooded pointer probably could be found. He looked to be all cur; but there was something about him that made me know that he wasn't. He had ways and wiles about him.

I have owned many good dogs, but Mike was a character. He was always surprising me with the things he did, which he had thought out, all by himself things that endeared him to me. For example, one afternoon we were crossing a field when we came to a rather cold dark stream with steep banks. Mike did not like the looks of it; but his heart must have kept saying,

"Whither thou goest, I will go." I managed to slip down the bank, cross the water with the aid of some limbs, and literally crawled up the farther bank. I then looked for Mike and called him.

Having estimated the problem, and disliking cold water, he had calmly walked away from the creek in a straight line, just as a high jumper or a pole vaulter would, in order to afford himself a speedy run for his takeoff. He went about thirty yards, turned, and came running full speed for the creek. There was a break in the trees so that I could watch him land safely. I was surprised how high he went.

A wild white-tailed deer has been known to jump forty-two feet; a horse, thirty-six feet; a man, twenty-eight feet. I am sure that Mike jumped between twenty and twenty-five feet, and he did so with certainty and grace.

The same week I took a friend hunting quail. Every time he shot, he missed. Meanwhile Mike disappeared. I was not surprised, as his russet coloring blended perfectly with those of the autumn. When I found him he was lying flat in a ditch, his head on his outstretched paws. He looked at me with eyes that seemed to express disappointment, chagrin, and even disgust. He was not able to take any more strong doses of missing! It made him sick; besides, all his work was going for nothing. Of course, I may have misinterpreted his expression; but it looked like humiliating regret to me. Indeed, Mike's expression was so forlorn it would not have surprised me if big dash tears had rolled down his cheeks.

As we approached an old rail fence one day, Mike sprang up to the top rail. It must have been at that moment that one of the top rails began to swing at right angles to the line of the fence. Just at that moment the hot and heavy scent of a covey of quail, almost beneath him, assailed Mike's nostrils. He crept forward a step to make certain, and found himself with all four feet on the swaying fence rail. Mike's game was to keep his balance and also not to frighten the covey. I can still see him, the picture of shrewd loyalty and devotion, holding his balance until I could come up. He was rocking perfectly.

On another occasion I missed him. After a few minutes he came creeping and crawling back to me. On reaching me, he whined, turned around and started back the way he had come. He paused, looking back to make sure I understood his message and was following. His gait was very peculiar. He was walking as if he were stepping on eggs. He led me to a big covey of quail. He must have known that I could not see him; so he came and got me!

One day Mike and I were out on a sandy road when a big crowd of frolicking young people came by. Purely in jest, one of them threw a pine cone at Mike. It did not hit him; but even if it had, it could not have hurt him. But it wounded his dignity; and he never forgot it.

Except for the one who had tossed the cone, all the others could enter my yard in perfect safety. But the one who threw the cone would stop outside the gate and call for someone please to "tie Mike up." Really gentle by disposition, Mike would not let anyone take liberties with him.

When I hunted in Pennsylvania, there were some ringneck pheasants there. We were allowed to kill only the cock birds, which are easily distinguished by their gaudy colors and their long tails. It is characteristic of these birds that they will often run long distances on the ground before taking flight. One afternoon, in a wild valley, Mike struck a trail. I knew at once it must be a pheasant because of the distance he was going. At last he came to a stand. I walked in carefully to flush the bird. After all our long walk, it was a hen! Of course, I did not shoot. As I stood idly there, Mike, apparently in anger, whirled on me and barked in the most disgusted fashion! There was no mistaking what he meant: "After all my careful work, what in the world is the matter with you?" Some dogs are certainly capable of rebuking their masters—if the provocation is great.

Once when Mike and I were hunting in a field of wheat stubble near a thicket of blackberry canes, he came back to me whining, and he seemed to be cringing. Something had scared him, and he was not a dog easily scared. I was wearing my corduroy trousers; and he took hold of the cuff of one leg, to pull me back, or at least to delay me. But feeling I should investigate, I literally dragged Mike through the stubble. As we drew near the briar patch, I heard what had frightened Mike; then I saw the snake, that ashen heap of death. I have lost dogs that have been struck by rattlers, and have located these lethal serpents by dogs which barked at them—being wary enough to keep their distance. I looked at Mike. In his eyes was distinct warning. I had dealt with dogs all my life, but what kind of a dog was this? I have had a good dog "take on" a wild boar that had personal designs on me. Yet I doubt if that brave dog was really defending me. With Mike it was different. He cautiously warned me against what he knew was deadly danger. Is it any wonder that I love and honor his memory?

Early in our acquaintance he gave me a good idea of his unusualness. Early one damp morning, I drove out in a buggy (I had no car) to hunt quail. Mike lay in the bottom of the buggy and a robe covered him and my knees. About a mile from town a heavy Osage orange hedge stood on the left of the road. As we were passing this, something happened—something for which I could not at first account. The robe had risen off my knees. Mike was standing up. As soon as I saw the trance-like look in his eyes, I knew that he had winded quail, and had pointed them from the buggy! For precaution's sake, I drove forward a few paces, where I got out of the buggy. But as he was still pointing, I had to lift him down to the roadway. He was still pointing, and as stiff as a board.

When his feet touched the ground he began a curious stiff-legged walk back down the road. Then he came to a perfect point. As the grass was rather thin, I saw the quail on the ground, a beautiful covey of about sixteen birds. When they rose and whirled over the hedge, I did not shoot—partly, I think, because of the strange magic of Mike's behavior.

On another occasion I took a friend duck hunting. Flight shooting was then permitted after sundown. I put my friend on a good stand and he blazed away for an hour. I shot only twice. But when dark came, and I started down the old bank on which we had been standing, I almost fell over a big pile of wild ducks. That was Mike's work. He had brought all my friend's ducks to me! He had original ideas about loyalty.

When the Great Depression came, I had three sons in college. I had already sold some heirloom furniture. Was there anything else that might bring in some money? There was Mike. Unfortunately a man of means had seen him work. He had several times approached me to buy him. Meanwhile the university treasurer kept bearing down on me. On a disastrous day I decided to let my dear Mike go. I felt worse than a sinner. While I was making the crate, Mike watched me curiously. When I put him in and nailed it shut, he must have had an inkling of what was coming. He lay flat on the bottom of the box, and looked at me with big misty eyes. I set the crate in the wheelbarrow, and rolled it down to the express office. I heard some subdued whimpering, but I really believe that Mike was weeping. Nor was he the only one. I left him at the office to be shipped out.

But I had hardly reached home when the enormity of my crime overcame me. I rushed back to the express office (although no train was due for several hours). "It's a mistake!" I exclaimed to the express agent. "I'm not going to sell him."

Not long after that I decided to stop quail shooting. By then Mike was getting old. The aspect of the approach of age is always sad with a dog as active and intelligent as Mike. While he was still strong, I could expect him always to meet me halfway down the avenue that led to my home. He apparently timed my arrival; but was usually an hour or so early, just lying there waiting. At other times, he would pull at my corduroy trousers, trying to get me started on a hunt, or would run down the avenue, barking, and looking expectantly toward the house for me to join him. But then came days when he did not meet me. And sometimes when I would seem to be getting ready to go for a hunt, he would lie in the sun by the steps, thump the ground with his tail, and look at me with a nameless wistfulness. He seemed to be acknowledging his own weakness, and doing so with tragic regret. His eyes spoke for him. Like King Lear, he was saying, "I am old now."

Then, too, Mike began to make mistakes in the field. One day he was holding a point on the briared bank of a ditch. I was sure he had a quail or a pheasant. But as I got near him he gave up the point, and turned back to me, his expression registering shame and apology. He crawled up to me whining, and rubbed against my boots, as if imploring forgiveness. He was abashed that he had been pointing an old land turtle! Yet the finest part of his life was yet to come. He had always loved children, and had been a great favorite with them. One of my grandsons was crazy about Mike; when, therefore, the boy's mother told me that another child was expected, I let them take him. "He might make a nurse for the baby." I said, never dreaming of the real import of my words.

In a pretty room on the second floor of my son's house all was made ready for the new baby. In the center of the room was the immaculate crib, all lacy and frilly. There was a mahogany footboard around the base. One day when the mother came into the room she was greeted by a low growl. Mike had taken possession of the little square box beneath the bassinet. Please don't ask me how he knew a baby was coming there. Perhaps he had dealt with a baby before, in another family. True, there was an unwonted air of suppressed excitement and expectancy, and he may have interpreted these. Do some animals, at certain times, have the eerie clairvoyance of premonition? At any rate, Mike planted himself under the bassinet, and would not leave. He had to be fed and watered there.

The mother was at the hospital two weeks. When she brought the tiny daughter home, Mike barked delightedly. And he took charge. Except for the mother, he would let no one else enter the room. When the baby cried, or even fretted, Mike barked. After some months had passed, and the baby began to crawl about the room, Mike would come close and lie down so that tiny Bonnie could sleep with him for a pillow. My daughter-in-law said, "I feel much safer with Mike than with a nurse."

When Bonnie was a year and a half old, she was allowed to run up and down the pavement in front of her house—but only if Mike went with her. He was not by then keeping up with the baby very well. He always stayed between her and the street. One day she threw a little rubber ball out into the road, and at once, like a fairy, ran after it. Mike was old then and not nearly so fast as he had once been. Two cars were coming from opposite directions. Mike, making the effort of his life, dashed between Bonnie and one car. She was saved, but he was struck and killed.

Mike was a dog that looked all wrong, but was all right. Ugly, he was loyal and smart. Many redeeming faults were his—those same human qualities that make people lovable. It is not hard for me to forget Savannah Count; but I shall always remember Mike.

Daisy and the Chimera

Rutledge had an abiding fascination with strange and foreboding creatures, and he variously used the word "chimera" to describe cottonmouth water moccasins, canebrake rattlesnakes, timber rattlesnakes, diamondback rattlesnakes, wild boars, and sharks. Here we have the gripping saga of a jaunty little setter, Daisy, and a giant diamondback. The tale is not one of bird hunting or wingshooting as such, but anyone who has spent much time following a bird dog in snake country knows the dreaded possibility of a dog-snake encounter in warmer weather. Moreover, both this piece and the one that follows ("Then Gabriel Blew His Horn") exemplify Rutledge's storytelling ability at its best.

There is little doubt that this story is either fiction or, at the very least, an exercise of literary license in the broadest sense. Still, any teller of tales who lacks the art of embellishment is immediately at a decided disadvantage, a problem that never gave Rutledge any trouble. Milstead might well have been an autobiographical representation of Rutledge, for he was a plantation owner, a great lover of dogs, an individual well versed in the ways of the wilds, and a man who would certainly have welcomed a tidy sum of money for a big snake. At any rate, the end result is a first-rate dog story, one that has heretofore been overlooked in anthologies but is sure to be enjoyed by those who delight in the accomplishments of man's staunchest friend.

Insofar as I have been able to ascertain, "Daisy and the Chimera" has only been published heretofore in *Bolio and Other Dogs,* although it is possible that the story first appeared in a magazine. Certainly this is the first time it has been reprinted in the past half-century.

————

The whole thing probably started on the day Vincente Blasco's motorboat ran out of gas when it was in the river opposite Norman Milstead's plantation. "I thought something would happen to you on your pleasure jaunts one of these days, Vincente," Milstead was saying as he met the little Italian down on the decrepit plantation wharf.

Beneath Vincente's piratic mustache gleamed white teeth. He could smile engagingly. "I need de gas," he explained. "My tank, heem is dry."

"Can't you burn moonshine?"

"Too much expense," Vincente explained seriously, with a gesture somewhat oriental and certainly comprehensive.

"I can let you have five gallons. Will you bring it back to me next week?"

"Yes; and bring you six for your favor."

"Look here, Vincente," said Milstead, a sudden thought coming to him, "I want to show you something. While your man is getting the gas, just come over here with me by this big oak."

Milstead led the Italian down a short stretch of riverbank, overarched with jasmine vines, dimmed by myrtle that exhaled fragrance as they brushed the bushes. They emerged upon an open glade under a monster live-oak— a vast tree that must have stood there for nearly two centuries. Over it clambered huge man-bodied vines; and growing on the marvelously long limbs, some of them parallel with the ground and not more than five feet from it, were fairy forests of vivid green ferns. Near the base of the oak the plantation owner paused.

They made an interesting contrast in manhood as they stood there together: the Italian, short, stout, swarthy, radiating a certain charm which came from quick apprehension, alert interest, deft precision in adjusting himself to any situation. Milstead was tall, grave, clean-shaven; a powerful figure, but spare. His hair was black, and inclined to curl a little; his eyes were dark blue. They looked rather piercingly from under beetle brows. Such eyes can be tender; but they can also be vindictive.

It was hard to get at the age of Vincente; possibly fifty, though his flair for living always made him appear younger than he was. But certainly he was older than Milstead, by ten, possibly fifteen, years.

"Some tree," said Vincente, his quick black eyes appraising the majesty of the monarch.

"I didn't bring you here to look at a tree," Milstead said; "you have seen plenty of big ones in Italy. But, Vincente, I want you to see what came my way yesterday. You're interested in natural history."

He stepped around the tree, leading Blasco by the arm. Pausing, he pointed to something hung against the rugged bark of the old patriarch. Another patriarch it was, and apparently of another world. Milstead expected an exclamation of awe from his visitor. But all he got was a chirpy whistle, perhaps of mild surprise.

"I killed it and brought it in," Milstead explained. "There is a den out near a place called Jones' Pond. One was killed there two years ago; now this one; a third has been seen. I fastened this one up here this morning to photograph him. Seven feet, nine inches he measures; and his weight is thirty-four pounds. He had eighteen rattles. It is what we call a diamondback. You aren't seeing things, Vincente. But you didn't leave anything like that in Italy."

If Vincente was impressed by these words, his reaction was singular indeed.

"Ah," he breathed, as if he hadn't really heard Milstead at all; and he stepped forward toward the snake and touched it with a delicate forefinger. "Ah, my friend," he went on, "it is a pity that he is dead. If he was alive, I could make you an offer for heem."

"Offer?" asked Milstead. "What in the world would you do in the city with a monster like that? The whole Police Department would raid your fruit-shop." "A serpent like this—deadly, terrible—he is what the people like to see. 'Oh,'" he mimicked, "'have you seen what Vincente Blasco has in his store on Broad Street? It is one of the wonders of the world. It is a sea-serpent. It is a chimera. It frightened me, but I am glad I saw it.' So they would talk," Vincente explained.

"They would come. That means trade. I hear, too," he added, "that rats have a fear of such a snake. I have too many rats. It would be a nice arrangement."

"Perhaps I can get you one," Milstead said. "What would he be worth? But I don't vouch for the nice arrangement part of it."

"I am no dealer in such pretties," Vincente answered; "but if he is as large as this one, and full of life, I give you feefty dollars."

"Next week," Milstead answered, "when you come by here on one of your trips, leave those six gallons of gas for me, and have fifty dollars handy in your rompers."

It was the first week of October when all this occurred; and it happened that at the time Milstead had little work on his hands. To ride the woods, to locate a big diamondback, and to capture him for Blasco—this seemed an easy and rather an interesting way to make fifty dollars. Besides, he would be ridding his own place of a creature that was a somewhat constant menace to man and to stock. Only the month before, he had lost a Jersey heifer from snakebite. The thing was worth trying at any rate. Besides, he could take his gun along and round up a covey or two. It was the first of the season, and his setter Daisy was sick for a hunt.

Two days after Vincente's visit, Milstead made an early start for what he believed to be the rendezvous of a fine covey of quail, and possibly of a diamondback as well. The nature of the morning did not appear quite in keeping with so curious and grim an enterprise. An autumn haze hung over the river, where the long lances of light from the rising sun made the mists sparkle. Into the purple tops of towering yellow pines stole the radiant beams; and from those crests were raveled away streamers of light.

Mockingbirds, returning to their lyric mood after a long silence, were warbling from smilax-crowned hollies and cedars. Carolina wrens called with wild, sweet abandon to one another. Milstead heard one quite near him, and another answering from across the river, a full half-mile away.

The world was steeped in a mellow peace, a balmy serenity. Mystical airs breathed through the quiet forest, in the circling arms of which Milstead's home lay. It seemed a morning for almost any other kind of an undertaking than the one that was afoot.

But perhaps, thought Milstead, Poe was wrong in giving dismal settings for his dismal tales. The effect of tragedy may be heightened by contrast; there is something satiric in the peril that is encountered in beautiful sunshine, with birds happily warbling, and with the sky gazing calmly down with the eyes of fathomless azure.

"I believe I can locate one of those things for Vincente," Milstead told himself as he journeyed out through the scented woodland. "Daisy can take care of herself all right. She knows a snake. I wouldn't come if it would risk her."

He looked at the snowy setter rambling through the roadside bushes as a man will look who knows and loves his dog.

As the forest glimmered in the dawn, it was a radiant, dewy world into which the plantation-owner rode. The pine trash on the road exhaled a spice odor of freshness and wild cleanliness. High in the lustral morning heavens the giant yellow pines soared, chairing softly to the rising sun. The wild-woods glinted, shimmered, seemed aware of the miracle that they themselves were. It did not appear the kind of world that might hold peril and tragedy. It appeared made for love and peace, for song and joy.

Milstead knew where certain great diamond-backs had their haunt. During the preceding summer his neighbor, Claude Marlowe, a woodsman of the pineland, had killed one that was little short of eight feet. Milstead had wondered at it; had examined it as it had hung on a persimmon bush beside the public road. And one of his hounds, happening to pass the place, began to show signs of extreme caution and mistrust; finally located the thing; backed away with the glint of ancient wisdom in his sagacious eyes, and ere he left the scene, howled lugubriously.

Paris Green Washington, a plantation Negro of a singular dearth of imagination, had reported that he had seen, near the same locality, a snake of the same species and apparently of the same proportions. Several other persons had had the dubious privilege of seeing one of these serpent wonders; and each person had apparently made his discovery in the neighborhood of Jones' Pond, a strange cypressed lagoon that lay on Milstead's place, not two miles from the house. He had reason to believe these Negroes and their stories, especially since each one admitted that his attitude toward the chimera in question had been one of extreme conciliation. Then, of course, there was this late serpent that Milstead had shown to his friend, Vincente Blasco.

"I'll get him one," he repeated; "and he'll be as welcome to it as fifty dollars will be to me. Besides, I've a sneaking interest in these babies that love so to play with their rattles."

He had tied behind his saddle a big burlap sack. Stopping by a group of young hickories, he cut one with a stout fork in its end. He had caught snakes before. Pinning one's head to the ground with the fork, he would hold him tight until he could get his hand around the thing's neck. Then it could be lifted and thrust down into the bag. The sack tied shut, he would leave his catch until he could return to the plantation for a wagon and a big box.

It may be thrilling, but it isn't exactly delicately discreet to carry a diamondback in a flimsy bag. A mere scratch from an inch-long fang may do damage that no amount of caution and effort can repair.

Out of the plantation's far gateway and into the lonely woods the man rode. The bay branches, drenched in fragrant dew, glistened, and exhaled a winy fragrance. The sunshine filtered shyly into these remote solitudes.

Milstead saw a buck, thin strips of velvet hanging in tatters from his horns, slide into a myrtle thicket. Woodpeckers were hammering in assiduous fashion, calling stridently whenever they let up on their carpentering. Cicadas began to shrill, but not so aridly as they would later in the day.

A half mile from the gate, Milstead turned off the road, literally taking to the woods. He had a curious feeling that the rare exotic beauty of the world which surrounded him had about it something sinister, something ironic, something satiric. He attributed his sensation to the eerie grimness of his mission. And it was the anticipation that caused his feeling. When he actually came on the snake, all would be well. All would be well. He began to wonder if it would . . .

Afar off now, in the open pinelands, appeared the lagoon, marked by its magical gleam of black waters, its moss-hung bald cypresses, its aspect of perpetual, mournful beauty. In those giant trees snowy egrets nested, so spectral in their loveliness as to be like spirits of the place. In the dark waters alligators lived their solitary, treacherous lives; and large-mouthed bass of unbelievable size managed to exist there by reason of their swiftness as dodgers of the huge reptiles. Wood ducks nested in the low forks of the cypresses; and often they were seen, as placid and as beautiful as the waters themselves, floating on that mirror-like surface.

To the right of the lagoon was a long savanna—a green plain of many acres in extent, where flag-flowers grew, and gaudy fly-traps, and alluring orchis flowers. It had a certain air of faerie peril, a beauty not quite of earth, an eerie loveliness not quite familiar, not quite smiling. It was toward this glimmering stretch of country that Milstead headed his horse.

It was the horse that gave him the first intimation that he had found what he was after. For a few yards Milstead noticed that his animal— a little red pony that he enjoyed riding because of his sure-footedness in the woods—began to show a gingerly sort of stepping that his rider interpreted to mean that the creature did not like the lush, quaking footing that the sa- vanna afforded. Milstead idly recalled that the pony had once spring-bogged down in a rice-field; and now he thought it possible that that far recollection had returned to him. But then the horse stopped. His head went up high. He trembled. His ears were cocked. He gave vent to a shocked and mighty snort, as if blowing spasmodically from him some dreadful odor. Probably that was precisely what the red pony was doing. He next began to quiver violently; and his whole attitude gave his rider to understand that they had both better be moving out of that place.

"It may be a snake," the man said slowly. "Well," he added half-aloud, "that's what I've come after."

He decided to dismount. There were no trees near. A strange, scrubby, little live-oak growing forlornly on the edge of a ridge of sand that crossed the savanna, seemed the only place where he could tie his horse. That he must tie him was evident, for by now the animal was positive that his life depended upon his immediate departure for somewhere else.

His rider slipped from him, leading him with much persuasion to the oak bush, where he tied him securely. The morning was warm. Milstead slipped off his coat, tying it to the saddle. Then he began to look about cau- tiously.

He whistled for Daisy. Then, for the first time, he noticed the dog stand- ing. Could it be a covey of quail? Could it be a woodcock, migrated early? It might be a snake. That it was, Milstead grew more certain as he watched how fidgety the dog was, and with what a curious gleam in her eyes she stared at the bushes ahead of her. Once she looked back; and there was that in her beautiful eyes that told Milstead to beware.

Down the ridge of sand he went, peering ahead under the sparse growth of huckleberry bushes. Suddenly a curious odor assailed him. He knew it must be an animal, but it seemed vegetable. It was like cucumber; yet its pungency was like that of bear scent. Milstead knew what it was. If he had been flamboyant in his way of thinking, he would have called it the odor of Sudden Death.

"I see it now," he said to himself. "It's about the kind that Vincente wants, too. It's rather larger than any I've ever picked up. It certainly is no plaything." Under the bronzing huckleberry bushes lay the great serpent— a regal reptile. He had lately shed his skin, and in his tawny gold phase he looked almost gaudy. Black and yellow and brown he gleamed on the white sand, lying there indolently in a huge S-shape. Milstead caught the glint from his cold unlidded eyes.

But, after all, a man is a man, and a snake is of a creation infinitely and remotely inferior. Against a sensible man, even the hugest diamondback, lacking the tremendous advantage of surprise, is helpless.

Milstead strode forward softly, his forked stick held before him. The snake saw the weapon coming; he seemed to bulge. Thrillingly his rattles began to sing their arid warning. Preliminary to taking his coil, the serpent foreshortened himself. His bulk seemed amazing.

Milstead could not help marking the thin, contemptuous lips of his antagonist; his baleful spade-head; his massive jaws, powerfully articulated. The Seminoles used to call him "The Great King," and this specimen justified that proud appellation.

The man had a curious feeling that he was intruding; though perhaps that is a somewhat natural emotion that any man may experience upon encountering a deadly serpent in the wilds. Really, Milstead thought, this was the diamondback's home, this lush savanna, this dreamy, stealthy place; the dim shores of this lonely lagoon—they were the serpent's by right of eminent domain.

"I'll have to get Daisy out of the way first," he said to himself. "This is strictly my little affair. She's found him, but she can't help me further."

Jerking a chain from his pocket, he walked around cautiously, fastened the snap to a ring in the setter's collar, and then led her to a safe distance, where he tied her to a stout bush. Daisy whined uneasily. Returning, he found that the great serpent had not moved. Milstead extended his forked stick, parting the bushes. A man must be sure that he's dealing with only one snake. These beauties often come in pairs.

Now the forked stick was close to the snake's massive head. There was a chance that the reptile would strike at it. Milstead did not want to infuriate it more than was necessary, though capture would assuredly madden it. With a deft maneuver, avoiding the spade-shaped head, he thrust the fork down strongly behind the massive jaws. The pointed ends of the stick were buried in the sand. The diamondback was securely caught.

As Milstead expected, the body of the snake writhed weirdly out of the bushes, his rattles whirring wildly. The powerful muscular body, contorted into fearsome coils of frantic maneuvers, turned and twisted above the coppercolored huckleberry leaves. Keeping the fork tightly thrust downward, the man approached. He had done this thing before. But something now told him to beware. Several times in his life he had had what appeared to be premonitions. He certainly felt one now. But there was Vincente, and his fifty dollars.

Stooping now, with his stick held tighter than ever, Milstead thrust his left hand down under the bushes. It touched the snake's back. It slipped down that gorgeous broad hide until the fingers were just behind the forked stick. Then they closed like a vise about the snake's throat. Milstead had the thing by the neck. He released the stick, and tossed it aside into the savanna. Then he tried to rise from his stooped position.

The effort caused him to stagger. He found himself suddenly struggling with main power to hold his grip on the diamond-back's neck; and he staggered when he lifted that massive writhing weight. But he steadied himself. He was apparent master of the situation after all. Then he took a step toward his horse.

The red pony had witnessed the whole singular performance; and there was no denying that he understood the entire affair—everything save what he believed his master's arrant folly. He now stood quite ready and also quite determined to make a bolt. This Milstead evidently did not perceive—or was too busy with another matter to take much account of.

The body of the diamondback writhed upward. Almost before his captor realized what was happening, the snake had coiled its immense body about his left arm; and partly because of pain, partly, certainly, because of anger, and wholly because it was struggling for its freedom, the reptile began to constrict the man's arm. At first Milstead, his eye now on the pony, was not exactly aware of what was really happening. Other serpents had done precisely the same thing before.

He was walking slowly toward his horse, talking to it to make it calm. He glanced down at his left hand, extended now away from him, and to his horror he saw that the rattler's head was moving; it seemed to have some purchase that the man could not control. At the same time, Milstead felt a certain dim but positive numbing of his left arm.

The diamondback was tightening his coil about the man's bare arm; that grip was deadening. It meant that the man's grasp of the snake's neck would inevitably weaken. It was loosening now. Milstead knew it. The great serpent appeared to know it, for he continued slowly but remorselessly to tighten his deadly coil. He was like a wrestler who gets a purchase on his antagonist.

Unless he could do something quickly, the sure thing to happen would be that the snake, freeing his head, would strike the man. Already that grim head was moving in the man's grasp. Milstead dared not reach round with his right hand; for, not knowing just what liberty the reptile had, he did not know whether he might not launch himself forward for an inch or two, sufficiently far for a fatal strike.

He thought of stooping down and laying the snake's head on the sand, and trying to crush it with his heel. But such a maneuver, with a serpent of this size and strength, would likely mean bungling—the rattler's pulling loose, and striking surely and with deadly effect.

Then there was the chance that the man might hold his grip until he could ride to the plantation for help. It would take only a matter of a few minutes. That seemed the best way out—if he could hold on. But that was the question. Milstead had encountered something too formidable for him. He felt himself outmaneuvered and, physically, almost overpowered; and, spiritually, sickened.

Few people realize the sheer animal strength of a serpent of this size. Milstead began to realize it. He would have to get help. The thing seemed to have him.

But he had forgotten for the moment that the horse was fully aware of the nature of the thing the man was carrying. As his master approached, the red pony backed away, snorting, straining at the buck hide thong that tied him. Even the stubborn live oak was bent almost over with the frantic pulling of the tethered mount. While Milstead was still five yards away, he saw that he would never ride home on that horse with that snake. There are some things that simply cannot be done. The man doubted if he could get up to the red pony, much less mount it and ride away. Clearly the horse considered that to approach was his master's intent; and with equal clearness he considered that such an intent was an imposition.

Milstead paused, talking to the pony the while. Well a horse knows the tone of fear; and it fills him with apprehension. There was the red pony, his head and neck extended, the thong that tied him taut as a bowstring. There was his would-be rider, a horrible thing in his hand, his arm banded by the cold coils of a chimera—a tortured man, trying to speak words of assurance.

There was the diamondback, momentarily insinuating himself out of the man's nerve-wrung grasp.

There seemed no help near for Milstead. He thought of the oily Vincente Blasco, and he cursed him in his heart.

Milstead looked about him for a moment, trying to locate a weapon of some sort. The long, sandy ridge spanning the pale green savanna offered nothing. The beauty of the bright woodland mocked the man. Flocks of blue-birds were warbling like aerial rivulets. The sunshine made the lovely savanna twinkle with myriads of lustrous lights. There was a fragrant, meadowy scent of dew and lush foliage and rare flowers awaft in the air.

But all this was irony. Here was a man fighting for his life.

There was a half-hitch tying the red pony to the oak bush. The same kind of tie fastened the thong to the bridle. Milstead felt a sudden overpowering need for that tough, pliable piece of buckskin. But whether he could get it, was the question. Undoubtedly the pony was about to break away. Whether the thong would break, or whether it would pull off at one end or the other, who could tell? The man had to have a part of that thong. He stepped forward toward the horse.

Of course the red pony now knew that his master was demented. He reared, plunged. Milstead walked toward him, but now he held his fettered left arm behind him, away from him. It drooped with exhaustion and with the dead weight of the diamond-back. He was almost to the horse now. The red pony blew out his breath in a long, amazed snort. He pawed bickeringly. His eyes were bulging large, and showed much white. His ears were shot straight forward at an angle that expressed both acute astonishment and vivid alertness.

Milstead reached his right hand forward to get it on the dangling loose tip of the half-hitch. The horse tried to bolt. The thong held. The horse curveted until he almost ran around Milstead. He bucked violently. He tore loose.

The red pony was free; and he appeared to appreciate marvelously his freedom. He flashed through the edge of the savanna, snorting loudly; he dashed away frantically, yet unwilling to lose any sight of what might be happening. With stirrups flying and clanking, he galloped off, looking back first from one side, then from the other, his head wildly high, his mane and tail streaming. A ship is by no means the only thing that sets its sails when it lifts anchor.

Milstead's horse was gone; the buck hide thong was gone; his best chance for safety was gone. But there was Daisy. Milstead, almost in despair, turned toward the setter. She might help him. Burdened by the ghastly chimera that was suffocating his strength, he staggered toward the faithful setter. She must have understood it all. How little, indeed, of all we do, and of all our difficulties, does a dog not understand?

With a spasm of renewed hope, Milstead tried to grip the serpent's neck more tightly. He came almost to where Daisy waited. He sank to one knee, extending toward his comrade his prisoned arm almost powerless in the convoluted strictures of its dread shackles.

"For God's sake, Daisy, help me, but don't let him get you," he said.

Daisy had all the delicacy of breeding of an English setter, and she knew the nature of this monster. But her loved master was in danger. What will not a dog attack for the sake of a human being beloved? If Daisy had cringed, Milstead would have been lost.

Suddenly she sank her teeth in the rattler's great bulging back. Instantly he relaxed his hold, writhing wildly. Milstead, feeling his arm more free, tightened his grip as the serpent released his. Meanwhile Daisy held on grimly. Her master reached down and untied her. Together, then, they bore the monster to the waiting sack.

"Turn him loose him now," he said. And Daisy did.

Into the burlap bag Milstead dropped his dread burden. Then he tied the mouth of the sack shut and dragged it into the sultry shadow of a little oak. For a time Milstead sat on the ground, exhausted. Daisy lay with her head in his lap.

The man regained his feet, breathing heavily, looking down on the hidden chimera that but a moment before had literally had him in its grasp. In the high pines near the lagoon, pines that now murmured and waved in an ecstasy of morning gladness, parula warblers chanted their elfin melodies. The sun gleamed and glinted across the savanna as if nothing had happened.

Milstead thought bitterly that the same melodies would have been lyrically chanted, the same sunlight lustrally gleamed, had the great reptile made an end of him. He had long since learned what every true woodsman knows: that under the beauteous garb of nature beats a heart that is relentless; for to him who sees aright, the countenance of nature has always about it something not quite intimate, not quite safe.

On the borders of the lagoon he caught the red pony. Retracing his steps to the place where the rattler lay, he carried his burden rather gingerly out toward the road, where he laid it in a heavy bed of gallberry bushes. To ride back to the plantation, returning with a wagon and a box for the captive, were matters of only a half hour. And in an hour Milstead had the huge diamondback free of the sack and safely in a commodious box with a wire front. But he built a little extension and put a second wire front protecting the first—or protecting those who were curious enough to investigate. The whole dread arrangement he put in an empty feed house, awaiting the coming of Vincente Blasco.

In a few days' time the familiar spluttering of the Italian's motor-boat engine was heard on the river; and, true to his promise, he delivered at Milstead's wharf six gallons of gasoline. He found Milstead somewhat grim and silent.

"How 'bout da beeg snake?" he asked. "You cannot catch so easy, I know. Maybe next week, next month?"

"You can get him today," Milstead replied in a most disinterested fashion.

"You got heem? Live? Beeg one?"

"Big enough," the other admitted. Vincente drew out his wallet. "I have feefty for you," he said, peeling off the tens from an astonishing assortment.

"Now, Vincente," Milstead said, "this thing you are getting is a dangerous thing, you understand?"

"I want him dang'rous," the little Italian answered.

"But no monkeying with him will do," the other warned. "You must keep people away from him, and you must stay away yourself."

"He not much to handle," Vincente said easily. "You catch heem, is it not?"

"Yes, I caught him."

"Easy?"

"Oh, yes," Milstead responded dryly. "I just lassoed him and dropped him in a sack."

Vincente, always a bit of an actor, suddenly made the deft motions of throwing a lariat, then of lifting with it something heavy that he had caught. "Like dat?" he queried, his white teeth flashing.

"Well, yes," Milstead admitted, grudgingly, "but with a good deal less effort."

"I will get heem now," the Italian said. "You ought to go into business," he advised, his sharp eyes gleaming. "Easy money."

"Thanks."

"You could catcha many beeg snake."

"I rather think, Vincente," Milstead answered, with a certain depth of meaning that the other could not fully appreciate, "that perhaps there are some things in this world not meant to be caught."

"Dat nice leetle dog," said Vincente, eying Daisy. "You sell heem?"

"Not for a million dollars," said Milstead, "and your moonshine business to boot."

Then Gabriel Blew His Horn

Gabriel of this story typifies the "huntermen" who loom so large in Rutledge's writings. Indeed, this is but one of many appearances the giant black trapper makes in Old Flintlock's tales. Second only to Prince Alston, Rutledge's "companion to my heart," Gabriel was a staunch sporting ally and, when it came to the ways of wild creatures, a man whose knowledge matched his stature. Gabe's constant companion was a nondescript hound, Lucy, a true dog of all trades. Lucy could tree a raccoon, 'possum, or squirrel; scatter turkeys so that her master could employ the highly effective tactic of calling them within shooting range as the flock attempted to reassemble; bay an otter; or give concrete meaning to the phrase "bring home the bacon," through cornering feral hogs.

Here the erstwhile companions, man and dog, deal with a majestic deer and one of the chimeras that Rutledge so loved to describe, a giant alligator. The unfolding drama is a chilling one, and in this case believable, for all the creatures described were found in the Santee paradise Rutledge called his "Home by the River." The piece does not even involve a bird dog, just a battered but beloved hound. Yet no close companion of canines can fail to be moved by its unfolding events. "Then Gabriel Blew His Horn" first appeared in the May 1929 issue of *Boys' Life* and then in *Bolio and Other Dogs*. More than two decades later, in June 1951, it was reprinted in *Progressive Farmer*.

———————

Gabriel, the giant Negro trapper of the Santee delta, had two possessions of which he was fond: one was the beautiful hunting horn that John Toland, of Philadelphia, had given him many years before when Gabriel had helped the visiting sportsman stalk the fourteen-point buck on Indian Hill, that wild and desolate track just below Navarino. So delighted had Toland been that he had asked his dusky guide what he would like best in all the world; and Gabe, who had for days been casting languishing glances at the polished horn that hung over the white man's shoulder, had indicated, with the huge shyness of a modest man, that the horn looked to him like a million dollars. Forthwith he was presented with it, and it became his most cherished possession. Associated in his affections with this ornament was his hound Lucy—a strange, beautiful, savage creature of aristocratic antecedents. Graceful was she, refined, with eyes of occult gleamings and ears that swept the grass when she trailed. Suspicious, at times ferocious, avoiding all men save her black master, Lucy was used by Gabe for a diverting variety of pursuits: to follow the wary ambling raccoons that paced by moonlight down the glimmering wood paths and through the silvery marshes, to take the trail of a flock of wild turkeys, to run violently into the birds, scattering them for Gabe, who then, with Lucy crouching breathlessly behind him, would call up one of the splendid birds to his doom.

Especially in the fall of the year, when the unmarked razorbacks of the pinelands roamed far to hunt acorns, Lucy was a godsend to Gabriel. For a good many seasons, because of the prowess of his dog as a follower, a finder, and a holder of someone else's swine, her master had never lacked for Christmas hams and bacon.

On several occasions, in the dreary morasses of the delta, Lucy had brought to bay the finest of all furred creatures of that region—the shy otter; and because of the skill of his hound Gabe was almost the only hunter in that great stretch of country who had, in one season, captured as many as five otters.

Lucy would take any trail that Gabe told her to take; and from any trail, however fragrant and alluring, she would immediately desist at the word of her master. A more complete companionship between dog and man could not exist; indeed, this one was almost unique, for to it Gabe brought that strange wise intimacy that he had with all animals—that peculiar fellowship and understanding that he shared with the creatures of the wild. This comprehension, turned to his account, was what made him the best trapper, hunter, and general poaching rounder-up of game in all that country.

In Montgomery Creek, near the ancient river-landing of Peachtree Plantation, Gabe kept his little cypress canoe tied up. With Lucy balanced nicely amidship, and with his battered gun laid along the thwarts, it was an easy thing for him to paddle over the broad yellow Santee, enter one of the great canals of the delta, and forthwith be in a wild-life paradise. Seldom, indeed, when Gabe recrossed was his canoe not heavily burdened with the spoils of the hunt: with a deer, a turkey, wild ducks, raccoons, otter. Of mere trash like rabbits, snipe, and woodcock, he never took any account. He could not afford to buy many shells, and he liked every one to count for something.

On that balmy day in late January there was nothing except the summery nature of the weather to suggest to Gabe that this particular day might have in store for him something unusual. Lucy sat eagerly in the little craft, now and then shivering with a little thrill of anticipation. There was nothing in that serene sunshine, that broad and placid river, the roseate mist that lingered on the far shores, to suggest that the day was to be a fateful one. Gabriel, his broad-bladed red cedar paddle sweeping the water deeply and noiselessly, drove his little canoe southeastward toward the mouth of Six-Mile Creek. He knew, for the week before he had seen their tracks sprawled awkwardly in the mud there, that a fine flock of wild turkeys was ranging the marshes of Navarino and the long wooded ridge behind them. And, save for Gabe, they would be undisturbed. Moreover, since their food supply was plentiful, their range would be restricted. No wild turkey is going to wander far from quiet and plenty of choice food, such as that lonely region of the great delta affords.

Rolling out of the immense swamp-country to northward, the mighty river, down in Gabe's territory, is an affluent and splendid stream, taking on some of the mystery and majesty of any great river as it nears the ocean. Often, on still nights, from his cabin on Peachtree, Gabe could hear the soft tumult of the surf on the beaches of Cedar Island and Murphy's Island. And always, as he paddled down the great stream, he was cautiously aware of that vast terminal ahead, the tides from which made themselves felt more than ten miles inland.

As Gabe turned his canoe into Six-Mile Creek, he flushed a flock of a hundred mallards. Northward they streamed over the delta, settling at last in a pond well known to the Negro hunter, who cautiously took note of their address. Other ducks thronged overhead—the first flights from the distant North having arrived for the great migration a few weeks later. Gabe saw rosy-breasted mourning doves wooing each other on the low sunny cypress limbs overhanging the warm waters. It was more like a day for fishing than for hunting. Onward the trapper paddled up the tortuous reaches of the lonely waterway, at almost every bend jumping ducks. Twice he saw minks, but the shy creatures dived before he could bring up his gun. It was a day for seeing game. Surely it would be a record day, thought Gabe.

Coming at last to a long field of wampee and low marsh in which he knew the footing to be fairly dry, Gabe ran the bow of his canoe into the soft bank, staked his paddle, tied the boat's rope to it, and he and Lucy went ashore. Hardly had he cleared the bank when, to his amazement, just out of gunshot, he saw a big-bodied deer standing in the short marsh, its head high, turned in his direction. It was evidently a buck, but it had dropped its horns; Gabe could tell from the stranger's butt-head that he must have just lately lost his antlers.

The Negro crouched, stole forward rapidly, trying to get to leeward; and behind him, apparently understanding the nature of the situation, Lucy slunk swiftly, her ears trailing the ground, her great eyes lighting with the excitement of the chase. After he had gone twenty yards, Gabe essayed to ease himself up to take a look. What he saw made him stand straight up: far across the wide marsh field a tall white flag was waving derisively. The buck was in a full run for the distant swamp. "We'll try him some other day," Gabe muttered, as he and Lucy turned off toward an old tree-grown bank that spanned a section of the delta. It was evidently down this bank that the buck had come, for here were his tracks—blunt toed and sprawling, showing his age and his weight. As Gabe was stooping under a little arch of tall wild blackberry canes, something gleaming on the ground caught his eye. It was a stag's freshly dropped horn. The Negro picked it up, softly whistling to himself. Even in his vast gnarled hand it looked huge. The beaded beam-base was not less than six inches in circumference. Tall were the six tines that sprang along the length of their massive support. About halfway up the beam, the horn structure flattened, so that the great antler was symmetrically palmated. A superb woodland trophy it was-and Gabe felt sure that he had, a few moments before, looked upon its former owner.

"'Bout September," he muttered, as he tied the single horn to his belt, "he will done have ordered a large size, and then Lucy and I will visit him."

The hound Lucy was at her best on this day. Gabe thought he had never seen her so keen, intelligent and obedient. A dozen times he whistled her off trails that he did not want to follow, and she gave them up with eager cheerfulness. Far down the bank, near the Three Sisters—three lonely pines standing up strangely out of the wide sea of the delta marsh—Lucy came upon a track that took Gabe's fancy. It was that of a big otter. Lucy's delighted excitement over her find showed how fresh the trail was. To make her take it, to follow her closely until she brought the maker to bay in some obscure ditch head or in some shallow pond, was the kind of thing that Gabe had done before. The fur of the otter would be prime. The pelt would be the finest prize that could be had on the whole delta. Gabe hesitated only long enough to look over the strange wild country surrounding him in order to get his bearings. Then he gave the hound her head; and, grasping his gun tightly, and pulling down his battered cap, he took out after Lucy as fast as he could run with caution.

Lucy knew well enough the difference between a deer and an otter: she knew that with the former she must merely hold the trail until she forced the skulking game out to her master; with the latter, speed was the thing. She must corner and bay the otter before he could get to deep water. And, though an otter can travel with really amazing strength and swiftness over land, water is its natural element.

Over the quaking beds of wampee and faded lotus Lucy flew, water flashing up behind her. She crashed through the dry marsh, plunged deftly through beds of bulrushes, leaped sluggish old ditches choked with water weeds, scuttered over gleaming stretches of oily-colored water. It was a hot race, and she was gaining on the lithe otter that, well aware of his peril, was racing for his life toward Sand Lake.

As well as he could, Gabe followed fast; and while he could not keep up with the swift Lucy, no other man could have done what he did. The league-long quagmire, he negotiated as if he knew the nature of the footing of every inch of the terrain. A man long used to the delta and its ways, his feet were in no uncertain degree sentient, so that he instantly knew from a touch just how to step on a certain tussock, or a matted patch of wampee pads, or a stretch of tall marsh marking an ancient ditch, now choked with aquatic growths, but still capable of plunging a man to the thighs if he did not know his business.

Beside a young cypress on a rotted bank Gabe paused for a moment to make certain of the line of the otter's flight. As soon as he heard Lucy, he quickly nodded.

"Sand Lake," he muttered, running forward again; "and this end is so shallow, she might bay him in it."

Gabe's tone was not so positive as it might have been: he knew that for Lucy to round up an otter in the shallow end of Sand Lake, among the cypress-knees and bulrush hummocks was no easy task. But he had faith in his dog, and as he ran he listened for that eager change in her tone that would tell him that she had brought the wily fugitive to a stand. Suddenly, however, an unexpected sound brought him to a halt. Halting, he listened to it almost incredulously; for it was a sound seldom heard on the delta in January. Yet the balmy day accounted for it. It was the bull-mouthed, subterranean, Pleistocene roar of a great bull alligator. Over the wilderness of the vast delta country came the dragon challenge—weird, terrible. As suddenly as it had begun, it ceased; and the silence that followed it was deeply impressive.

"He is in Sand Lake too," said Gabe to himself, apprehension in his eye now, and in his voice; "I better call Lucy off that otter. 'Gator love a houn'," he muttered, as he put his gleaming horn to his lips.

The dreaming delta had listened to the joyous yelping of Lucy, had heard Gabe sloshing along after her, had thrilled to hear the grand and ominous bellowing of the bull alligator in the misty dim confines of Sand Lake. Now it listened to a shouting silence. For the mellow peals of Gabe's horn, there came in answer only that strange sibilant stillness that one hears when silence falls over a marsh country. Gabe blew only twice. It usually was necessary to sound his horn but once. Lucy would hear him, he knew; and if she heard him she would come—if she could. But her voice was still; and the bull's roarings had ceased; and the rich horn music was muted. Far back in the gray swamp that moldered beside the ancient river, an old owl, stirred from his noontide sleep by the noises from the delta, roused himself to give a melancholy derisive whoop, drowsy and cynical. Then silence brooded once more, immense and solitary.

Gabe knew that the otter had escaped; and he likewise knew that Lucy was either cornering obediently back toward him, or else had encountered the dragon of Sand Lake. Knowing that she would return to him on her own track, he went forward on hers, whistling now and then, calling, but losing heart every minute. What had happened at Sand Lake, Gabe was too late to see; but the signs that he found there told him all. As he emerged from the fringe of tall marsh and surveyed the lonely shores and the dreadful placid waters of that strange lagoon, he felt the horror of the beautiful hateful place. Here were the sprawled tracks of the otter; his belly and his tail had dragged in the soft mud. Here were Lucy's tracks. Then Gabe came upon a place where the shallow water was muddy, and in it were murky red tinges.

He saw where the otter had turned and scuttled off down a deep arm of the lagoon. There were hound tracks entering the water, but there were none coming out that he saw. Of that point, Gabe made absolutely certain. It took him a full and toilsome half hour to make the circuit of the mysterious lake. Deer tracks he found, and those of a roaming black bear; tracks of mink, otter, great blue heron; and wary king-rails. But there were no alligator tracks, and there were none of Lucy save those that entered on the south side. Gabriel, when he had come back to his starting point, sat heavily down on an old cypress log to grieve—to grieve and to vow vengeance on the old saurian that, somewhere beneath those calm and terrible waters, had mercilessly murdered the best friend and the only companion he had.

Even the cherished horn meant less now, for it would call Lucy no more. The calm sunlight of the late-winter day, the aromatic air, the tranquility of this remote sanctuary of the almost inviolate delta—all these were a mockery to Gabriel, who sat looking across the Lethe-like waters of Sand Lake. It was a touching tribute to Lucy to have a man like Gabe mourn for her.

A weary mile the trapper toiled back to his canoe that he had left tied in Six-Mile Creek. Slowly he paddled homeward, hardly noticing the wild life that he startled from creek-edge and from those misty water arms that retired among the marshes. But for the fact that his arm brushed it, he would have forgotten about the huge antler stuck in his belt. This he now laid in the boat just where Lucy had been wont to crouch. The antler afforded him a little comfort for the present and hope for the future.

But it was a desolate cabin to which Gabe returned; and the welcome of his wife did not change his fixed trouble. He could, he knew, get another puppy somewhere and raise it; but where would he find another Lucy? Meanwhile, he thought, back on the melancholy wasteland of the delta, the grim bullalligator, an abominable creature that was nothing but a submarine brigand and a marauder of the most murderous and heartless type, still dominated with his cold-hearted and sinister might the entire region of Sand Lake. One such bull, Gabe knew, haunting such a place, would take fearful toll of all creatures coming there to drink: of the deer, the wild hogs, the water birds, and even the beautiful otter that Gabe considered the prize game of his whole country.

The old adage, "While there is life, there is hope," Gabriel translated into his philosophy, when it ran something like, "While there's a chance for revenge, life's worth living."

On a rack of deer-antlers in his dim little cabin, Gabriel hung his polished horn, feeling for the moment that, having used it so long to call Lucy, he might never care to use it again. On the broad yellow-pine mantel over the fireplace he laid the huge antler that he had picked up on the wild bank. To Gabe, it was like an invitation to some high social affair, and he put it where he would be reminded not to forget to accept in due season the genial summons.

Yet spring came on apace; there were crops to plant; the fecund Santee country blossomed forth once more in its semitropical luxuriance. It was no time for hunting. Then followed the heat of the summer, with the almost daily thunderstorms. Gabe was busy with keeping down the ambitious crabgrass. His canoe lay idle in the mouth of Montgomery Creek. One day a log floated by, and, catching against it, tipped it so that it filled and sank. A week or so later, Gabe discovered it thus submerged, and he pulled it up on shore. The water leaked out, but a bucket full of sandy mud remained in the stern.

In this warm wet soil some gay aquatic plants soon sprouted; and in a short time thereafter Gabe's canoe resembled a flower bed. It was likewise a good index to his indifference to his craft and all appertaining thereto.

But autumn came, as it has a way of doing; and though by the first of October there was no frost, there were golden tinges here and there in the forests; migrants were arriving from the North; the crops looked ripe. Many trees showed in their foliage a fading spark of life, which slowly gleamed with a definite uncertainty. But what really made Gabe sure that fall had come was a clean-rubbed buck that he saw in the pinelands. He just happened to walk him up in the tall broom sedge, and the deer rocked away lithely. The Negro marked his shining horns, and he knew that on the delta there awaited him a stag of truly lordly proportions. Gabe, thinking of the dropped antler and having a quaint way of putting his thoughts, muttered to himself: "Dat genman on the delta will done order a larger size hat this season. Dis buck was wearing a cap, but my frien' by Sand Lake wears a high hat. I must call on him."

So it was that the next day Gabriel, at the full of the tide, in the pearly brightness of an early October morning, gun in hand, sauntered down to the landing where his canoe had been raising a fine crop of wampee and lotus. The plants had withered somewhat, but they were still decorative. Gabe grinned at them. But he was about to pull them all out, together with the mud to which they clung, when he shrewdly guessed that the mud was sealing a few rather generous cracks. He therefore launched the craft as it was, seated himself in such a way as to take care of the sickening list of the thing, and forthwith headed across the dreamy tide. All things looked bright and fair; but he felt his loneliness. The place in the canoe where Lucy used to sit was vacant. And even Gabe felt the difference between a merely empty place and a vacant one. He held his good old gun, however; and at the last minute he had decided to wear his hunting horn. It hung gleaming now from his shoulder.

Instead of heading for Six-Mile Creek this time, Gabriel held his canoe almost dead across the river, making for Fairfield Island. It did not take long with his smooth and powerful paddling, to bring the canoe safely into an old canal. There Gabe tied it, and then climbed slowly to the crest of the ruinous bank. Before him lay the immense wasteland of the delta—a vast shimmering country, beautiful but not forbidding. League after league rolled the yellow marshes; tall lotus-plants waved their sunflower heads; dusky clouds of blackbirds swarmed over the dripping beds of calamus and wampee.

But the trapper was not so much taking in the scenery as he was planning a little campaign. Far to the southeast his keen eyes scanned the dim gray wall of trees that marked the boundaries of Sand Lake; northward from that point was the dark Pine Ridge, in the fastness of whose shades many a deer was wont to lurk. But often the deer of the delta lay out on the old banks that sagged a melancholy way through the huge morasses of the marsh-lands. It was Gabe's game to cross the delta on the big bank of which he now stood, to range the Pine Ridge stealthily, and then to turn southward toward Sand Lake. Somewhere along this route he hoped to encounter either the grand old Navarino stag or else the bestial dragon that had destroyed Lucy. Thus in Gabe's mind there were two images: one very fair, of a superb buck with lordly antlers; the other repellent and abominable, of a monstrous murderer. And these two images well expressed the dual nature of the strange delta— one of them, beauty and grace and wild charm; the other occult, treacherous, gloomy, and disastrous.

Leaving his canoe tied in the canal about a half-mile from the river, the black hunter started down the long broken bank for the Pine Ridge. He felt not only solitary but abandoned; yet he had his trusty gun, and he had his beautiful silent horn.

Brightly gleamed the wide landscape; quietly slept the water in the old ditches and ponds; sweetly breathed the air over that solitary waste. The marshes kept their soft vigil of silence. In the fifteen square miles of delta country stretching away into mysterious distance Gabriel was the only human being. Indeed, Negroes seldom cared to visit the delta. Indian graves had been found there, where once the Santees and the Seminoles had roamed; and so weird were many of the wildlife calls and screams heard from that disastrous land that it was natural to believe it to be a natural abode of hants and nameless hobgoblins. Besides, had not Amos Boykin, one of the best Negro woodsmen of that whole region, mysteriously vanished on a trip to the delta? Of course there were those who hinted that his disappearance was accountable, for he had long sailed on a stormy domestic sea, and beyond the delta lay a new freedom, and possibly a new wife. But Amos was never heard from again. Gabe knew the delta too well to put much faith in the weird stories told of it; but he knew that it has natural perils in its treacherous quagmires, its venomous serpents, its mazy by paths.

Yet he was so deft of foot that he made the dangerous passage of the old bank without mishap; and an hour after he left his canoe, he was on the airy and fragrant Pine Ridge. Perhaps there are not many lonelier and lovelier places in America than that solitary stretch of virgin woodland, elevated from the delta by a strange low wane of the terrain. Here are giant yellow pines more than a century old, their isolation making them immune from the lumberman. Here tower great man-bodied hollies, sixty feet high. Here in sunny solitude patriarch live oaks spread their colossal arms.

Gabe began to be careful when he came near the live oaks, for in the autumn of a good acorn year, there is hardly a better place to search for a buck than beneath live oaks, of the sweet black acorns of which deer are inordinately fond.

Yet the black hunter, though he came upon deer tracks, saw nothing promising until he came clear of the deep shade of the oaks. There he found fresh tracks that he could almost identify as those of the stag he had seen on that far-off day when Lucy had been with him.

Moreover, the tracks were so fresh that some of the fragments of up-turned soil clinging to their rims were still damp. Following the trail like an Indian, Gabe fully expected to find it turning northward, for most deer of the delta bedded down for the day in the cane patches and the marshy hammocks that fringed the shadowy flanks of the Pine Ridge. To his surprise Gabe found the tracks turning southward. The stag was heading for the great open marshes of the Sand Lake country.

Nor was it unusual for a mastermind of the wild to keep his own counsel and to do something original like this. This was no common deer, but some splendid solitary, worth all the effort that even a veteran huntsman could bestow upon him. Gabe felt that things had broken in his favor when the buck had wandered off into comparatively open country. He might be able to follow his track and rouse him out of his bed; or if this crowned monarch had not deigned to lie down, he might stalk him. In any case the business was going to be exacting on the hunter. With a pang Gabe remembered Lucy. If he only had her now, he would stay right where he was; then, putting her on the track, he would count on her bringing the great buck to him. His loss was still bitter.

Gabriel, who did his hunting deliberately, now prepared to load his gun. His weapon was a crude single-barreled affair, but in this woodsman's hands it was deadly. When he left home he had slipped in his coat pocket three buckshot shells. But now as he felt about in the selfsame pocket, all he could discover was one shell. He also found a hole in one corner, just big enough for a shell to drop through. Somewhere along that old hummock spanning the delta, these shells had slipped from him. He had only one—and the chance of a lifetime perhaps waiting him in the wild field before him.

Gabe fondled the shell before he slipped it into the barrel.

"You got to do it all," he said. "Don't you fail me."

Then, taking a hitch in his belt, settling his cap down tightly over his eyes, and making those inward resolves that a sportsman does when a critical moment is ahead, the dusky hunter took up the trail of the great Navarino stag.

For the ordinary man such a quest would have been quite hopeless; but for Gabriel it was like finding an old friend in his own home. The Negro knew every bulrush bed, every smothered ditch, every patch of yellowing marsh in the wild country ahead. Moreover, he knew exactly where he would be likely to come on the stag. He had an instinct for locating game. A true hunter is one who can think after the thought of a wild creature.

Past Raccoon Bay went the stag and Gabe; past Bear Wallow; southwest toward Jackfield; then dead east for Sand Lake. As yet the tracker had had no sight of the deer; but he was not disturbed; such a stag moves deliberately; with many pauses and much shadowy skulking. If the trailer keeps the wind from the deer to him, if he can hold the track, and if the deer is without suspicion, the hunter will come on his game at last.

As Gabe neared Sand Lake, he was troubled by memories; but the great creature he was following he now knew to be so near that ancient pangs gave way to present thrills. Within two hundred yards of the solitary lagoon he thought he heard a splash in the water. Then unmistakably came the sound of a leap in the shallow water. Could the big buck have made him out? Another sound came: it was like a smothered groan. It might have come from a rooting razorback, or from an old marsh-raccoon, which often emits strange noises. Gabe crept forward. He reached the tall marsh fringing the lake. He insinuated himself craftily through it, making no more sound than a swamp rabbit. He saw the dull gleam of the placid waters. He saw the melancholy shore-line down which he had followed Lucy's last tracks.

Then suddenly he saw the great stag, up to his knees in water, apparently drinking. And he was well within range of Gabe's gun. Never in his long experience as a hunter had Gabe seen such a superb stag. Rugged, masterful, with massive craggy antlers, he was the proud monarch of the vast and lonely delta. As Gabe slowly raised his gun for the shot of his life, he muttered: "Dis is the grandpa of the one Mr. Toland done shoot." But, though Gabe's finger was on the trigger, and though his gleaming black eye held the brass sight of his weapon straight on the stag's heart, something halted the whole dramatic proceeding. Gabe saw that which made him lower his gun slightly.

The buck was not drinking though he had his head down. The trapper noticed for the first time the painful list of that proud crest. He saw the fore-feet planted forward; he noted the muscular rigidity of the body. Something had the deer. At that moment the stag began to turn in the water, groaning deeply. At the same time he struck with his polished fore hoofs at something in the water. A complete half circle the buck made, so that now he faced the shore. He was trying to make the land. But the bull alligator of Sand Lake had him. The beast had caught him high up on the right leg, just where it joined the body. In a grim and terrible grip of death the old Minotaur had the imperial stag. The beautiful beleaguered thing labored one step nearer shore, dragging his bestial assailant. But the effort was too great, and the stag almost collapsed. By this time the whole head of the alligator was visible.

Downward from the deer's heart Gabe shifted his aim.

"I done 'member Lucy," he said softly to himself as, with the sight of his battered gun fairly on the gator's eye, he pressed the trigger.

What followed was a wild mêlée. The bull let go his hold convulsively, and in extreme agony began to turn in slow, blind, painful circles, reddening the water as he turned. The stag leaped for the shore and for safety, in a moment being lost in the whispering wastes of the huge marsh country. Such was his vitality that even such a wound as he had received he could sustain. Slowly down the margin of the lake walked Gabe until he came close to the place where the huge bull, plainly visible in the shallow water, had ceased to move. Gabe waded in, grasped the old monster by the tail, and dragged him ashore. Then he sat down on the same log on which, nearly a year before, he had grieved for Lucy. Kind hearted was Gabe, but he found this vengeance sweet. He felt triumphant. Reaching for his horn, he put it to his lips and sounded a far-calling and plangent note. And though he gulped slightly to think that there could be no response to his resounding summons, he felt sternly satisfied.

A slight stir in the marsh beside him made him turn. He sprang up as if a specter had set upon him. Something leaped up on him. He sat down on the log weeping, with Lucy in his arms—maimed, disheveled, hollow-eyed Lucy, but the dog he loved better than anything else in life.

"I know you would come," he said, while the hound snuggled to him as if she were trying to get in his very heart. "You would come to me out of he'ben or hell if I will jes' blow."

To have her back was enough for Gabe. How she had escaped the bull's first lunge; how she had swum to a hummock of marsh on the edge of Sand Lake, and, more dead than alive, had lain there hours; how, her strength returning, she had begun to get food for herself; how, all those months, she had haunted this dread region, in the hope that Gabe would return to her—these were matters that Gabe could never with certainty know. Some of them he, indeed, surmised. But the loved and lost had been restored: that was the joy that filled the black hunter's heart.

Had you seen them traversing that wild bank homeward, you would have marveled to see how Gabe carried Lucy most of the way. It was not that she could not travel very well herself, but only that otherwise Gabe could not make sure enough that she was really with him once again.

Part Two

THE MAGIC OF GROUSE

Rutledge did not grow up in grouse country, but much of his hunting life was spent in regions where the drummer of the woods was in residence. He often enjoyed sojourns in the high country of neighboring North Carolina, where his half brother, Fred, lived. Then, as now, partridges (as the mountain folks called grouse) were found in decent numbers in the vast expanses of the Nantahala and Pisgah national forests. Even more significant were his numerous grouse-hunting experiences during the three-plus decades he spent teaching in Pennsylvania. Those years embraced the prime of his manhood, and it was also a period during which he wrote wisely and well.

Here we have a selection of eight of his finest writings on grouse, along with our only sampling of Rutledge's poetry. Lovers of sporting literature often seem unaware that Rutledge was a prolific poet who wrote hundreds of poems and published dozens of book-length collections of them. Many dealt with outdoor subjects, and while poetry is singularly out of fashion in today's world of outdoor literature, it seemed appropriate to include at least one example of his efforts in this genre. Whether in poetry or in prose, Rutledge writes of the noble bird with a feeling and flair reminiscent of Burton Spiller or, among modern scribes, George Bird Evans.

The Partridge

Taken from the November 1920 issue of *Field & Stream,* this is one of a number of poems Rutledge wrote for this popular sporting magazine over the years. It might also be worth noting that another hallowed name in the annals of American sporting literature, Nash Buckingham, also dabbled in poetry, particularly early in his career. Poetry is out of fashion among today's sportsmen, and I'm not at all sure that is good. Sport is, after all, an ongoing romance with the natural world, and the literate, thinking hunter should appreciate how the essence of that love affair can be captured in poetry as well as in prose.

———

With him the woodland wonders come;

Their beauties in his flight depart;
Or like music fading sweet
They linger in the listening heart;
For all that wanders and is wild,
With faerie charms remote and dim,
Luring like rich autumnal lights,
Seems gathered to the soul of him.

By the lost wood he brings a soul;
A spirit to the glen he gives;
The silent and forsaken hill
To sudden rapture wakes and lives
As off he speeds upon those wings
That deftly thread the thicket's way;
Or does he merely cross the road?
The day becomes a magic day!
Of mountain-silence he's the tone,
The voice of hushed, seraphic places;
The meaning of loneliness

That glimmers forth the forest's graces;
The haunting scenes of mountains grand,
The radiant peace of wonder-woods,
The mystery and marvel old
Abiding in the solitudes.

The hill crest pines have runes of sleep;
The bawling brook has urgent speech;
The ocean's old unrest is loud
In ruling anthems of the beach.
But in this bird the wildwood sings
The only lyric to impart
A sense of all the silentness
And music of sweet nature's heart.

Grouse of the Little Hills

First published in *Field & Stream* in November 1929, this piece also appears in *An American Hunter.* While a teacher at Mercersburg Academy, a position he held for thirty-three years during the prime of his manhood, Rutledge constantly pined for his beloved home, Hampton Plantation, in the South Carolina lowcountry. Each Christmas vacation he and his family would return, pilgrims to the place of Rutledge's upbringing, and every visit renewed Old Flintlock's resolve to save his ancestral home for future generations. Meanwhile, except for these cherished holiday interludes, he relied on the sport provided by Pennsylvania to salve the burns of homesickness and in some degree sate his hunger for sport. Pennsylvania hunting ways were different, as was to some degree the game available. Yet he already had familiarity with grouse, and he loved the rolling hills and secluded valleys of the Appalachians that were their favored habitat. In this story, set in the "Little Hills," he brings his feel for place and his sheer delight in being afield into play in telling fashion.

This story is a personal favorite of mine, perhaps because there are multiple mentions of a place name, Needmore, which is also given to a remote rural section along the Little Tennessee River in my highland homelands of western North Carolina. Yet, commonality of geographical appeal aside, once you read it I think my reasoning will be clear.

———————

While, in the low country of the Carolinas, there is as fine deer hunting as is to be had anywhere in America, there are no ruffed grouse there; and I have always felt that the ruffed grouse is the wariest, the swiftest, and the most beautiful game bird in the world. The bronzed magnificence of old gobblers allures me; so does the gleam of sunlight on the tall and craggy antlers of the whitetail; yet a hunting season for me remains incomplete unless I can have a day or two with grouse. Most of my hunting of this grand bird has been in the mountains of Western North Carolina, of Virginia, and of

Pennsylvania. Usually, before taking such a hunt, I hobnob with the natives; for occasionally one will be found who knows his game birds and animals.

To hear Dave Mellott talk, you would think the ruffed grouse no real bird at all, but a phantom of the first water. I encountered Dave in the hardware store a few nights before the season opened. You know how the hunters and all the would-be hunters foregather to talk it over before the bombardment begins, and each one sends everybody else to the place where game has not been seen. "A gunnerman," says the old Negro proverb, "will always lie."

But Dave really seemed inclined to tell me where I might find some grouse. "I don't mind giving the thing away," he said, "because I can never hit a grouse. It seems that by the time I git my gun up, the blame birdie is out of sight. It don't ever 'low me no chanst."

"All you need, Dave," I said, "is to practice being a little quicker."

"I could git a whole heap quicker," he answered, "and yet never git my sight on one of them things. When I hunts, I hunts; I ain't out to compete with no lightnin'."

And yet Dave is a real hunter; he isn't the kind of sportsman who thinks a bullet is a little bull, and who discovers whether his gun is loaded by looking down the barrel while manipulating the triggers. But he just can't be bothered with grouse. "Ain't no sense in a bird flying so fast," he told me with some indignation. "Any shot that ever overtakes him will have its tongue hangin' out!"

"Tell me where you saw these grouse, Dave, if you aren't going after them."

"It's in Fulton County," he answered, referring to that strange wild country in southern Pennsylvania close to the Potomac River—a county in which there are thousands of acres of primeval land but in which there is no railroad, no jail, no poorhouse. "You go past Needmore, then on by Cuckoo, past the Meadow Ground, and Indian Spring, and that there place they call Bird-in-Hand. It's right there, though it's a lie. Leastways I ain't never got no bird in hand there. Them little hills right by that country store that sells more bootleg than groceries—that's the place. Them birds walk right across the road there by the store. But when they see me cumin', they don't give me no chanst. I reckon they know who I is," Dave ended, laughing; "but they wouldn't take no account of you."

As the great First Day approached and I made the momentous decision as to where I should go, I determined to take Dave Mellott's word and to try for the grouse of the little hills. I had a memorable day of it, and shall here record what appealed to me as its most interesting adventures.

The last night of October had hung mist-wreaths on all the trees; while mantles they were, that turned softly to pink and to gold as the still morning of the First Day brightened over the world. It was daybreak as I crossed the high ridge of the Tuscaroras and dipped into the fragrant, wild valley which hasn't changed very much since the days when Cornplanter, the Indian chief, found it his happy hunting ground right here in this world and this life.

Here and there, in the lonely vale, I could see tiny spires of smoke rising straight into the dewy morning air. Were the hardworking mountaineers rising betimes to go to labor, or were the little home stills right on the job? I hesitate to ask so unpatriotic a question; but I can testify that every cabin and farm house that I passed had about it a prevailing odor: it was that of apple-jack. In my car I had with me my old dog Starshine; but I never called her that. She was Star or Shine, according as my memory functioned on the first or second syllables of her name. She snuggled beside me on the front seat, her head flat on the window-sill, her eyes gleaming, her black nose twitching. I don't want to go so far as to say that she "made game" every time we passed a farmhouse; but she certainly took a deep interest in those auras of distillation.

Past Needmore we sped in our Detroit Demon. Even a hunter can afford a flivver nowadays. Into Cuckoo we sailed. Cuckoo was asleep, and stayed so. If ever Cuckoo rears a distinguished son, he may become backdoor-keeper at the Dead Letter Office. On we bounded, Bird-in-Hand bound. People have different ideas about the high moments of life. Perhaps mine are humbler than those of most people. But a drive early in the morning on the First Day, through a romantic, fragrant valley, seems to me about one of the keenest and most harmless pleasures that can come to a mortal.

I almost passed Bird-in-Hand, and would assuredly have done so but for the fact that here the valley closed in on the road; not high hills marching together, but strange little hills that had cantered away from their mother mountains and had stopped here ages ago, in a little, huddled group. These were the hills Dave Mellott had told me about. Here was the place in the road that the grouse used as their public playground. I was where I belonged.

Though the sun was now firing the dark fringes of pines that rimmed the hilltops, the inhabitants of Bird-in-Hand still snoozed. What's the use of waking if you can be sleeping, and if there's nothing to do if you get up? Parking my car in the city square, the same being a hitching yard with one post, I got Shine out, made sure that I had the shells I wanted, and started down the misty road toward the foot of the first little hill. I knew that my car would be safe there for a month or two, for that metropolis isn't exactly overrun with city slickers. A fact that never fails to give me high hope for the future of our land is that there remains so much utterly wild and charming country.

Some fifty yards from where I had parked my car, I came to a wild grapevine on the mossy fence bordering the way. It had dim clusters of fruit. Farther back there were discernible groups of sumac bushes, dully red. Studying the trees, I found them to be chiefly evergreens; but there were hickories as well, and oaks, and alders along the stream that babbled back in the shadows, and thickets of birch and chestnut-sprouts.

The place looked like grouse, and it smelled like grouse.

Hunters know what I mean. I know I am talking to men who know, not with men who think that a trailing vine is one that follows a scent for miles; that a running vine is one that gets up and goes if you come too near; and that it is a pleasant pastime for the true naturalist and sportsman to hunt for and to bring home the spots that the fawns have dropped.

There was light enough to shoot when Shine and I got fairly into the woods. The leaves were damp, so that we made little noise as we went up the aromatic little glade between two of the hills. We collected a rabbit en route—a poor thing to do early in the day. I thought I heard a grouse fly up ahead of us, but I could not be certain; nor did the dog give any evidence that she was aware of the presence of the prince of the woodland. Our glade ended in a wild shambles of grapevines, exhaling delicious odors. But the grouse were not there. I turned up a slope and climbed to the crest of the ridge.

I had barely time to get my breath and to locate myself when, from the hollow beyond, a grouse flew up and came toward me. I saw that he was going to pass over me. He was traveling fast and high, but he fell to the shot and Shine retrieved him unruffled—the noblest game bird of the whole world, I believe. He is the true aristocrat. Much as I love grouse hunting, I seldom kill one without misgivings. But my philosophy comes to my rescue just there and tells me that a kind of Providence established game birds and animals for our especial use; and we do not live truly like nature's own sons if we do not use all the bounties that she has so liberally and with matchless forethought provided for us. There is always something ludicrous about these people who thoroughly enjoy their lamb, their beef and their chicken, and then devote the energy thus acquired to damning the poor hunter because he kills a deer or a wild goose or a grouse.

The bird I had just shot was a cock, in his prime, with perfect plumage; his ruff was exceptionally heavy and black. I wondered what had made him get up, for my dog and I had been too far off to frighten him. Then I heard someone walking. Evidently another hunter was in the wooded gully below me. If so, might it not be a good plan for me to continue along the ridge, parallel to him? He might flush another grouse, and the bird might take the same course as the first one. Probably the man was a Dave Mellott kind of hunter to whom the flight of the grouse was one of the wonders of the world.

Up the ridge I went, keeping pace with my grouse-flusher. Hardly a hundred yards from where the first show had been made, I heard the soft thunder of the rise of another bird. Whether he had seen the line of flight of the first bird, or whether it was just my luck, I can never tell; but the second grouse came over my head at precisely the same angle as the first one. This shot was made also. I had a shamefaced feeling that the performance was too mechanical to be sporty. But I wasn't gravely troubled, for the day was as yet young and I had a pair of mountain pheasants.

As these two grouse rose and came up the hill toward me, beating their way masterfully up to the treetops, I had, even while getting ready to shoot, a chance to watch their flight. It does not appear that anyone can ever regard it as anything but thrilling. In our attempts at locomotion, we improve our cars, our airplanes. But the grouse, countless centuries ago, perfected a flight that has the finality of finished art. It is graceful, swift, powerful, and yet strangely enigmatic. It attains what the finest automobile strives for: formidable power immediately available and under the most delicately adjusted control.

I do not know that it is a better flight than that of the quail, but it is far more impressive. And because the grouse is a bird of the forest and must needs do constant maneuvering while in flight, I think he handles himself more deftly than the bobwhite. In the flight of the larger bird there is endless variety. Especially interesting to me are three features: one is the occasional silent rise, the big bird taking wing with hardly a sound; one is the instinctive habit of putting an obstruction between himself and his pursuer, and the other is his love of often going almost straight up to clear the trees and then tearing away over their tops, as if he were running the hundred yards in the Olympics. Indeed, the flight of birds alone would afford a man a lifelong study.

Believing that I had about used up my luck in the matter of having a stranger shoo grouse for me, I left him and turned back, going down the hill and across the road. Here, under a swarthy hemlock of massive proportions, Shine had her first opportunity to show that this was her party as well as mine. She found where a grouse had been walking that very morning. Plainly her behavior said so. She first stopped dead, her eyes fixed in a glassy stare; then she unlimbered a little. Her tail wagged; she broke point, but moved forward like a circus-dog walking on eggs. Once she looked back at me in order to ascertain if I fully realized the importance of the business at hand. I tried to look sufficient and reassuring. She crossed the little stream that purls about the hemlock's roots. She stopped by some alders. She went on noiselessly to a clump of wild raspberries that had draped an old fallen log. Here she froze right. I tingled. You know the feeling.

It was pretty thick ahead, and I didn't know just where the bird would go. I decided it would have to be a quick shot. But who can ever be certain, unless he actually sees his game on the ground, just what will get up when his dog points in a thick place? I expected one grouse. To my consternation, three got up. And they got up as a covey. I'm ashamed to confess it, but I thereafter joined the Dave Mellott class. I did select one bird, but just as I had my sight on him he melted into a young pine; and when I looked for another victim, all were gone. I deserved scorn, and the look Shine gave me expressed it sufficiently. A fly is sometimes too much for the strength of a fish; and a grouse's fly is often too much for the strength of the sportsman. But these three were still somewhere in the little hills.

Probably one of these grouse offered me a shot a half hour later. But I had the same chance of getting him as a Democrat has of getting an office in Pennsylvania. I walked under a spruce, and he went hurtling out from the dusky branches over my head. I fired wildly. Shine eyed me commiseratingly, as if to suggest that she was mortified to find me slipping. My feelings did not improve, nor did hers, for during the next hour or so we struck no game at all.

It was now near noon, and I was pretty well back in the little hills. It was a long way to the car. I decided to hunt back toward Bird-in-Hand. Shine managed to discover a small flight of woodcock in a boggy thicket, and three of these we secured—solemn, tiny gobblers, with all the dignity of high officials upon them.

A mile farther on we came rather unexpectedly to the borders of a wild field that must have been used at some time as a pasture. It was bordered by a stone fence over which wild roses wept, and grapevines trained, and teaberries hung in clusters. I felt that there ought to be a grouse here. And there was.

Shine stood him from the top of the old crumbled wall, and he went rocketing off across the old pasture. I was afraid that I had waited too long to shoot, but he fell like a plummet; a head shot, I discovered later. Not long after this grouse had been secured, I reached Bird-in-Hand. It was still somnolent, as it always is. A stray cow seemed to be trying to eat the upholstery of my car. Otherwise it was unmolested. In it I packed away my game and my gun; then Shine and I went into the store.

"Well," said the proprietor, "how many did you git?"

"I didn't do so well," I answered with a hunter's evasion.

"They ain't so plenty this year," he volunteered, "and they say their fur is mangy." To him, hunting always meant hunting rabbits.

"Did you ever see any grouse near here?" I asked.

"Grouse?" he questioned uncertainly. "What kind of a bug insect is that?"

But I did not answer, delighted that the presence of the grouse of the little hills was not known even to the lord proprietor of the place. I made a few purchases for Shine and me. Then we took the homeward road, fully determined to revisit so pleasant a country.

Still-Hunting Sir Ruffneck

This is one of Rutledge's more obscure pieces, thanks no doubt in part to its offbeat approach. Yet it exemplifies his varied approaches to sport and willingness to experiment. The article first appeared in *Forest & Stream*, November 1918, and subsequently in *Days Off in Dixie*. It suggests that the casual hunter or someone who lacks the advantages of a bird dog can still enjoy hunting grouse. I heartily agree, inasmuch as the first thirty or forty "pottiges" I took, all of them during my adolescence in the Smokies, came by chance. Some came while rabbit hunting, but most opportunities took place in the course of squirrel hunts. Doubtless I will expose myself to the potential for criticism for shooting grouse that were walking through the woods, but rest assured that to a twelve-year-old boy for whom a brace of bushytails was a prize, no compunction about "ground swatting" existed. Later I became more sporting and less the bloodthirsty youngster, and I would note that a fair number of these "on the ground" grouse were shot with a .22.

Rutledge took a different view and would not have approved of my efforts in early adolescence. He suggests merely letting grouse wander within range, then flushing them for a wing shot. It isn't the most productive type of hunting, at least in terms of a heavy game bag, but there are few things better suited to quieting the troubled soul than a day of the sort described here.

The man who likes to take a day off in the autumn to range the woods for the ruffed grouse is not likely to have a bird dog trained on grouse. Some regular grouse hunters have such dogs; but the average man who loves the recreation of the woods has not. However, his lack in that respect need be no discouragement to him; indeed, from some points of view it is a positive advantage to have no dog. Even the best dog is noisy in the woods, and thus he puts all game on guard against the approaching hunter; unless the dog be of the best type, his hunting of grouse will be a haphazard matter; unless the country be of a suitable nature, and unless the grouse happen to be in a mood to lie to the dog, there may be great difficulty in securing shots over pints.

While I do not deny the companionship of a dog in the woods, he is not al-ways desirable. Still hunting with him is not possible; and it is of still hunting Sir Ruffneck that I want to speak. It is a much easier matter to still hunt the ruffed grouse than it is to still hunt quail. Indeed, where the cover of fields is heavy, the latter task is impossible. I have heard men say that they could do it successfully, but I believe they must have had a few pet coveys "gentled" to come to a whistle and eat out of the hand. When the frost-blackened ragweed is knee-high and the dry foxtail grass has arched over, it is often a hopeless matter to find and to follow quail. Besides, hunting quail without a dog has no advantages. Most men get as much enjoyment out of watching the action of the dogs in the field as they do in tramping the fields and bag-ging the game. Some must get their sport out of watching the dogs, for they find it impossible to bag the game. But still hunting the grouse is practicable even for the man whose work does not permit him to become thoroughly acquainted with all the remarkable characteristics of this extraordinary bird.

The ruffed grouse drums at all seasons of the year. This sound is probably a love call and a challenge to rivals. It may be compared to the strutting of the turkey; we know that odd sound that the gobbler emits when at the zenith of his bombastic strut. Sometimes the drum of Sir Ruffneck is, I think, merely an expression of his feeling of lordship over the lesser creatures of creation. This is probably what it means in autumn. This expression of superiority on his part permits man to take a fall out of his pride; for, after a little experi-ence, one can follow the drum, locate the grouse, and probably get a shot at the prince of the woodland as he whirrs off his vine-draped rock or off his ancient mossy log, half-buried in leaf mould in the heart of a sequestered thicket.

But while the grouse can be approached if thus located, it is a difficult matter to ascertain the direction from which the drumming comes. On still fall days, when the dropping of a single lazy leaf attracts notice, a grouse may be heard drumming in his soft, dim, throbbing, penetrant way. Is it on this slope of the hill, or across the hollow? Is it down the ridge, or is it up? How far off is he? It is very easy to err in attempting to answer these questions. And on the right answers will depend the success of your hunt. The thing to do is to stand still, listening until you are sure of the direction whence the drumming comes. Then walk a hundred yards in that direction, pausing to hear the drum. When you are sure of your direction, then try to determine the distance. I confess that this is most baffling, especially if the atmosphere is damp, for then the sound will have its natural muffled quality enhanced. But at least the hunter knows that if he keeps on in the right direction he will eventually flush the bird. He should be ready to shoot at any time. While stalking one grouse, he may flush another; or he may flush the one he is after much sooner than he expected. If the drumming ceases, especially if it ends abruptly in the midst of a drum, he may be sure that the bird is probably aware of his approach. Not one man in a hundred can crawl up to a drumming grouse. I do not refer, of course, to the grouse of those regions where the lack of hunters has rendered the birds tame and fearless, but to the alert, sprightly, crafty, elusive grouse of our settled regions, where for a generation at least sportsmen have roamed the woods.

Of course, a man cannot depend on a grouse to accommodate him by drumming. He must have other ways of locating his game. The most natural of these is by sitting still, looking, listening; moving on after a time, to take up the silent, crafty watch at a different place in the woods. This kind of hunting just suits some men. I remember taking a friend deer-hunting in the South. We rode out to the stands in a wagon. I posted him on a log on the edge of the road. "Stay here," I said, "until we get back. It may be a couple of hours." He subsided amiably on the log. "Just my kind of hunting," he answered. When we returned he was fast asleep.

Where the woods are level, the hunter will have to do his still hunting at random until he finds a grouse; then he may be able to discover what brought the bird to that particular place. If some attraction in the shape of food is visible, the inference is that more birds are near. The hunter should sit still and wait. The great principle of all still hunting is to let the hunted rather than the hunter make its presence known. If the bird is an old cock, he may be a wanderer; for in the autumn the old males range erratically, and one may be found miles from a comrade. I once shot a grouse along a creek flowing through a farming community; the mountains, whence he had come, were five miles away.

Where the hunting is done on hillsides, where most grouse-shooting is naturally to be had, the still hunter should begin his day by seeking to ascertain whether the grouse are ranging high or low. Though they sometimes are distributed over various altitudes, it often occurs that they frequent the high sides of the ridges, or else are all down near the bottom. It saves a lot of tramping, not to mention disappointment, if the hunter will take time and patience to discover where his birds are feeding and ranging. Then he can spend his day either uphill or downhill, rather than spend it traveling back and forth in a fruitless search.

The still hunter of grouse must be a patient man, and he must be one capable of limiting his ambitions. After sitting for several hours, feeling that as they glide by he is losing his chance of bragging to the people at home, he must not be discouraged. He should always go on the principle that to every patient man the chance comes. More than once I have had a very empty morning stillhunting, and a very full and sporty afternoon; indeed, several times I have saved the day after sundown. And what I can do the average hunter can do.

The chances that the still hunter for grouse has are not limited to the chances of Sir Ruffneck himself. If he is not too exacting in the matter of the kind of game he desires, while sitting quietly on his rock or log, waiting for grouse, he may also be waiting to see a mountain covey of quail, a fox-squirrel, or a gray squirrel come within range; or perhaps a rabbit that another hunter has started will come jumping sedulously along. I have known foxes, wild turkeys, and even deer to be killed by men who were still hunting grouse. I take it that while few men like to "kill them all," every man likes to take something home, lest the children think that Dad is a back number, and lest someone else who has been counting on a game dinner will have to rearrange her menu.

Men in the woods will act almost as they do at home; I mean that their natures will betray them or will save them. Whatever you do, try not to be a buffalo in the woods. I have a friend who is a giant of a man; in business, he "butts the bull off the bridge." Unfortunately, he carries his ideas of success into the woods. On a still day he can be heard for miles, tearing through the brush, calling his comrades at the top of his powerful voice, dislodging boulders that go thundering down the mountain, getting all out of breath and "overhet"—to what end? Presumably because he thinks the mere expenditure of energy can win in the game of hunting. Never. Silence, craft, keenness of hearing and vision, patience: these alone bring home the bacon in the game of still hunting. Don't crack a twig in the woods if you can help it; don't talk above a whisper; don't shout—whistle if you have to signal; don't wind yourself by going too strenuously, for if you do and get a shot you will probably miss. Take the sport calmly, quietly, determinedly. Be an Indian.

Knowing the favorite foods of the grouse in the hunting season, the still hunter will naturally frequent these places where the bird's food is found. Grouse, like quail, feed early and late, and they usually walk to the feeding ground. How often have I sat near a tangle of grapes and greenbriars and heard the hesitant approach of grouse. They usually come singly; they learn early that each individual must take care of itself. At such a time it is not enough for the hunter to make no sound; he must not move his head or his body, for the eye of a wild thing is as quick to detect movement as its ear is to detect sound. He must let the bird come well within distance; then, unless he wants to watch it feed or wants to take a chance on others corning up, he must flush it and shoot. I have no use for the man who will shoot a grouse in a tree or on the ground. He ought to get his recreation in some other way. He kills the bird and the sport at one shot. Some allowance is made, of course, for those who use a .22 rifle. That surely is legitimate, especially if the bird be taken in the head. Anything else is disgraceful.

In bagging the grouse on the wing, much depends on the nature of the bird's rise. The intelligence of the grouse is well known, as is its favorite method of illustrating that intelligence by foiling the sportsman by a baffling rise. Also, if there is a tree to be put between the hunter and the hurrying bird, Sir Ruffneck will put it there. In still-hunting, therefore, the hunter, having located a grouse, should look the situation over carefully; decide where the grouse will go if flushed and where the hunter wants it to go. In short, one of the arts of still-hunting consists in flushing the bird in a manner that is advantageous to the hunter. Don't flush at random and take a chance; try, at least to flush craftily, designedly, and make as certain as you can of your shot. Should the bird flush wild, or should you miss, don't guess as to where he will come down. Watch to the very last glimmer of his wings. Mark him down. Note particularly whether he veers to right or left. The chances are that if his flight is high over sprouts and trees, it will be long and somewhat wild; if through the woods it can usually be followed with considerable accuracy. And always be as tireless in your pursuit of him as you were patient in your waiting for him to come to you.

Grouse of the Cloudlands

Initially published in *Field & Stream* in March 1933, this piece subsequently appeared in *An American Hunter*. Its setting is one of Rutledge's favorite Pennsylvania haunts.

The hunter who turns from deer and turkeys of a level and swampy country such as the magnificent preserve of the Kinloch Club to follow the ruffed grouse in high mountains will find that a good deal more is demanded of him in a physical way; indeed, before the opening of any grouse season, I begin to tramp the hills so as to get accustomed to the climbing. The shooting, too, is of a nature radically different, in that the sportsman has to make allowance for all those angles that are due to the game's often precipitous rise or volplaning descent. Yet when a man has once tasted the tang of ruffed grouse hunting in difficult country, he will always hate to let a season go by without at least one day in pursuit of this wise and beautiful bird in his fastness in the lonely hills.

It has never seemed to me that enough could ever be written about the ruffed grouse. The nature of this grand bird is so above reproach that it must always be classed among the royalty in the great community of wild life. Its romantic wild haunts, its patrician habits, its princely bearing, its cyclone speed upon the wing, the marvelous skill with which it unerringly executes its aerial maneuvers, its poise and rare distinction of carriage, its keenly bred woodland intelligence, the beauty and appropriateness of its tawny plumage—whatever aspect you may take of this noble wild thing, you will find it perfect. Without irreverence I may truly say that it took God to imagine the ruffed grouse.

Lately I have been following his wildwood majesty in the land of the sky—that is to say, on the very crests of the high Tuscaroras in southern Pennsylvania. And as my experiences have brought me some new ideas about this favorite game bird I should like to share these woodland memories with my fellow sportsmen.

In this part of the country grouse are always very scarce, always very wild. If in a day's tramp I rouse half a dozen, I have done well; and if I get a couple of shots, a lucky boy am I. Never have I killed the season's limit; and I am just as well satisfied not to have done so.

Come to these cloudlands with me, leaving home before daylight on a foggy November morning. It's three miles to the foot of the mountain, and two miles more over a rough road around its immense humped shoulder. When I come to where a little stream babbles across the road, I stop my car. It is as yet the twilight of morning. The woods are still. The good smell of damp leaves is like a tonic. Far across the Little Cove, on the shadowy bench of the next mountain range, I hear a fox barking. A horned owl hoots a sardonic reply. There, in the dim sweet woods, I feel close to the heart of things. In a sense, every sportsman has pioneer blood in him, and the frontiers are always beckoning and calling him on to adventure. Take your pharmacy away, and give me a morning in the mountains.

With the first streaks of dawn I begin my long climb. There is no road or trail, and I just have to ease my way through thickets of birch, laurel and rockoak, interlaced with wild grapevines. Before I have gone a hundred yards from the car, and while it is still too dark to shoot, I walk right up to a cock grouse. I am in a thick growth of tall timber at the time; and while I merely catch an impression rather than a view of the lordly bird, I can tell that he has executed what I should call his spiral rise. To reach the tops of the lofty trees so that he may zoom away freely, a grouse often climbs abruptly, almost perpendicularly, sometimes dizzily swinging in a circle. Here, gentlemen, is perhaps the very easiest shot in all the world to miss. It takes advanced calculus to determine where the bird will be on that spiral at any given moment. I suppose Captain Bogardus would never have missed such a chance; but the problem has me going for fair.

A little higher up the mountain, with better visibility now, I flush something else, and it gives me a qualm to see it disappear over the lofty ridge above me. It is a gobbler going off his roost. Hearing me coming, he suddenly remembers that he has an engagement for breakfast far, far away. And I'm not invited.

But it's grouse I'm after, and I'm in agreement with those sportsmen who believe that a real wild grouse is as hard to bag as a wild turkey. As *Bonasa umbellus* is unquestionably the most warily intelligent of our native American game birds, he must be hunted mentally rather than physically. Elusive on the wing, he is equally so in his habits. Even where grouse are known to be, a hunter, unless he uses his head, may tramp the woods all day without flushing a single bird.

In my experience, I have found these woodland princes to be very sensitive to weather conditions. I have known many amateurs to think that a windy day ought to enable them to approach wild game easily. They suppose that the noise in the forest will camouflage their own approach. As a matter of fact, a stormy day is the worst kind of day for hunting in the woods, especially for following grouse. All game is nervous under such conditions, and the grouse appears to be supersensitive. When the wind has been rioting through the disheveled autumn forest, I have had grouse flush full two hundred yards away. I think game uses its eyes to perfection when its sense of hearing is handicapped. The hunter is under the double stress of having to "sort out," in a second, the sounds made by his game from the general tumult of creaking trees, scurrying leaves and whistling wind. For hunting grouse, stormy weather is a good time to stay at home, or you might spend such time in a duck blind in some quiet cove.

When it comes to rainy weather, if you are an amiable sponge and can stand the soaking, you may have some sport if you do not look for your grouse on the ground. They do not like wet feet and feathers any more than you do. Practically all the birds will be in the trees—in pines, hemlocks, spruces and other evergreens. There does not seem to be any rule as to the height at which a grouse will perch; he is a sensible fellow and wants shelter from the rain. I have flushed birds in showery weather from dense white pines not over fifteen feet high, and likewise from patriarch trees, the lowest limbs of which were at least fifty feet from the ground. In woods in which conifers are found only here and there, the skillful grouse hunter will visit these trees, especially in wet weather. And is there a sportier shot than one at a big cock rocketing out of a tall evergreen?

As the grouse takes to trees in the rain, so he is likely to be found there after a fall of snow—especially if it be the first one of the year. In good grouse country, the day after a snow, I have not found a track; but I have flushed a good many birds out of the evergreens.

Just as windy weather makes these birds excessively wary, so in time of snow they are likely to be wild also. Their natural cover is for the time obliterated, and they compensate this handicap by being more than ever alert. Indeed, except where snow lies on the ground all winter, a snowfall affects all game in the same manner: the beasties and birdies grow suddenly canny. I have known amateur hunters to set out in a snow or after a snowstorm, expecting to have to hail a truck to bring back their kill—yet return all wet and empty handed. While a snow ought to enable you to see your game farther off, at such a time it hides more craftily, and it can see you farther off, too.

Grouse, like quail and wild turkeys, feed in the morning and the late afternoon, employing the midday hours in resting. On ordinary days, from eleven o'clock until about two they just loaf—being far more sensible than we are. A knowledge of what they are doing during certain hours of the day will always afford the hunter an intelligent guide for finding them. In the morning and the late afternoon don't hunt them where there's no grouse food—no sumac, hawberries, berries of the tea-bush and the wild greenbrier, wild grapes and the like. Where the food is, there will the grouse be also.

For his noontime siesta the grouse, like the quail, seeks a sheltered sunny place, preferably where there is sand or soft loam in which he can dust himself. However, this attention to his toilette is more assiduously followed in summer than in winter.

On the crests of all these great Tuscarora ridges where I'm having this morning hunt there is a wild chaos of great boulders—serried ranks of them scattered here and piled there since the days of creation. Yet they are beautiful too in their placid strength of stone, their outlines softened by an overgrowth of mosses and lichens; and out of their crevices grow plumed pines and hardy rock-oaks.

It is when I am within fifty yards of the summit, catfooting it over these rocks, that a big cock grouse gets up off to my right from a clump of rock-oaks which are still holding their tawny foliage. These right-hand shots when the hunter is teetering for a balance just aren't so hot. With the first barrel I make an elegant miss; it's perfect. The second brings down the cock, and he pitches headlong to the rocky hillside. In grouse hunting, and perhaps in all hunting, a man ought to make a kill early just to give him a little confidence—just to remind him that the thing is possible.

After retrieving my bird I climb to the mountain crest, arriving there a few minutes before sunrise. There's no fog up here. All is still, warm and bright; and before me lies the vast panorama of the Cumberland Valley, with its distant blue mountains on the farther side vividly silhouetted against the red sky. This is a most solitary place; yet even here are traces of man. In the first place, a rude trail used for ages by the Indians runs along the entire length of this immense range, from the Susquehanna to the Potomac, a hundred miles or so at least. Then, a half century ago, a man named Kirschner, with more ambition than judgment, decided to clear a field of some sixty acres on this wild mountaintop—despite the rocks and despite the severe acclivity.

Man and field have long since disappeared. The field is now a wonderful pine thicket, with open spaces grown to sumac and tea-berry, the whole overrun with wild grapes and bittersweet vines, which, of course, are favorite foods for the grouse. Indeed, I never saw a place more calculated to attract this princely bird, yet far up here in the cloudlands, more than two thousand feet above the valley.

As I am all alone, and as I have no dog with me, I am doing a kind of still-hunting. This is fascinating work, and it keeps a man on edge every second. Just as I pass the tumbled ruins of an old stone fence I see a grouse make a little run on the ground fifty yards ahead of me under the dense pines. He does not rise, but dodges behind a clump of pines that have collapsed with the fall of the old chestnut that supported them. I walk warily, hoping to negotiate the vital distance. You know what I mean. In woods fairly open, if you can get within a certain yardage of a grouse, you can nearly always have a chance at him—even if it is but a second's chance.

Just here I should like to comment on the question, Does a ruffed grouse need a run before rising? I was lately taken to task for saying that he did not. I think this little preliminary run is the result of nervousness. His first impulse is to seek some immediate shelter from the ambush of which he can observe his pursuer and so the better decide his strategy of escape, and also to secure a vantage-point for rising. The wild turkey, a ponderous, even an awkward bird, needs such a run; the vulture nearly always employs it. But the grouse does not have to. He can rise in full flight, like the quail. He can make his start from beneath some bush or clump of laurel, from a stump or an old log, from a tree or a mat of vines, with no preliminary start. Indeed, this patrician reminds me of a car that has no low or second gear. He has all the latest equipment: streamlined body, freewheeling, floating power. He never "makes a start" in the ordinary sense, but dashes into full flight instantly. Nor could a startled hummingbird more deftly thread the thicket's mazy way than he.

When I get within thirty feet of the grouse, he's up, he's roaring off through the pines—he's gone! I don't even get the gun to my shoulder. One thing, however, I notice, as surely you must have many a time: the grouse spreads his tail when rising, and keeps it spread until he gets well away. It's a marvelously sensitive rudder too. When in full flight above the treetops, a grouse generally has his tail closed; and at that angle his neck always looks curiously long.

It's time now for a little rest and a smoke, and I sit in the mellow autumn sunshine at the foot of a burly old white oak, my position commanding a view of the long slope of the pine thicket toward the valley. I am looking under it, not over it.

After a half hour the stillness of that high mountain is broken by a dainty, wary step. I hear it on the leaves just at the fringes of the thicket. More than a hundred yards from me two grouse walk into view. I think this bird can look curiously different in different postures. When off guard, it walks low to the ground, with body parallel to the earth; but when alert, it straightens up in almost startling fashion, standing strangely slim and high. This same posture is assumed by a watchful grouse on a tree.

These two birds I see are beautiful things, true children of nature, joyous and free. Some spirit of festival must be on them now, for they partly spread their wings and tails, make little playful runs, pause to get the full effect of the balmy sunshine. At last one flies up on a sumac bush for breakfast. The other lies on his side in a little sandy place, ruffling his feathers until he looks twice his normal size. Well, what is a hunter to do about such goings on?

Having located grouse on the ground, as I have done, it is necessary for me to look the situation over carefully if I hope for a chance. In short, it is for me to decide now where the birds will go if flushed from a certain direction, and whether that direction is the one I want them to take. But it has always seemed to me a difficult thing to drive any intelligent game bird or animal. Such a creature will probably have ideas of its own—some of them highly original. When after these mountaintop grouse I have to be especially strategic in the line of my approach, for if a grouse is walked up from a certain direction, and is thereby persuaded to kite away over the edge of the immense hill, there's no telling where he will stop. He isn't going to fly into the next county, but he's going farther than the hunter will care to pursue him.

Leaving out of the question the mother grouse when diverting the attention of the intruder from her brood, and the tame grouse of the North Woods, the question of how far one of our regular ruffed grouse will fly has always interested me. Of course, a good many factors enter into the situation. I have seen a grouse fly not more than thirty yards; he was not much startled, perhaps, and he saw choice cover near. At other times I have watched a grouse fly clear across from one mountain to another, a distance of at least a mile, and disappear going strong. I believe that in such a case the bird may have some particular refuge in mind, and there is a chance also that he is taking a certain joy in flight.

In the hunting season, in reasonably level woods, with cover pretty well distributed, I have found the average fly of one of our grouse to be between two and three hundred yards. Indeed, for many years I have made it a practice, after flushing one of the birds, to count my steps forward. When I have come two hundred yards, I get ready; and unless the grouse gets up within the next two hundred, I begin to swing around. Of course, if he gets up at first with extreme wildness, he may be after a nonstop record; but I think a hunter can usually tell when a grouse is going to make an oversized fly. Due allowance, too, must be made for this bird's habit of starting in a straight line and then, toward the end of his flight, veering craftily and with great sharpness to right or left.

After this digression, can you remember that we are stalking two fine birds that we have seen on the ground under the shelter of the fringes of the pine thicket? I slip back through the pines a hundred yards, then ease downhill for another hundred, until I am just about on a line with them. Now comes the stalk. It is always a difficult thing for me to get within shooting range of this bird.

When I am still fifty yards off, the one on the ground makes a little dashing run; the one on the vine tangle stands up straight, all his feathers drawn in tightly. Who is it that thus intrudes at sunrise into their hilltop Eden?

Of course, I have dreams of making a double. These dreams! The bird on the ground suddenly smashes away in full flight, a serried array of greenery between us. In fact, I never saw him after his rise. The other bird decides to be unconventional. A quarter of a mile behind me, on the ridge crest, is a rockoak thicket. He will fly to that. With a roar of wings he is up and away, high over the pines, and swinging past me on the left. I lead him about two feet. As the gun speaks he closes his wings and shoots like a broken meteor earthward.

I have always noticed that a grouse shot on the wing seldom falls to earth straight downward. So great is his velocity that it carries him far on. This is a cock with a brown ruff—something of a rarity. He lies on the sunny pine needles, with hardly one of his beautiful feathers ruffled. Some sentimentalist would exclaim, "Oh, the pity of it!" But my philosophy of hunting teaches me that an inscrutably wise Providence put these game birds and animals here for the pleasure and profit of our pursuit. And I remember too that a grouse killed cleanly by a gun meets a fate more in keeping with its noble nature than one caught in the darkness by some predatory prowler or murderously torn by a goshawk.

These grouse of the cloudlands call this high solitary place their home. On the coldest and stormiest days of winter they have this warm pine thicket, with its kindly slope toward the south, its shelter, its abundant food. Of course, they occasionally stray toward the valley. But this is their citadel, and a lordly one, too—primeval, with no smoke, no noise, no hurry; no odors save nature's hale and fragrant ones; close to the clouds, the sky, the stars; and overlooking a magnificent panorama of valley, with dim ranges and ranges of mountains beyond.

The charm of this splendid bird never fails, and his presence imparts to the woods in which he dwells a romantic wildness akin to wonder. He seems the tone of mountain silences, the voice of hushed and virginal woods. The silentness and the music of nature find in him adequate expression. I never see one without his making that day for me a magic day.

Patsy and the Princes

First published in the September 1935 issue of *Field & Stream,* this piece is one
of Rutledge's best-known bird-hunting stories. It later appeared in *Hunter's
Choice* and *Fireworks in the Peafield Corner.*

———

The daughter of Carolina Frank is a princess by right. I became Patsy's
owner when she was only four weeks old, and she already showed her
blue blood and all it means in a pointer pup. Sensitive, patrician, and affectionate, she was not happy unless she could curl up in my lap by day and
sleep on my bed at night.

She was high-strung to a degree. When she first barked, the sound of her
own voice almost scared her to death. One day she retrieved an old tin can
and brought it up the front steps, and the noise it made when it got away
from her made her tremble. Most pointers have a very businesslike tempera-
ment, but Patsy was as gentle as a setter. You know, some gods are ladies and
gentlemen; and some just aren't.

While she was still so young that weeds would throw her down and briers
were impassable barriers, I used to teach her to trail by shooting a starling and
dragging it around the yard, turning her loose on the scent. At seven weeks of
age she was broken to my .410 gun, was trailing, and was pointing staunchly.

Her behavior with rabbits puzzled and amused me not a little. Apparently she considered them legitimate playmates; and when one fled at her
approach, she would stand and gaze after it with a most woebegone expression, as if she felt that her little comrade had deserted her. On the scent of
birds of all kinds she displayed a stern demeanor, as if she had discovered her
mission in life. But she wanted to romp with rabbits, and they wouldn't play
the game.

It has never seemed to me necessary to take a bird dog into the wilds to
train him. Most of the work can be done right at home; and the sooner it is
started, the better. Of all qualities in a bird dog pup, give me nose. By careful
and intelligent handling, almost anything can be done with a young bird dog
that has a good nose. Affection and gentleness on the part of the trainer count
far more than any harsh measures yet devised. If your pup has an indifferent

nose, he will never amount to much in the field, even with blood, looks, and pedigree in his favor.

Establishing oneself in a dog's confidence is the foundation of training. For example, if a man ever lures a dog to him affectionately and then beats him, that dog's trust will be shaken forever. I never whipped Patsy for anything. It took a little patience to teach her that stockings, old shoes, and rugs are not meant to be lugged into obscure corners of the house and there chewed up; but I knew she was only a baby, and she learned quickly.

No man would knock the block off his year-old baby for pouring a cup of milk on the living-room floor; but many a man will nearly kill a puppy for some playful trick or some little infraction of domestic manners. Start them very young, and treat them gently and fairly. They like square shooters just as well as men do. A bird dog is just like a boy: let him run wild for the first part of his life, and you establish chances against his ever settling down to reliable behavior.

Patsy was two months old when the season for upland game opened in Pennsylvania. Now, you know how it is when you possess a puppy of that age at such a time. You think: "He can't possibly give me any sport this year. This child could never take it. Perhaps later I may take him out a few times, and next year he will be a real dog. I may send him to a trainer, or to some friend in the South, where the season lasts until March. It's hardly right to take this babe into the woods."

Such thoughts might have been mine had Patsy not been so different. As the first day approached, and my activity with gun, shells, alarm-clock, and hints of what things a hunter likes for lunch apprised my wife of the coning of the Great Day, I made my revolutionary decision. I would not only take Patsy out, but I would take her into the big mountains, after the prince of American game birds—none other than the ruffed grouse, the mountain pheasant, the *Bonasa umbellus* himself—partridge of New England. My knowledge of Latin is about as hazy as that of the average sportsman, but I do know that *Bonasa umbellus* means "the shadowy bull that runs away." Well, scientists may call it running, but I call it flying, zooming, hurtling. "Running" is too tame a word to describe the thrilling precision of that apparently incontinent flight.

I once asked an old Negro in the North Carolina mountains why he never shot at a grouse on the wing. With the broad drawl peculiar to the people of those mountains he said, "Becus when I'se hyar, he's thar." I suppose the marvelous flight of this prince of the woodlands has afforded more just cause for American sportsmen to doubt their ability as marksmen than most of the other game targets put together.

On the first of November, if the day breaks clear, there is light enough to shoot at six o'clock. To my wife's amusement, I usually get up at three-thirty. Often, after a long drive from home, I have sat in the car for an hour, waiting for it to get light enough to shoot. Once, while thus waiting, I saw a grand fox chase across some open mountain meadows. Seven hounds were trying to determine just how fast a fox can run. In the dim dawn the circus came right by me; and the fox was a silver fox, as black as coal—the only wild one I ever saw in the Pennsylvania mountains.

On this first of November I arose at my usual heathenish hour. I carried Patsy downstairs to the kitchen. It was to be her first early start! I laid her in a corner, and then busied myself with getting breakfast. Soon I saw that she had gone fast asleep again! With night still huge and ominous outside, Patsy looked pathetically innocent and little, and I felt somewhat like a brute over this matter of risking her in the wilderness. But my heart was hardened, and I took her with me.

On the fifteen-mile drive up Path Valley, she lay fast asleep beside me, content to go anywhere if she could be with me. To a dog, a man is either a god or a devil. I have a notion that if we'd act more like gods toward our dogs we'd get a lot further with them. I am no authority on gods and have no personal interviews to report, but my understanding is that they are kindly and tolerant, especially toward their inferiors; whereas devils are full of anger, hatred, malice, and all other kinds of rascality. Certainly every puppy begins by conceiving his master to be a god; it is that master's business never to do anything to make that dog change his mind.

I stopped my car in a lane leading from the highway into the mountains. Patsy snored contentedly. Under the circumstances I felt like the Dutchman who, seeing his beagle hound running a skunk across an open field, exclaimed, "What chanst for me to get sport today already yet?"

The day promised to be mild and still. A filmy haze lay over mountain and valley. I heard a red fox give his rasping bark. A horned owl weirdly intoned his eerie notes. Over the mountains day came all pink and pearly. It was time to start.

I took a drink of hot tea, then gave Patsy a snifter of the same, and we started; that is, I started up the lane, carrying my grouse dog under my arm. By the time we got into the brush on the lower benches of the mountain, there was light enough to shoot. I set my puppy down, and together we began the invasion of some of my old grouse haunts—pine thickets, old orchards, laurel glens, deserted pastures where smothers of grapevine cover old stone walls, abandoned mountain fields where grow the sumac and the wild rose and the greenbriers, on the fruits of all of which grouse delight to feed.

As my preliminary training of Patsy had included encouraging her to range out, in the twilight of the dawn I was happy to see her keeping about thirty yards ahead of me, a white fairy in those dusky solitudes. A light frost was beginning to melt, making conditions ideal for Patsy to pick up a trail.

After some fifteen minutes we came to a gentle slope, on the incline of which was a pile of dead pine brush. While thirty yards away from this my little princess hesitated; then she drew to a dead point. A damp air was breathing from the pine tops toward her. What did she have? There are plenty of quail in these coverts, but my mind told me that she had a grouse; and it was the first one she had ever winded. If she had hunted grouse for ten years, she could not have acted more perfectly.

Easing around until I got behind her, and scanning the country ahead to calculate just where his lordly majesty would go when flushed, I walked in carefully. When I came to Patsy, she did not break point, but she did look up at me, as if saying "I've got something; I only hope it's what you want."

Passing her, I walked slowly up toward the brush-pile.

Three grouse hurtled out, each choosing a different direction. I have always found it a most difficult thing to make a double on grouse when several get up together. When I try it, I usually miss all of them. One of these was perceptibly larger than the other two; an old cock he was, and when he thundered up he headed for his mountain home. As he bore to the left, I had to lead him; I also shot above him.

There is always danger that a man used to shooting quail will under shoot a grouse; for the quail generally goes straight away, not much higher than the gunner's head, whereas the grouse may rise twenty-five or thirty feet before straightening out for his real flight. Added to this is the fact that the grouse is not only rising but often going uphill, so that a combination of circumstances, creating difficult angles, has to be met.

I try to get the right angles and the allowance for leading, and all that; but here's a bird that really does not wait for you to figure out how to shoot him scientifically. With me the matter is always more or less of a haphazard affair, with some dead reckoning thrown in. If the grouse falls, I always feel more lucky than smart. Some game can be killed with geometric precision, but hardly the grouse.

By good chance, this old cock got in the way of my shot, closed his wings, and pitched downward with great velocity. I called Patsy. But at the sound of the gun she did not break point! No, sir; there she was planted. Walking back, I patted and praised her; then I picked her up and carried her to where her first grouse lay. She tried to retrieve him for me, but he was too big. Stumblingly she dragged him toward me.

All this called for some special demonstration on my part; so I sat down, took my baby in my lap, stroked her sensitive head, and otherwise gave her to understand that she was behaving like a champion. She kept sniffing delightedly at the big bird, and I knew that from that day forth I was to have a grouse-minded dog.

Wandering a little higher into the hills, we came to a rivulet gushing along among mossy rocks. Here were kalmias and great thickets of greenbriers under the oaks and hemlocks. Patsy, who had now traveled about a mile, was showing signs of getting tired. Several times I stopped for a few minutes to rest her. Coming to a dense patch of laurel, I sent Patsy in for a scout, I could see the open woods on all sides of this thicket, and kept watching for my dog to come out. But no dog.

"It must be a point," thought I, sidling ahead through the dense greenery. All was silence. I didn't want to call for fear of flushing something out of range. I had a sudden apprehension about a rattlesnake. This is bad country for snakes, though they are rarely abroad after the first frosts. Besides, if a snake strikes a dog, the dog always gives notice by a sharp yelp. No sound had come from Patsy. I was puzzled, and was greatly relieved when I saw her standing with both forepaws on an old dead chestnut log. She was almost hidden by the overarching laurels.

At first I thought she had come to the log and, finding it too much for her, was waiting for me to help her over. But then I caught in her eyes that dreamy look dear to every lover of a bird dog: she was fast on point. I walked in carefully. When I got to Patsy, I stopped to stroke her head and stepped over the log. Nothing happened. Well, I thought, an old dog is often fooled; what can you expect from a youngster?

A little circling among the bushes brought me no results. I returned to Patsy. "Lady," I said, "'scuse me, but you're a liar."

Still the elf held her stand.

"Now, ain't that sumpin?" I muttered, and began to glance around for a land turtle, the scent of which will sometimes mislead even a champion bird dog. But nary a turtle.

I picked Patsy up, and to my surprise she was as stiff as a little statue! Her whole body seemed to resent my interfering with her business. The dream light never left her eyes. I set her down, and she continued to point, only this time she took two steps to the left and she seemed intent upon the log.

Just then I heard a slight movement in the dry leaves in the shelter of the old chestnut log. In another second, two grouse tore away from the side of the log, where they had been all along, as Patsy had so faithfully been trying to tell me. They went down the mountain. At fifty yards, as they hurtled into a smother of hemlocks, I let drive rather blindly, and could see no result of the shot except a single small feather drifting idly downward.

"If I had done half as well as you did," I told Patsy, "we'd have all we are allowed in Pennsylvania in one day."

With no faith that I had done anything, I came to the place where my dead grouse should have lain. As I expected, there was no sign of it. Here was a perfect shambles of logs and limbs, the debris of a lumbering operation. I had a hard time getting along, and it was much worse for Patsy. Just as I was on the point of carrying her out of this hopeless thicket she came to a stand. As she was under a deep tangle, I laid down my gun and literally had to crawl to get to her. Two feet in front of her nose, wedged under a log, was my grouse! When he had struck the ground, he had had life enough left to dash to hiding, but he was now dead. I retrieved him and my baby champion.

"It's the limit," I said, meaning both kinds, and, picking up my gun, started back for the car.

Patsy is but one of many bird dog puppies that I have started very early. If this can be done normally and gently, it's the thing to do. Of course, I have been fortunate in living on the outskirts of a village, and quail nest right by my house. But many fundamentals can be taught a puppy without actual access to live game birds. Most of the books about training bird dogs have a good deal to do with reclaiming vagabonds and reforming criminals. But if you will get a puppy of patrician blood, make him love you, and start him on his career while he is still toddling, most of the difficulties that come with the breaking of a year-old, senseless, half-wild dog will never appear.

A bird dog has a real mission in life. Make this clear to him during the first three or four months of his life, and the chances are that, instead of having to show him further how to hunt, from them on he will be teaching you the finer points of the game.

The Prince of the Woodland

Although quite similar in title, this is not the same as "Prince of the Wood-lands," another well-known Rutledge story that can be found in *Hunting and Home in the Southern Heartland: The Best of Archibald Rutledge.* It previously appeared in *Days Off in Dixie.*

While the majority of Rutledge's grouse hunting was done during his years of teaching in Pennsylvania, he did occasionally find time to take to the hills of neighboring North Carolina. His half-brother, Frederick, lived in Asheville (where he wrote and published a little-known book, *Fair Fields of Memory*), and through him Old Flintlock likely would have had ample hunting and social contacts. It is in the Tarheel high country that this piece opens, but in reality it is a wide-ranging look at the habits, idiosyncrasies, and biology of grouse.

Rutledge indulges in more than a bit of literary license when he talks about "thirty-pound wild gobblers in the pinelands of the South." They simply don't grow that big in such regions, although the rare bird of the eastern subspecies will reach that weight in the rich agricultural lands of states such as Iowa. Nonetheless, this is an eloquent tribute to a game bird that truly is a "Prince."

––––––––––

Two of us were sitting on an old mossy rail fence that sagged its way through the deep woods of Western North Carolina. We were smoking and our guns lay across our knees. Suddenly, with no warning at all, a cock grouse whirred out of the laurels directly behind us, and went flashing away down the hillside. My friend, who was sitting on the right, turned on the fence, threw his gun to the left shoulder, and, at seventy yards, far through the glimmering vista of forest light and shade, brought the proud cock's flight to a headlong collapse.

"Man alive! How did you ever do it?" I gasped.

But he could not answer; for he was the more surprised of the two of us; nor has he yet quite recovered from the astonishing shock of pleasure that he experienced. And that was seven years ago.

That story is but one of the thousands that could be told to illustrate the tricks of the prince of the woodland; for in this respect he is probably superior to all game birds. So many members of the great game family rely for their safety on keeping their distance from man; or, when surprised, on a flight which carries them far out of danger. The bobwhite quail depends to such a degree on his protective coloring that he may sometimes be picked up in the grass, out of a clump of bushes, or from among piles of autumn-strewn leaves. But the ruffed grouse does not greatly rely on his coloring; perhaps he is conscious of his size, which more readily betrays his presence. Nor does he wholly depend on his flight, which is indeed worthy of his—and man's—deepest respect. Rather he relies on a certain resourcefulness, an ability to use his wits, a positive genius for making the manner of his escape suitable to the nature of the circumstances and the form of the danger which confront him.

Aside from beauty of plumage and a princely bearing, another point on which the ruffed grouse takes the palm from every other game bird in North America is his sheer pluck. This is not said inadvisably; for after calling thirty pound wild gobblers in the pinelands of the South, after shooting mallards and black ducks over decoys on the East Coast, after bagging the sporty bobwhite quail in the covers of several states—in fact, after a long and not unprofitable experience, I am fully convinced that a brace of fine grouse in the sportsman's jacket, after a day in laurelled gorges and along the borders of autumn-tinted, second-growth woodlands, is more genuine game than all the other game that can be bagged. He alone by his superb gameness justifies the use of the word "game" as applying to all the birds of his class.

But it is not only of the ruffed grouse as it is brought home in the game bag that I would speak; nor yet of it essentially as an object of sport, but rather as the extraordinary romantic and picturesque figure of the woodland that it is; for the ruffed grouse is first a distinct individual and then an object of sport.

The nature of this bird is so above reproach that it must be classed among the royalty of the community of wild life: its haunts, its habits, its unfailing high spirit, its great speed on the wing, and the marvelous skill with which it executes its aerial maneuvers, its beauty of plumage and rare distinction of carriage, but above all the keenly bred woodland intelligence that invariably accompanies it—all its characteristics are admirable, except, indeed, to those poor sportsmen who find in its tricks and in the baffling nature and velocity of its flight a cause for grievance.

The grouse is as peculiarly a bird of the woods as the bobwhite is a bird of the open. Yet grouse take not unkindly to certain aspects of civilization. Thus, they are frequently to be found in old hillside fields, overgrown with pines and cedars; in mountain orchards, and in those desolate tracts of scrub-growth that mark the trail of the lumberman. But the very nature of the grouse demands a certain wildness in its surroundings; and where all such essential elements are lacking, the birds will not be found. The grouse loves laurelled stream-wet gorges, sunny tracts of second-growth chestnuts and oaks, glades of maple, birch and ash, and pine-grown old fields adjacent to the hills or mountains, where the sumac flames, where there are dogwood berries to be had, and where clusters of wild grapes have been sweetened by the early frost. In general, despite the fondness of the grouse for taking refuge from pursuit in hemlocks, pines, and other evergreens, it much prefers woodlands that are grown with deciduous trees. But the summer range of the grouse naturally differs from the autumn and winter range. In summer it is to be found over a wider territory and at higher altitudes. And since at this season its food is animal rather than vegetable, it will be found oftenest on the ground, searching for crickets, beetles, and the larval forms of woodland butterflies.

As soon as the autumn sets in, the princely bird delights to resort to sunny southern exposures and is frequently to be seen along the bases of the hills and mountains, among scrub pines and cedars, and along mountain streams entering the valley. In the late autumn, when all the leaves are down, he is fond of resorting to gullies and to those dry beds of summer streams which descend the hills; there he can generally procure an abundant supply of wild grapes and greenbriar berries. In the fall, Sir Ruffneck—do not confuse the term with another which never could apply to him—begins to be a vegetarian; and then, at feeding time in the early morning or late evening, he is most likely to be found in some dogwood tree, under some grapevine, beneath fruitful oaks or chestnuts, or along some old woodland fence, where the clusters of scarlet sumac flame and the heavy greenbriars offer beneath their shelter bunches of succulent berries.

In the winter, the grouse is transformed from a terrestrial to an arboreal bird; for, when the snow covers the ground together with all the varieties of food which it might offer, the grouse becomes dependent on such berries as may remain clinging to bare vines, and on the buds which the trees seem to put out for his especial benefit. Thus, in the winter, or at least while snow is on the ground, our grouse is a bird of the trees; though he often leaves his tracks in the snow and occasionally will spend a bitter night buried snugly beneath it.

For ordinary roosting, the grouse usually chooses a low, bushy-topped evergreen and perches on the matted foliage rather than on a limb. Often, he is not above reach of a fox, and always roosts within easy climb of a weasel; and this habit of his is surely one reason why his tribe does not increase more rapidly in those regions where he is afforded adequate protection from hunters.

Except in flight, or when walking, unconscious of the presence of the observer, the ruffed grouse is not frequently seen; its protective coloring is as perfect as the bobwhite's. Occasionally it can be detected on a log, or in some tree in which the foliage is not dense. When on the alert in a tree it presents an extraordinarily perfect picture of wariness and wildness. On the limb of a spruce or pine the little prince will stand erect, stiff, and motionless, his feathers held so compactly against his body as to give him a slim appearance. If dogs are working about under a tree, the grouse will crane his shapely neck and peer at their maneuvers. There is small doubt that he considers them foxes; and knowing that they cannot climb, he will stay where he is and watch them with curious interest. At such a time, it is sometimes possible to approach within photographing distance of a ruffed grouse. Some poor sportsmen take advantage of such a situation to shoot the glorious bird, and some of them would be surprised to learn that they ought to be ashamed of themselves.

Nothing gives a better idea of the skill in flight and the game qualities of the ruffed grouse than the fact that it has held its own against almost incalculable odds. It probably has more enemies than any other game bird; and among these are the subtlest and most intelligent of the stalkers. Aside from its wild enemies, it must face the hunter, and by whom it is followed relentlessly into the deepest fastnesses. Poor marksmanship matched against its skill and speed in flight explains one fruitful cause of the survival of the grouse. Among its chief enemies in nature are the fox, the skunk, the wildcat, the weasel, the mink, the bald eagle, the golden eagle, the Cooper's hawk, the pigeon hawk, the duck hawk (peregrine falcon), the red-shouldered hawk, the barred owl, and the great horned owl (*Bubo virginianus*). Even the raccoon will sometimes succeed in taking the grouse at night. And the subtle mink must also be ranked as a destroyer; for, while not frequently ranging in the territory of the grouse, he will never pass one by.

In the Big Allegheny Mountains of western Pennsylvania I have been told by old grouse hunters that foxes destroy great numbers of the birds, especially the half-grown ones and the grown ones of the first year. One reliable hunter told me that, in following the track of a weasel over soft snow, he had come upon the carcasses of seven ruffed grouse, each lying under a little evergreen tree. In each case, the night prowler had sucked the blood, eaten shreds of flesh from the wound in the neck, and had then abandoned the bird. In two or three instances there was telltale evidence on the snow of the bitter struggle that had taken place; but in the baffling darkness and attacked by surprise, the woodland prince could not but succumb to one of the stealthiest and, for its size, one of the strongest of animals. Of course, the owls and foxes are night hunters, and they take heavy toll of the ranks of this splendid bird. In fact, in some regions the ruffed grouse constitutes one of the chief factors in Reynard's regular diet.

The calls of the ruffed grouse are peculiar in sound and they are singularly few in number. It may with justice be said to be one of the silentest of birds. The drumming of the cock, which is a call answering several purposes, is, of course, made with the wings. It has an almost weirdly vague yet penetrating, throbbing quality. Like the crowing of a gamecock, it is sometimes a challenge, or at least a proud expression of an assurance of general supremacy. Again, it attracts the female in the rapturous mating season; but it is not essentially a mating signal, a love note; for it may be heard at all seasons. It is most frequently heard in the spring and in the fall.

This is one of the sounds of nature to be marked and remembered. To locate the direction from which it comes is difficult; and to judge its distance away requires woodcraft of a high degree. It is probably more baffling in these two respects than the ventriloquistic note of a great horned owl, or the whistling of the wings of wild ducks, passing invisibly after nightfall. Drumming is the only sound made by the ruffed grouse that can be imitated. Therefore, this bird, mercifully, can seldom be called to a blind.

When suddenly alarmed, it gives a little clucking sound, pitched in the same tone as that given by the startled bobwhite quail. Also, when the young have become scattered, the mother calls them up with a series of short, sharp, insistent, clucking whistles. Occasionally, the grouse will give a querulous call while in flight. But none of these notes is often heard. On the wing, but for the whirr of the heavy primaries, the ruffed grouse is generally silent; and in sailing or volplaning at amazing angles, his wings may make no more sound than a bat's. A big grouse can fly low over a hunter's head without making enough noise to attract his attention. But on the other hand, I have heard an old cock, dropping with incredible velocity from the top of a high ridge to a far, hemlock-darkened gorge below, go literally roaring down the mountainside, the wind shrilling through the hollow arcs of his wings as it does through the bald eagle's when he drops like a bolt on his prey.

When wounded, this bird makes no sound of protest; though when one that is winged is pursued through bushes and over logs, it is likely to cluck excitedly. I have always considered this silence as in a degree indicative of his princely blood, though it is a distinguishing characteristic among all truly game birds. The greatest complainers are the harriers of these birds, and in particular the duck hawk, which screams shrilly when wounded.

Other variations in plumage are sometimes observed. I secured a large cock grouse in November, 1913, which displayed a heavy chocolate-colored ruff, quite unlike the typical black ruff. Some will be bagged which are exceptionally dark, others unusually red. Those found in the North are "booted," as a provision against intense cold, while the "pheasants"—same species—killed in the mountains of the South have clean legs. As to size, there is not much variation throughout the wide range inhabited.

The flight of the ruffed grouse is essentially a flight of the woods, as opposed to the bobwhite's, which is generally a flight of the open; and though I do not disparage the flight of the quail or deny his ample ability to take care of himself in the forest as well as in the field, his flight is far less impressive than that of the grouse. The latter's is all ease, grace, buoyancy, and amazing speed. It seems to gather force and choose direction without pause or effort. And all the while he never forgets to put the biggest tree or the only evergreen in the neighborhood between his vanishing form and the eager sportsman's leveled piece. The prominence of such a baffling obstruction is seldom noticed by the hunter until the wily bird has effaced himself behind it. The distinguishing characteristic of the grouse's flight is its infinite variety; for, as no two places in the woods are ever exactly the same, and as the bird's manner of flight must, at least to some extent, be made to conform to the nature of its surroundings, he is obliged to use resourcefulness in effecting his escape. And this he has developed to an admirable degree.

The only game bird whose flight is truly comparable to that of the ruffed grouse is the woodcock; but the latter's flight, while often swift and enigmatic, frequently offers the sportsman a dead easy shot. The woodcock seldom purposely screens himself behind trees, and his getaway, while baffling in dense thickets, is quite easy and tame in the open. Moreover, the woodcock in flight generally seems to be looking for a suitable place to alight, while the ruffed grouse, once started, apparently has not the slightest idea of stopping anywhere this side of day after tomorrow. Whether it be reality or not, the end of his flight seems to be a sudden check, a dive as it were into a fallen treetop or beside an old log, or a quick gliding upward to the shelter of an evergreen. In short, when he decides to take to cover, he does it like a man taking shelter from a hard shower or from flying bullets.

Yet this splendid bird soon learns when it is among friends and protectors. There are authentic instances of wild grouse that would come from the woods at a call, would eat from the hand, and would allow themselves to be picked up without displaying any fear or suspicion.

From these and similar instances it may be inferred that, in spite of the latent wildness of its nature and of its love for conditions incompatible with those of civilization, the ruffed grouse can be domesticated; at least, it can be tamed and reared successfully. But so far experiments with it have been desultory; though the time is coming when, if the bird is to be preserved in its present range, it will have to be bred and distributed as quail are now. Of the two birds, the grouse is the more hardy, and is never winter killed. Their nests run apparently equal risks of destruction; wild animals and forest fires accounting for the loss of the partridge's, and the crow and the mowing machine for the bobwhite's.

Every sportsman who has hunted the ruffed grouse has his story to tell of the best shot he ever made or saw or heard of. There is a singular and suspicious dearth of stories recording the worst misses, though, conscience knows, there is an abundance of authentic material.

Once, while going through a thicket of pines and cedars, I walked under a wild dogwood tree which was bare of leaves. I had passed it and was in the act of stooping under the low-sweeping boughs of a pine when a ruffed grouse, which had been sitting down on the limbs of the dogwood, whirred out and darted away behind the dense cedars. From where he was sitting, I could have reached him from the ground; and he was directly over me as I passed. Why did he not fly out at my approach, as every other wild bird would have done? Why did he deliberately sit in that bare tree, waiting until I was stooping under a pine? In plain terms, he had too much sense to fly out in front of me. He saw his deadly peril; he weighed his chances carefully, deliberately. He waited for the favorable moment, until he had me at his mercy. Then he dashed away safely to liberty. That is one reason why, in shooting grouse, I never feel that I am taking advantage of this extraordinary bird; for, measured by the times he has taken cruel advantage of me, and of my race of sportsmen, I am one of his very heaviest creditors. Nor can I reasonably hope that our score will ever be settled.

The grouse, then, is a bird of wonderful resources; there is no counting on exactly what he will do. He acts from intelligent motives relative to his interest; and without more than instinct, no bird could do the audacious things he does and "get away with them." But, as has been hinted before, *Bonasa umbellus* is a prince, a creature of divine rights and powers, a super bird. And he is far more the master of the situation than the sportsman who pursues him.

His presence never fails to impart a romantic wildness to the woods which he inhabits. The charm of his beauty never wanes, and the sportsman's appreciation of him as an object of his pursuit is constantly increasing. As the bonny quail expresses admirably the spirit of brown stubble fields and frost withered fencerows, so the prince of the woodland embodies the haunting charm of whatever is wildest, most beautiful, and most elusive in the forest.

It's the Scotch in Them

This piece originally appeared in the February 1939 issue of *Field & Stream.*
It shows that Rutledge had a sound all-around knowledge of working dogs,
with the play on the Scottish nature of the dog's name, Bonnie, figuring
nicely in the story's title. Incidentally, Rutledge's felicity with titles—it produced memorable ones such as "Miss Seduction Struts Her Stuff" (referring
to a turkey call) and "The Lady in Green" (a gifted lady hunter)—shines
through as well. This largely forgotten piece has not, I believe, heretofore
appeared in book form. Bonnie and her brave master match wits, unevenly,
with the "Herd Bull," as Rutledge styles a giant specimen of the grouse tribe,
but they do succeed in writing a fitting and fulfilling close to another season.

Some literary bimbo once complained of Scotchmen that you could never
find one with his mind "in an undress." He might just as well have been
talking about *Bonasa umbellus,* the lordly ruffed grouse. During all the years
I have hunted this bird in southern Pennsylvania I have never seen one look
awkward, never seen one taken unawares. He is as full of vivid resource as a
matchmaker is of craft, and as a debutante is supposed to be of innocence.

Beyond doubt there is something peculiar, something remarkable, about
the boys who hunt grouse. During those long months when the season
is closed, they talk in worshipful tones of the Prince with the Ruff; they
frame pictures of him, and two that I know write poetry to him. They love
and admire this bird they hunt. One old grouse hunter, who lives so close
to the mountains that deer come by droves to feast in his buckwheat field,
maintains that no one should ever feel proud over killing a grouse; that the
element of luck is so great that thankfulness is the only proper emotion. Even
when given a pointing dog, a reasonably open shot and a wily grouse, the
hunter rather than the grouse needs your prayers and sympathy.

Among the experiences I have had with this wary Scotch mountaineer,
none is more memorable than the one that befell me the time I met the Herd
Bull. Now, this grouse was not a legendary one that had eluded hunters for
years. I saw him, named him, and shot at him all by myself. I call him the

Herd Bull because he was by far the most enormous cock grouse that I have ever seen.

My encounter with him was not altogether unexpected. One November day, just at sunrise, a friend and I were hunting in Allen's Valley in the mountains of the region I have mentioned. This valley lies just west of the Big Tuscarora Mountain. You can reach it by the Fire Tower Road or by way of Cowan's Gap. Swampy, secluded, desperately thick, it offers as fine a refuge for game as there is in the whole region of the Alleghenies.

Our plan that morning was to separate, make our way down the valley about two hundred yards apart, and meet at the old bridge for lunch. My pal, who would much rather have me roll a grouse than do so himself, sent me on the old road that passes the deer camp.

"Be mighty careful," he warned me, "just as you reach the bend with the heavy growth of teaberries on your left; I jumped a fine one there two days ago. If by chance he's back home, he is likely to come out in the road and give you a fair chance at him."

The morning was just frosty enough to make me blow on my hands every now and again. Fortunately the woods were still, whatever sounds there were being readily audible. Hardly had we started when a buck and his doe made a terrific racket as they ripped out of their beds in the laurel to my left and went up the mountain to enter the State Game Reservation.

The old road down which I was cautiously walking had been made for hauling lumber out of the valley. But it had been in disuse for nearly ten years and was now hardly more than a dim path. A turbulent mountain stream crossed it every few hundred yards, and where beavers had dammed it I walked a log made dangerously slippery by moss, or waded it hoping the icy water would not discover the hole in my leather boot.

Nearing the place of which I had been warned, I stopped to check on my shells. Yes, that was right: 7½'s in the right for a close fast shot in the thicket, and 2's in the left for a long drive in the open.

On either side of me were low laurel bushes, above which rose dense thickets of dogwood and mountain birch, with here and there families of small white pines; little of the big timber remained. The growth made it almost too thick for shooting, but the road itself was ten feet wide, and the bends in it were very gradual. In such a place every step sends a thrill through a hunter's spine, for he can never tell just when his chance will come or of what nature it will be.

Whether it was because I stepped on a dry twig or because a gray squirrel dropped a pine cone from a dead chestnut tree, I do not know; but suddenly there was thunder on my right. Distinctly I glimpsed a grouse as he zoomed off low to the ground, heading for the State Game Reservation.

What really took the stage by storm, however, was the great cock grouse that climbed for thirty feet to clear a white pine between him and the road. He skyrocketed; he dived into the road, side slipping dizzily; he careened from the left side to the right, and in blazing speed cut a right angle in the left and hurtled headlong through a pine. Gentlemen, with both barrels I missed him! A better man might well have tumbled him, but the Herd Bull really offered a shot only for an Annie Oakley. Some of those angles he maneuvered would have made a quail's head hang down in shame.

My chagrin decreases and my admiration increases each time I think of that gallant and spectacular escape of the Herd Bull. Nor was it the dazzling maneuver of the old boy that impressed me most. It was his huge size. Truly, he was a giant among grouse. That fact should have made him easier to hit, but it had not made it easier for me.

Most of my grouse hunting has been done without a dog. The only time a dog is really essential, I believe, is when you cripple a bird, for in his ability to duck under logs and discover a hiding place in a few seconds a crippled grouse is masterly.

Just last season it was my good fortune to discover that an English setter I had bought the year before as a three-weeks-old baby was becoming a grouse dog. Even as a puppy Bonnie was gentle, inquisitive, careful, obedient. After cutting her teeth on quail hunting, she turned to the lordly grouse with comparatively few errors, all excusable.

We never got an even break with that first grouse she pointed, when, early last season, I was again in Allen's Valley with a friend. The woods were still faintly bright in autumn gold and reds. Striking her leisurely even pace, Bonnie would hunt for ten or fifteen minutes and then return for further orders.

Another hunter must have put up the grouse, for he came from behind us and was above the tree-tops as he passed. He was too far to shoot, but I could see him sail down toward a laurel patch two hundred yards ahead of us.

"Now, Bonnie," I said, more to myself than to her, "here's your chance. Just work as if you were hunting quail, except that you must be three times as careful; and when you catch his scent, point at once—don't try to creep up on him." Fortunately the little setter was able to work upwind. So busy was I watching her that I had failed to keep pace with her advance. For a few minutes she disappeared from sight. And then I saw her. There she stood in a little patch of sunlight, fast on point, a beautiful picture of sport and grace. So crouched and frozen was she that I thought she had approached nearer her splendid quarry than she had intended. My job now was to get within range before his winged highness left his cover as a projectile leaves the muzzle of a cannon.

Manifestly the grouse was in a patch of laurel just shoulder high; on either side the brush was even lower. It was my chance. The only thing left to do was to get cranberry sauce.

When I was within twenty steps of the dog, up went my grouse: My ears told me he was quitting the country—but where was he? Frantically, with my gun half way up, I waited for him to appear. When at last he did appear, he was sixty yards away, a hopeless distance through the thick cover. Bonnie, not hearing the gun, came to me for an explanation. Speaking in self-defense, I told her, "You've got to expect those things when you hunt these birds. We're in the Big Leagues now."

The grouse had escaped in this wise: running to the edge of the laurel thicket, he took wing and roared off not more than a foot or two from the ground, thus concealing himself from the hunter until he calculated he was safe; then he veered up over the tree-tops to display his prowess flauntingly. Bonnie's first grouse was a smart one—it was the Scotch in him.

While he was supposed to be entirely a dweller of the mountain, and nothing seems to delight a grouse more than an old pine field on the very top of a big rise, especially if there are wild grapes close at hand for his breakfast, once in a while one of these wily birds will work his way into the valley, following an old fencerow or a stream with wooded banks. I know of one fine cock grouse that was killed five miles from the nearest mountain, having evidently followed the Conococheague Creek out of Path Valley. Now, while a grouse may on occasion leave his home, he is careful to carry with him the head and the wings that compel your high opinion of him. Even when in strange country, and apparently lost, he never loses his head.

Last season one of my sons and I were hunting quail in Path Valley. This valley lies east of Tuscarora Mountain, and is in no place more than a mile wide. Even today, still so wild is this region that it is not uncommon to see a mighty bronzed gobbler launch himself from one mountain to beat his way across the valley. Deer cross constantly.

The puppy we had with us was completely nonplussed by a high wind sweeping across parched stubble. It was not surprising, therefore, that we walked into a covey of quail of whose presence the puppy was blissfully unaware. They made for a nearby fence-row, grown to sumac and bittersweet, both laden with bright berries. On the other side of this fence was an old apple orchard, which was just midway in the valley, approximately a half mile from either mountain.

We eased up to the fencerow fully quail-minded. Imagine my surprise, therefore, when out from the fence burst *Bonasa umbellus*—a grouse in all his glory. The thing happened to me much as it did on one occasion to my friend, Asbury Lynch. Said Asbury, "That grouse, he just onscrewed his toe-nails to mow off the pinetops, but I leaved him have it."

After my grouse was on the ground and the excitement over, our puppy pointed manfully. Such pointing is not essentially different from the prisoner's pardon which arrived shortly after the execution had taken place. The grouse may have been crossing the valley, or he may have just been feeding far from his home; but to judge from the way in which he started, he had a mighty definite idea about where he was going.

It is only natural to think of a creature in relation to and in connection with its native habitat, and this is true even of human beings. We think of the king cobra and India, the lion and Africa, a Swiss and the Alps, a Dutchman and a beer garden. And it is difficult to think of ruffed grouse without picturing great craggy boulders, ancient lichen-covered fellows, balanced precariously on the steepest climb of the mountain; old hillside clearings; or dense pine thickets, where your only hope is to drive a grouse to your companion, who is flanking the edge; or wild gorges, where the trunks of fallen trees, wild grape-vines and tangles of greenbriers force you to climb, crawl and cuss before you are half way through them.

My friend Asbury tells of a man who, in trying to sell a particularly barren plot of ground, declared that all his land needed was a little water and a couple of good men. The prospective buyer replied in disgust, "That's all hell needs." And all you need in grouse hunting is the strength of youth, the wisdom of age, great patience and lightning in your trigger finger. At best these will give you a start in the right direction.

I say "great patience" because these mountaineers are so puzzling in their habits; today they will all be on the very crest of the mountain, and tomorrow they will be in pine thickets almost in the valley. One hunter told us that last year he hunted all one day without seeing a grouse; that just at dusk, as he was leaving for home and fireside, a covey of eleven went over him and fanned out on a ridge that he knew almost by heart.

There was insufficient light that evening; so he returned "soon in de mawnin'," loaded down with shells and expectations. He found not one grouse on the entire ridge.

On the last day of the past season I was hunting with a friend and Bonnie in a wooded valley called the Little Cove. The afternoon wore away without the sign of a feather, and you know how fast the sun sets on the last day. There was but a half hour of daylight left when we heard a grouse rise, then another, and then another.

"Darn it, Bonnie, be careful!"

In front of us was a section of the mountain that had recently been cut over, and fallen tree-tops screened our view. And then that sound began again: four, five, six grouse in all.

"Dammit, dog, this is the last chance!"

Neither my friend Jack nor I saw as much as a tail.

"Now, Jack," I said, "they must have gone straight ahead. We'll have to work fast. Suppose you hold the old road in the bottom of the ravine, and I'll see what I can kick out of these fallen tree-tops on the left-hand slope."

One grouse had not gone far. Electing to clear a small grove of white pines, he had to cross the road manned by my companion. Jack drove him just at the right second, and he pitched down in a cloud of feathers.

At the crack of the gun two more birds left a tall pine, well out of range. Fifty yards farther on I heard one break away almost over my head; he went back toward where he had been jumped. I took one snap shot at him, missing cleanly. The light was nearly gone. Suddenly Bonnie made game; she did not point, but slowed her short choppy gait and began a crouching purposeful walk that means, "Hunter, watch your step." Moving up rapidly, I was within forty feet of the grouse when he got up, heading straight down the ravine somewhat in front of my companion.

I wonder if grouse aren't flying faster these days. This one burnt the wind, weaving slightly to left and right. By providence or chance my right barrel caught him amidships. Such was his momentum that it carried him fifty or sixty feet down the mountainside. It was a proud little setter that retrieved him.

A grouse apiece for two happy, weary hunters is a prize that carries with it all the glamour of the wildwood; they can hang up their guns with a memory that will warm and thrill them every time it comes to mind. And so, as the sun went down that evening, we turned toward our car, thankful for the sport and the luck that had been ours. And should we not be forgiven if there was mixed with that thankfulness just a touch of pride?

"What's that you say, Bonnie? Dog, be patient; only a few months, and the season will be here again. According to all reports, there are plenty of grouse left in the covers. If we have a good spring for hatching, birds will be plentiful. Yes, you're getting to be a right smart grouse dog. No, I don't mean all those things I say about you when a grouse just won't hold to your point. Some bright November day we will slip up to Allen's Valley and match our wits with those of the Herd Bull. And since grouse are Scotchmen, he must be the big chief of a highland clan."

My Last Grouse Hunt

The title of this piece may well be misleading, inasmuch as the story initially appeared in the March 1941 issue of *Outdoor Life* and subsequently in *Hunter's Choice* and *Fireworks in the Peafield Corner.*

One would like to think that, in the three decades of life he had left, Rutledge again went afield after the bird he so loved. Admittedly, once he moved back to his beloved Hampton Plantation, he left the locale that furnished the setting for most of his grouse stories. Yet he knew the high country of North Carolina well, had relatives living in the Asheville area, and wrote more than once of sport in the Appalachian regions of the Old North State. Whether or not he hunted grouse again, this piece is a fitting conclusion to this section, for it offers a poignant, powerful tribute to a game bird that was a lot like Old Flintlock—rugged, independent, possessed of noble traits, and a lover of wild and lonely places.

———————

Unless he happens to have taken a hunting trip into a far country that he knows he will never visit again, it is seldom that a man realizes that any particular hunt is his last one. But it happened to me; for the time came when I who had lived in grouse country for more than thirty years, was compelled to move into a country where grouse are as rare as the flowers a wife gets after the honeymoon. On the South Carolina seacoast, to which I moved from the mountains of southern Pennsylvania, only one grouse has been seen in the last 150 years. Of course, you can hunt him there if you want to; but you will not find him.

I feel certain that a lot of the boys feel just as I do about a grouse: when all is said and done, there is no other bird in all the world that is his equal in that perfect combination of beauty, speed, wild woodcraft, and a certain patrician elegance. If Helen of Troy had been a bird, she would have been a grouse.

Like most hunters, I have hunted far more grouse than I have ever found; shot at more than I have ever killed. The greatest number I ever got in a hunt was three. But always, if I could bring home one of these patricians of the wilds, I'd feel like some kind of a champion. And now, now I was to take to the hills for my very last grouse hunt. When we are conscious of doing anything for the last time, an especial light seems to come over everything that we feel we shall not see again. It was so with me when, that mid-afternoon in late November, I drove the two miles to the mountains and got out of my car, all alone, for a final ramble.

These mountains, the Tuscaroras, are not lofty, but they are rugged and heavily wooded. Ages of erosion have formed alternate ridges and hollows on their slopes. Down nearly every hollow trickles a little stream. Here and there are great smothers of wild grapes. Occasionally one comes upon an old deserted clearing, where stand gnarled apple trees. But there is no open shooting. It is all of the woods variety. And there is not what I should call level shooting; that is, when a bird is flushed, the hunter, in trying to bring him down, has to take into account all the uphill-and-down-dale angles that the fugitive's flight will naturally follow in accord with the terrain. When grouse live in a country that stands almost on end, you have to do some fast figuring—and you have to have a lot of luck—to get them.

It was about 3:00 P.M. when I started up the mountain. There had been a rain earlier in the day, and the clouds still hung heavy. There was some mist in the woods; and as there was no wind, I knew there would be more fog ere nightfall. Up an old timber road I went, hardly making a sound on the damp leaves that strewed the ground. Past pine thickets, dogwood copses, jungles of greenbriers, I eased my way up the slope. As all this territory is fairly good grouse country, I was on the alert to shoot; but the woods were silent and apparently lifeless. I came to the edge of an old abandoned orchard, where, thirty years before, I had killed my first grouse. There was the same old haw tree by which he fell.

Beyond the orchard I knew of a wonderful growth of wild grapes. There I could nearly always flush one or two grouse. I began to walk faster now, as the woods seemed to be getting dusky. Coming through a birch thicket which ended where the grapes begin, I heard a great roar in front of me. Fifty yards away a whole covey of grouse got up—five, to be exact. But they did not fly as a covey. Three fanned out wide and went far up the mountain. Two hurtled off to right and left and then bore down the mountain. In that whole season I had not seen so many birds together. But there was no chance to shoot. Thirty years earlier I should probably have blared forth with both barrels—in the fond and juvenile hope that my good gun would somehow rise to the occasion, and would miraculously do more than it was made to do. But I have reached a time of life when I just don't shoot at game that is out of range; and long years of pretty steady going in the fields and woods have taught me something of the meaning of range; that is, the certain capacity of a gun or a rifle.

It was now nearly four o'clock. Mists were filling the hollows.

I had hardly more than an hour to hunt. On this last day there was to be no late afterglow; just a quiet closing in of foggy darkness. The first thing I had to do was to make a decision: should I follow the three birds up the mountain, and then try to flush one of the others on my way down? Or should I turn homeward, incidentally hunting for these latter two? Taking a hitch in my belt, I headed up the mountain.

Practically all my grouse hunting has been merely walking them up. I have hunted with good dogs, but never with a good grouse dog. The birds of the region I am describing rarely lie to any kind of dog, however careful he may be. The man who has to find his own grouse generally is careful to observe how far one has flown, the approximate line of his height, and the kind of place on the ground where he is most likely to hide. It pays the hunter to watch a flying grouse as far as his eyes can follow him.

Of course, it's to be remembered that the bird will not always alight on the ground; if there's an evergreen in his path, he may stop in it, probably high up; likely standing there slim and erect and hardly looking like a grouse. It is generally thought that educated grouse do not light on bare trees; yet I once saw three come to rest on the perfectly bare branches of an old sycamore.

When I have the approximate distance a grouse has gone, and his direction of flight, I follow him, but I try never to go straight at him. Wild game is always able to recognize a hunter who acts as if he were on the warpath. As I never walk directly toward a grouse, so I never try to sneak up on him. That is a maneuver that will scare the wits out of him. My general attitude in approaching game is that of elaborate and rather goofy indifference; I try to act as if I were idly looking for posies, or dreaming of some lost love of the long ago. The hunter who is stalking, if he shows himself at all, should always try to create the impression that he is doing anything else in the world but hunt. By this sort of trickery I have often been able to walk within twenty feet of a grouse, whereas, had I stormed down at him, he probably should have kited out of cover while I was still fifty yards away.

If you want a real chance at your grouse, don't let him say of you, "Oh, my gosh, here comes that killer!" Always persuade him to say unconcernedly, "I wonder who that booby is, wandering around vaguely?"

The three grouse that had gone up the mountain had, as I have said, fanned out. I decided to try for the one on the left. With damp leaves spread over slippery rocks for a footing, I had to take it easy; besides, the upward incline was here about 45 degrees, and I could not take the hills as I once did.

Figuring that my grouse had gone not more than 150 yards, and knowing the approximate direction that he'd taken, I passed the grapevine tangle and came out to where huge poplars grew and where stood the serried, spectral ranks of dead chestnuts. There was little undergrowth here; but the dark sky and the double shadow of the mountain and the great trees made visibility very poor.

As a matter of fact, I began to doubt that I could really see a grouse, even if he got up close to me. A patriarch chestnut log, prone on the wild hillside before me, attracted my notice. If I were a grouse, that's the kind of place where I'd like to hide. Nearer and nearer I came. Was he there? I felt certain that he must be. Corning up to it so that it would be on my left, I paused. Have you ever noticed how likely a wily grouse is to get up, not while you are walking, but if you stop; or, having stopped, you start forward once more?

Was he there? If he wasn't, what kind of a projectile was that which stormed from under that log and went hurtling up that dim hillside? For a dazzling combination of apparently wild and incontinent abandon, which in reality is thrilling precision, give me a grouse. This bird was going uphill, close to the ground, and quartering a little to the right. He would.

I shot a foot above him and nearly two feet to the right of him. His great flight was ended. I found him lying on a bed of colored leaves—a fit resting place for this woodland prince. A beautiful cock he was, with an exceptionally deep ruff. Through the dusky woods I turned down the mountain. I had in mind those two grouse that had gone downhill; but it was very late, the forest looked foggy, and all the trees were dripping water distilled from the rising mist. A certain gloom, typical of a rainy November twilight, reigned over the world; but it did not get me. My last hunt for grouse had been successful.

Halfway to my car, in the dusk beside the trail I noticed a remarkably straight young dogwood. As one of my hobbies is making walking sticks, I stopped to examine this one in order to see whether its big lateral root would afford a handle. Laying my gun down, I got on one knee, and began to rake away the leaves from the root. Not far off was the stump of a big pine that had recently been cut. About twenty yards away was its withered top on the ground.

When he had me just where he wanted me, and not till then, a second cock grouse tore out of that dead pine top and zoomed straight down the mountain. While still kneeling, I managed to get my gun up, had a flashing certainty of getting a bead on him, and let drive. I remember wondering whether, even if I had him dead to rights, the shot would have enough velocity to overtake him. Miraculously, it did. In semidarkness I retrieved my second grand bird, a cock also, and a little larger than the first.

Far off in the valley the lights in the village began to twinkle through the mist. Through the lone woods in the deepening dusk I walked. Until I die I hope to hunt; but my days with grouse are over. Yet still in my dreams I am after them: I see the autumn hills, I smell the damp fragrances of fallen leaves, I hear the sudden thunder of those aristocratic tawny wings.

Part Three

A BEVY OF BOBWHITE TALES

Were Archibald Rutledge alive today, he would undoubtedly bemoan the sad fate of the bobwhite. Although he had no way of knowing it, the time Rutledge spent in the South was the heyday of the noble little bird so beloved by the region's outdoor writers. Some of America's finest sporting scribes—among them Nash Buckingham, Havilah Babcock, Robert Ruark, Charlie Elliott, Charley Dickey, and Henry Edwards Davis, as well as Rutledge—praised the partridge (as the bird was normally styled, at least in South Carolina, when it wasn't simply called "bird") in tales that are both timeless and delightful. Sadly, these grand men were writing of a world and a way of hunting that now threatens to vanish forever.

Just a short time ago I was reading a privately printed autobiography, Cato Holler's *Adventures of a Lifetime,* in which a man who was ninety-four years of age as he wrote (in the 1990s) posed a poignant question: "Will the Bobwhite's Song Disappear?" It may well happen. Gone, likely never to return, are those unpaid gamekeepers of yesteryear, tenant farmers. So are overgrown fencerows; a penchant for leaving corners of soybean fields unharvested; and dedicated hunting and trapping of the quail's inveterate enemies, 'coons, 'possums, and skunks. It is now against federal law to shoot raptors, yet two generations ago, in my own boyhood, every hawk was considered a "chicken hawk" and was shot on sight. I am in no way advocating the drastic step of ignoring federal law, but I am willing to state that anyone who today argues that sharpshin or red-tailed hawks are endangered is about as blind or deluded as it is possible to be.

Sometimes it seems that a whole set of circumstances, ranging from "clean" farming practices to the modern mindset (even dedicated 'coon hunters now release their quarry rather than shoot it), have as their singular focus eradication of the brave little bobwhite. To be sure, the laudable Conservation Reserve Program has restored quite a bit of suitable quail habitat in the Midwest, in good rain years parts of Texas have great bird numbers, ongoing research at Tall Timbers and in a number of southern states continues to offer us insight on the plight of the quail, and efforts such as Quail Forever and the National Bobwhite Conservation Initiative are fighting the good fight. Therein lie glimmers of hope.

On the flip side of the coin, though, consider the experiences of a good friend of mine who made valiant (and expensive) efforts to restore viable bird numbers in the South Carolina lowcountry where both Rutledge and Babcock hunted. He tried everything—controlled burning; food plots; careful avoidance of being too clean in farming, trapping, and similar efforts—only to decide, after the better part of a decade, that he was losing ground in an ongoing exercise in futility. Some days you would hunt a whole day, behind great dogs, and find but four or five coveys. Even then, the odds were that at least two of the coveys would get up wild and set wing for the nearest impenetrable hell hole.

Rutledge could never have dreamed of such circumstances. He lived in a time and a place where bobwhites singing on fence posts in April were an integral part of the sounds of spring, where the howl of the coyote was never heard, and where big coveys were sure to be found in every frost-tipped broom-sedge field come late fall. He hunted Mr. Bob regularly, bird dogs were always a part of the Hampton Plantation scene, and this most delectable of game birds was as much a part of his festive holiday table as haunches of venison, roast wild turkey, and stuffed ducks.

Alas, those circumstances prevail no more. Going if not gone, save in a few areas where management practices which are as expensive as they are intensive, is the bobwhite in the lands where Rutledge hunted. Yet we can enjoy the world of quail hunting as once it was, albeit vicariously, through a bevy of first-rate bobwhite tales from a man who dearly loved a staunch point or a cleanly executed double. The enduring stories that follow will take you straight back to the days of bobwhite hunting as once they were.

The Baby Toddles

As Rutledge's fellow scribe and South Carolinian, Havilah Babcock, once suggested, anyone who follows a bungling puppy afield as it earns hunting stripes is sure to "cry a little and laugh a lot." In this piece, originally published in the August 1922 issue of *Field & Stream,* we share the trials, tribulations, and ultimate triumph of a canine toddler as it learns the ropes.

The days of forty-bird coveys, at least in this part of the country (I live in the state, South Carolina, which Rutledge called home), belong to a world we have lost. However, the magical moment when a puppy comes of age, be it with a whopping bevy of birds or the mere handful of wild and exceedingly wary wingsters that is today's lot hereabouts, belongs to the ages. Here Rutledge, in his inimitable fashion, shares one such moment with us.

"How many birds do you think there are in it?" I asked Jake.

"Forty if there's one," he said.

I believed him; for Jack owed me nothing, and he is not a farmer. To a farmer—at least one who does not hunt—a covey of quail always has forty birds, just as to an amateur deer hunter every buck weighs two hundred pounds.

"There must have been two coveys together," I suggested.

"Then they've been together for a long time," he said, "and don't you know how birds quarrel when two flocks come together? These acted like one covey."

"Are you guessing, Jake, or did you count them?"

"Well, I'll tell you. I first saw one bunch of five or six run across the old road by the sawmill; then I counted twenty-nine birds cross. Then after I had come up to the place, several others that I had not seen flew up. There must be forty."

During the autumn Jake does some rather skilful trapping; and while he never wastes a shell on a quail, he condescends to notice the birds. I knew therefore that he was not describing to me meadow larks or killdeer, as some other hopeful informants have done. These quail were evidently out by the old saw mill by the creek; and as that particular region was singularly hunterless, I felt certain that the covey must be intact. It seemed as if a regular heyday or mayday of a time was ahead.

But I had no dog. All I had was Star; and to be very exact, the day I heard about this quail camp meeting Star was three months old. What I had managed to teach him was to love the sound of a shotgun; to delight in picking up the English sparrows that fell before it; and to know that I would whip him if he didn't mind me. The youngster's education was beginning; but he had a long road to travel ere he reached stately doghood. He had never been in the field; but in my yard he had made life rather lively for an old barred rock hen and her brood. These chicks he persistently, even monotonously, pointed; and as he would come to a stand, his right forefoot would come up prettily. Several times I saw him lose his balance while going through this performance.

But to return to the big covey. My decision about it was speedy. I would repair that very afternoon to the old sawmill; and Star would repair with me. I would do most of the repairing; both while we were in the field, and then upon the pup, after our return home, I supposed.

Three miles in our Ford roller-skate brought us into the birdy country. The landscape is typical of the fruitful regions of southern Pennsylvania. The old road was bordered by old fences grown to oak-bushes, sumac—now aflame with autumn-colored foliage and clustered berries—blackberry canes, and the like. On the right lay a cornfield with the brown shocks waiting to be plundered by the farmer; on the left lay a field of wheat stubble and ragweed; and if there's a better feeding ground for quail, take the lead and I'll follow fast. Beyond the wheat field was a slow-winding creek, overhung with sycamores and shellbarks. A heavy woodland lay at the far end of the corn field. It was bird country. I was a bird hunter. But what about the bird dog?

During the drive Star had lain on the seat beside me. He looked small enough to crawl into the pocket of my hunting coat. He was not at all sure that he liked riding in a Rolls Royce. When I looked down at him, his eyes seemed rather bright, undetermined, and apprehensive. He made me feel that I ought to be ashamed to bring a baby out on a tear like this one.

When Star and I alighted from the car, it was four o'clock of a late October afternoon. The air was still and damp with a penetrating fall dampness. The tattered gold of the frost-killed foliage hung motionless. It was the kind of afternoon that made me know that wheresoever the foot of a quail would tread, thereupon verily should be left a hot scent. On such an afternoon a trained dog has it easy with birds. But what could I expect of my tiny companion? Honestly, when I set him down in the road and saw him shiver; when I noted the alarming difference in size between him and the roadside briars, when he gazed at me as if I was his last friend, and he had just lost me—then I began to think that it might have been wiser had I left the infant at home. Nor were my feelings soon reassured; for in the wheat stubble which we now entered, Star was submerged. He was so little that a dewberry vine threw him headlong. After that encounter he listed to leeward. I felt as if I was not hunting birds but trying to kill off the makings of a good dog. However, we managed to beat out the stubble pretty well. The birds were not in it. Then we turned toward the creek. The long and level rays of the red sun were firing the woods and on the gliding waters were writing scattered messages in many colors. Through the damp woods we trudged, Star enjoying the respite from the tall ragweed. We came down to the edge of the creek, and there the pup drank fearsomely from the mighty waters which stretched full twenty feet broad before him. It was while Star was assuaging himself in this pure Volstead fashion that I heard a sound which never fails to thrill a sportsman. I heard quail moving in damp leaves; distinctly I heard the excited chittering of the covey.

"Jake's covey," I said, "forty birds; and if they fly past me, they will likely knock me down with the blast of the wind from their wings."

I did not move; I looked and listened. It is a grateful feeling to have, when one is well nigh licked—the feeling that perhaps after all there is going to be some shooting. At last I made out the birds. They were on the farther side of the creek. They had evidently come down to drink before going to roost. What were they about to do? Would they travel over land to the roost, or would they fly? Old birds love to fly to the roost, especially if they think there is trouble to them if they stay on the ground. Star, unconscious of my great discovery, his little shaggy setter sides bulging barrel-like, turned his intelligent but childish face and looked at me drowsily. The baby was sleepy. The sun was about down, and he wanted to crawl into his box at home.

Whatever was to be done had to be done quickly. The misty October twilight would soon fade. The birds would be gone. Stooping down I picked up Star. I would wade the creek and flush the birds. Before I stepped into the water I tried to locate them once more. But they were gone. They had not taken wing. They had given me the slip. To give a hunter the slip is a quail covey's readiest accomplishment, especially at sundown, and more especially when a man does not have a dog. Oh for a real dog! As I waded the quiet stream, Star shivered in my arms and snuggled very close to me. I was afraid he might be asleep before I reached the farther bank. It was dusky there under the sycamores. A screech owl swooped down over our heads and snapped his bill at us. Fresh fallen shellbarks on the bank gave the air a spicy tang. I love October twilights, with their winy fragrances, their haunting mists, and the gloomy gold of their waning forests.

Reaching the farther bank, I walked carefully toward the spot where I had seen the quail. Of course they were not there. The low bushes and few briar canes were not dense. Gently the bank sloped away eastward, and as I looked toward its top I saw the fringe of light which marked where it joined a field where grew broom sedge. It was perhaps sixty yards from the creek to the broom sedge. "That's where they are," I said to myself; "but I should have been an hour earlier. They've walked up this slope and have gone out in that field to roost. Star, old fellow, we're on the hotfoot now for some fun.

Then I stopped to think. If I went blindly on, the chances were that I would miss the birds. It seems an easier thing to blunder on birds unaware than to follow them deliberately and to flush them. The time allowed me was very short; the dog allowed me was likewise. A man, however, must always yield to a dog in at least one respect: his nose is poor. I remembered that Star, sleepy and tired and snuggly as he was, and apparently helpless, had a nose. Therefore I decided to trust him to take me to those twilight birds that had just done the vanishing act to perfection. I put the puppy down where I knew the trail must be; and in a moment he had the scent. It must have been strong, for the pup waked up amazingly. He started up the bank; I followed like the inferior being that I really was in this business. Star took the very trail that I should have followed without him; but when he came within thirty yards of the sedge field, now glimmering before me in a soft red afterglow, he turned abruptly to the right.

"Hold up, boy," I said, "you're on the wrong trail. They've gone up this way."

But the baby seemed sure of himself. He crawled under a bush; he struggled with a fallen briar; but he went on—sure of himself. I was so interested that I came to the margin of the old field before I realized it; and I discovered that we were full fifty yards farther to the hillside. When Star got to the brink of the grass he did a thing that is indelibly imprinted upon my memory: he lay flat down on his little water barrel. Something told me that he was on a point. I saw him shiver; and this time it must have been from the excitement of drinking in all that dewy aroma that the big birds had just left. I think a dog's pleasure in scenting game is certainly as keen as our seeing it. Star lay still and enjoyed himself; I slipped up my safety and stepped forth into the still bright world of the lonely sedge field.

A big cock quail got up under my feet; another whirred out of the grass. They headed straight over the field and against the clear skyline. Then other birds got up, just by twos and threes. They seemed deliberate. Without stirring from where I first fired, I was able to down five birds. Nor had little Star stirred. I might call him a setting star were I a believer in puns. I thought he was simply bewildered by what he had led me into; but perhaps he may be given the credit of understanding he should not break point while birds were before him.

All the birds that flushed alighted not far off in the field, and almost immediately they began calling. Star and I advanced upon them; and the shooting was easy and yet fast. The skyline was fading; the birds were big ones; and they now seemed to realize that getting away was the part for them to play. Nevertheless, the chances were many; and the limit for the day was soon reached. As I picked up my last bird, I looked for Star. Until that moment I thought he had been close at my heels. He was not in sight; but a few yards off I heard a queer little mournful howl. He thought he was lost in the tall grass, and was duly notifying me of his plight. I gathered him in my arms; and soon we were retracing our way across the stream and toward the car. "Star," I told him, "when we started in here this afternoon, you were an ignorant cub; now you're a made dog. If you hadn't turned to the right on the hill back yonder, I never would have found those birds in time to salute them, and Star, I take my hat off to you, you and your parents of good blood and breeding; we know each other now and mutual confidence is established."

And that's the true story of the baby's first outing.

The Enemies of Quail

First published in *Sports Afield* in July 1959, this piece is something of a departure. Rutledge was first and foremost a storyteller, a man who firmly believed in literary license and made full use of it to embellish his tales. Yet he was also an astute, highly perceptive amateur naturalist, and it is no accident that he was a recipient of the coveted John Burroughs Award for excellence in nature writing. Here we see ample evidence of his keen observations, and the information is so intensely practical, so timeless, that anyone who bemoans the sad plight of the quail would do well to read and reread this piece. Indeed, I personally feel that many theory-filled biologists could profit from the readily understandable common sense to be found here.

While not the largest, and in some respects inferior to a lordly bird like the ruffed grouse, the bobwhite quail stands first in the hearts of America's hunters. When farming was less mechanical than it now is, quail probably were more numerous, and extended over a wider range. Nevertheless, the bobwhite has shown the steel in its nature by meeting the challenge of modern farming and multiplying.

This beautiful, and I might say perfect game bird, naturally has its enemies, as every other creature has. Of these, I suppose we must include man, for except in sanctuaries the quail is hunted wherever he is found. Yet it is a strange biological fact that man's invasion of the covey may well have a beneficial effect.

In Dr. Axel Munthe's famous book *The Story of San Michele* he described the plague in Florence. The feature that impressed him most was the utter abandonment with which people threw themselves into one another's arms when men and women were dying on doorsteps, in the streets, even in theaters. The reason was plain. Nature was saying: "The race is dying. Increase and multiply and replenish the earth."

The same principle works in time of war or any other disaster. People rush into each other's arms as they would never do in any ordinary time. Nature impels them to do so. And so it certainly is with quail. If you have a covey of standard size—12 to 16 birds—and don't hunt them or permit them to be hunted, there is a good chance that none of them will ever mate and nest. The following year you may have the very same covey. But if you shoot into them, break them up, scatter them—then the old biological urge takes hold of them. They, too, feel that the race is in danger; and as soon as the mating season comes, they will pair off and rear two new broods, and occasionally three.

But it is not of man as an enemy of quail that I would write. Many men protect them; others, by planting the crops on which these birds love to feed, keep them in safe country. I know a good many farmers who deliberately let a fencerow grow up in weeds, briars and bushes, so that quail will be afforded protection, especially in time of snow. Of the men who hunt quail, all true sportsmen will always leave at least six or seven birds in a covey. I have been invited to a hunt on quail preserves where there was a rule that no hunter should kill more than two quail out of one covey.

This did not seem to be a sensible rule, for no consideration was given to the size of the covey. One might have twenty birds and another might have six. As a rule, I should be in favor of leaving more than six or seven birds in any one covey; because in hunting these birds, it is not possible when they are in flight to recognize the sex. The sex, of course, can easily be distinguished if the birds are on the ground. The cocks look a little larger, and have so much more white about the head. But in the melee of a covey's rise, all the birds look alike.

Disregarding man, who is often a good friend to the quail, let us consider its natural, and therefore inveterate, enemies. Of these, strange as it may seem, I would put the house cat first. A cat is one of those animals that has a dual nature. You look at Tabby lying on your hearth, and you might consider her the most gentle and harmless of creatures. But late in the afternoon her wild nature awakes. She will slip out of the house and prowl your garden. If a field is near, she will go there as a nocturnal huntress, giving her sinister attention to anything she can catch—especially birds of all kinds, and rabbits. Of the birds, quail are perhaps the favorite quarry.

However well fed your tame cat may be, and however much of a homebody it may appear, a few moments outdoors, especially if a garden, field, or wood lot be near, will transform it into a regular wildcat. And it is amazing how far such a supposedly tame creature will travel. I have seen many a "tame" cat more than a mile from where it belongs, stalking game. I have seen several of my own cats in this dual role, and as a lover of quail their behavior set me against the whole race of cats—at least in rural or semi-rural areas.

While living in a fair sized village, on several occasions I have been shocked to see my old house cat bring in a quail. Some cats, of course, go wild, taking permanently to the woods and fields; and these, wholly dependent on their own efforts for their food, develop a sinister cunning, and become the very worst predators of all.

It may seem strange that I do not put the true wildcats—the bobcat and lynx—ahead of the ordinary tame cat as a dread enemy of quail. But the truth is that the wildcat is a creature of the deep woods, and rarely goes into fields, though he may travel old roads and trails. But his natural haunt is a thicket, his den a deep hole under a stump or in the cavity beneath the roots of a hurricane-thrown tree.

On the other hand, except in the rarest of exceptions, quail will not roost in the woods. They seek out a dry marsh, a stubble field, or a big area of grass. In fact, at twilight I have seen a covey rise from the edge of a patch of woods and fly far out over a favorable field. If quail especially like a certain roosting place, they may frequent it night after night. They never roost on the same spot, but in the same general area. I have found as many as sixteen "roosts" within a space of half an acre.

It might be supposed that game birds, such as quail, pheasants, and wild turkeys, all of which nest on the ground, would fall easy prey to predators during the nesting season. But wise nature intervenes. She makes at least three provisions against such a disaster. First, whether designedly or not, she fills the woods and fields with a confusing myriad of scents and fragrances. I have seen one of my fine old bird dogs, working upwind in a path, pass within six feet of a setting quail without noticing a thing. Under those conditions in the autumn or winter, he would have winded that quail twenty or thirty feet away.

Again, if a ground-nesting bird becomes suspicious that she may be followed by her scent to her nest (and this is especially true of the wild turkey, the scent of which is almost as strong as that of a deer), the mother bird will fly to and from her nesting site. It is a touching thing to see a prospective mother so protect her eggs.

In the third place, I have heard it said (but I cannot prove this except by conjecture based on observation) that in the spring and summer, a ground-nesting mother bird gives out less scent than usual, or else has the power to hold in the scent by compressing the feathers close to the body. Whether this is really done, or can be done, I am unable to say; but certainly neither hounds nor bird dogs appear able to scent game birds or animals in the spring and summer as they do in the autumn and the winter. Moreover, if dogs could work as well in hot weather as in the regular hunting seasons, the consequent destruction of game birds would surely become almost immediately apparent.

If, as I think, the common house cat is the worst enemy the quail has, the second, probably because he is so widely distributed, is the opossum. As soon as dusk falls, he begins to travel; and he forages all night. A possum has a good nose, and for his size he is very strong. He is especially fond of eggs of all kinds; and birds that nest on the ground are in constant peril from him. He will not only destroy the eggs but will kill the nesting mother. I once had a tame turkey hen killed on her nest by an opossum. I was sure of his identity, for I caught him in a trap beside the turkey he had killed. Then, too, I had seen his tracks.

A possum covers so much ground, and is so adept at getting over and under fences and through dense cover, that I consider him one of our worst predators, utterly worthless, and a constant and evil enemy of quail.

About 60 miles north of where I live there is one of the greatest quail countries of North America. Many millionaires from the North rent thousands of acres there to enjoy the sport. I personally have never seen so many quail anywhere. On a brief hunt one winter's afternoon I put up 12 coveys.

But a few years ago this concentration of birds caused a gathering of their enemies, especially of foxes. Year by year the quail decreased in numbers. This decrease was attributed to the foxes, which seemed to abound everywhere.

So serious did the situation become that the renters of several large properties talked with me seriously of giving up the sport. About that time an epidemic of hydrophobia assailed the foxes. Highly infectious, this disease is nearly always fatal. In that district, foxes were almost exterminated.

Within a single year, men who rented large quail areas told me that the birds had suddenly increased at least 100 per cent; and they did not hesitate to attribute this upsurge in the number of quail to the disappearance of the foxes.

I confess that until this time I had not considered the fox as an outstanding enemy of quail. He is, of course, carnivorous, feeding on birds, rabbits, mice, rats, squirrels; and occasionally raiding a chicken yard. But because he is primarily a creature of the woods, I had often thought of him as harder on the ruffed grouse and the wild turkey, which are birds of the woods, than on quail, which are essentially birds of the field. Quail will take refuge in woods, and will dust themselves in sand along the sunny edges of thickets and wood lots, but they feed and they roost in fields. Of course, under cover of night, foxes traverse fields, and come close to farmhouses and buildings, where they might well encounter quail, and I do not think they would pass a quail by. But I do not think a fox specializes in quail; and in the delicate balance of nature, he probably, by feeding on predators, does as much good as harm.

Whether the foxes that died of hydrophobia because of the great numbers of quail in their habitat had therefore become regular feeders on these fine birds, I have never been able to determine.

In fields where quail nest are usually found skunks, rats, and mice. All these will destroy quail eggs; but fortunately, as soon as one clutch of eggs is destroyed, the mother quail, turning around in the grass until the place becomes a nest, will begin to lay again.

And it should be remembered that little quail, like little grouse and wild turkeys and other game birds that nest on the ground, are precocial. That is, they belong to that group of birds that are "ready to go" as soon as they are hatched. They do not seem to have a fledgling stage, an awkward age. As soon as they hatch, they almost immediately leave the nest; in fact, I have seen baby quail running around when they were so young that snowy fragments of eggshell were still sticking to their backs! And when they are barely out of the nest, at a single note of alarm from the mother, with swift intelligence every one will hide. Once when a mother was giving her warning cry, I picked up one of her babies. It cuddled down between two of my fingers, and hid there!

While he might not pass by a nest full of eggs, I have never considered the raccoon a real enemy of the quail. He is a dweller in the woods; and as a rule, he haunts the edges of ponds and marshes. He loves fish, frogs, shellfish; at times he feeds on acorns, but he is rarely found at any distance from the water.

There are certain hawks that are enemies of quail; but the bobwhite is so swift to take cover that I do not believe that many are taken by these marauders. I have seen coveys and single birds attacked by the pigeon hawk, the Cooper's, the marsh and the red-shouldered. I once watched a marsh hawk vainly beating his wings on top of a briar patch, in the dusky safety of which a covey was securely hiding.

In my experience, there is only one condition which makes a hawk a distinct and constant menace to quail. That is when deep snow blankets the ground. In these times, strange to say, their assailer is a buteo, one of the milder-mannered hawks such as the red-shouldered or the red-tailed. Many of these stay in cold and snowy countries during the winter, whereas the fierce accipiters, of which the Cooper's is typical, are more common in my section of the South.

I suppose the swift and devastating duck hawk would pursue a quail; but he is more inclined to pursue larger game such as the ruffed grouse and the wild duck. However, once over a desolate sea marsh I watched one pursue a Wilson's snipe. By his dazzling speed and his expert dodging, the snipe escaped. It may be added that in open country few birds, whatever their swiftness, ever escape this superb marauder.

I mention the notorious menace of a buteo to a covey of quail. I have watched it often with deep misgiving; and on occasion have brought my rifle into play against this aerial corsair.

When a deep snow comes, with perhaps a glaze on it, a covey of quail will try to outlast the cold and exposure by harboring along a bushy and briared fencerow. Of course, with so glaring a background, they are easily seen, particularly from the air. A big hawk, of one of the species that is reputed to be mild-mannered, will locate the covey. Then he will take up his watch on a leafless tree nearby. Day by day this same hawk will kill and eat at least one quail. I have often known such a predator, at such a time favorable to him, to destroy the greater part of a covey of quail, and at times to take the last bird. When I knew what was going on, I would correct the situation by creeping up on the marauder through the snow-covered woods with my small but quite effective high-powered rifle. I know that professional ornithologists may tell you that these big buteo hawks are harmless to game. But I know what I have seen; I know also that these powerful and hungry hawks have not read the books that declare that they will not harm any game species.

As he is of wide distribution, merciless nature and wise in a minatory way, I believe that the great horned owl is a constant and dreadful enemy of the bobwhite. The only rift in the cloud is that this grim tiger of the wildwoods is comparatively rare. It is unusual for more than a pair to inhabit a certain stretch of woodland. They love woods that are lonely and wild, and timber that looks primeval.

It may be that his smaller cousin the barred owl will take an occasional quail, but he is nothing like the menace to this fine bird that the great horned owl is.

The great horned owl nests in the winter, while the coveys of quail are still intact. Once, beneath a nest of such an owl, in the fork of a giant oak, I found the remains of at least eleven quail, and these had been freshly killed. A hunter once told me that he had come on one of these fierce predators eating a wild turkey. I do not know if he killed this great game bird, but he was quite capable of doing so.

For many years in the wild mountains of southern Pennsylvania I used to hunt that lordly bird the ruffed grouse. Like other game birds they had their favorite haunts. There was one place in particular, full of greenbriars, wild grapes, and a few old apple trees of a deserted orchard where I had, until this certain year, been able to find grouse—not one or two, but twelve or fifteen. But this year they had vanished.

I revisited the place several times, but never saw a sign of a grouse. I did, however, find where two had been killed. Some of the feathers of these grouse were rolled in a ball—a typical owl manner of regurgitating indigestible matter. I also discovered that two great horned owls had taken up their residence in that little swampy valley. Before I left there, I managed to make way with these two marauders, whose lives were one long career of murder.

The following season the grouse returned to their loved little retreat. I believe that when horned owls move into a locality, most birds move out.

A last enemy of quail I shall mention is found only in the southeastern part of our country. This is the lordly diamondback rattlesnake, growing to an extreme length of nine feet. He is a persistent feeder on quail, usually the mature birds, which he captures by scent at night. I once opened one of these huge serpents whose body appeared bulgy. It contained three undigested quail.

The timber rattler and other forms of this species have a much wider range, but I doubt if they molest quail to any degree, if at all. But the lethal diamondback is a dangerous foe. Other snakes destroy quail by eating their eggs; among these are the black snake, the chicken snake, and the corn snake.

The quail, like the white-tailed deer, takes kindly to civilization. In this respect they are the opposite of the ruffed grouse and the wild turkey. These are true lovers of the wilderness.

If you have a rural or semi-rural residence that might harbor quail, or a farm, or a regular quail preserve, if you love the bobwhite as I do, you must keep his enemies under control—the housecat, the opossum, the fox, certain of the predatory hawks, all egg-eating snakes, the great horned owl, and the diamondback rattlesnake. These last two are not likely to be found near you unless you live, as I do, in the heart of the wilderness—which can be both frightening and beautiful.

Wintering Bobwhite

From *Field & Stream* for November 1919, this little essay shows that Rutledge was interested in and knowledgeable about game management. While landowners and biologists alike are still trying to figure out just what factors underlie the game little bird's sad state over much of the South, few would argue, even though four generations have come and gone since these words were written, that what the author suggests is anything other than sound and sensible.

———

The charge has sometimes been made that, while the average farm owner will not permit hunters to shoot his quail in the autumn, the same hunters will do more to protect the birds during the winter than will the natural champion of these birds. Like many general statements this is true in certain cases only; and wherever it is true, I think it is due less to neglect on the part of the farmer than to a failure to appreciate the vital needs of bobwhite during the heavy snows of winter. The average hunter knowing well the nature and the habits of the quail appreciates the position of the coveys when a blizzard comes. The average farmer may not. All that is necessary, then, seems to be to have owners of places put in possession of a few facts concerning the nature of quail, and also the best means whereby these fine birds can be safely brought through the severest spells of weather.

A good range for quail always has three elements: a grass, stubble, or ragweed field in which to feed and roost; a ravine, gully, briar patch, swamp, or woodland into which to retire during the siesta period of the day; and water. During the summer months there is, of course, no lack of cover; and food is everywhere abundant. At this season the bobwhite feeds on small fruits and on grasshoppers and numerous kinds of insects, many of them highly injurious to agriculture. For example, he eats the Colorado potato beetle, the cinch-bug, the cucumber beetle, and the cotton boll-weevil; and when we use the word eat, we mean that the bird's appetite and capacity are such that he will eat vast quantities of these harmful creatures if he can find them. As autumn comes, the food changes. It then becomes, of necessity, vegetable. Grains of various kinds and seeds of varieties too numerous to mention them constitute bobwhite's diet. His favorite grains are buckwheat, rye, wheat, oats, millet, and corn. Among the seeds that he enjoys are those with the three-sided mercury, foxtail grass, crab grass, witch grass, sheep sorrel, and the like. At one meal a bobwhite will eat hundreds and even thousands of these seeds that, developing, would double a farmer's work. Throughout an autumn and winter, several coveys of birds (say four of about fifteen birds each) will easily destroy 500 pounds of the worst weed seeds that can be found. These facts may be well known; but they are such that they will bear repeating. And they serve to confirm our judgment in the high economic value of the presence of bobwhite on the farm. His aesthetic value need hardly be emphasized, for there lives no man or woman with soul so dead as not to love the sight and the cheerful penetrating whistle of this friend of the fields.

In the winter, then, the covey's food supply consists of gleanings from the stubble fields, and of such weed seeds as he can pick up. Life for the birds is a simple matter if there is such a place to feed—that is, until the snow comes. It has been repeatedly demonstrated that bobwhite can stand without injury temperatures far below zero. In fact, cold can hardly kill the bird if he is in his normal condition of health. And it may be added bobwhite is subject to very few ailments. The worst one, and the one with which we must here deal is the fundamental and natural one of hunger. If he lacks food, he loses vitality; then it is that exposure may kill him.

Let us take a concrete example. A covey has been getting on well despite cold weather. There has been nothing to cut off the food supply. The first light snow has merely taught the birds how to get along in it, and how to feed on the grass-tops that have not been covered. Then, about the middle of the winter a heavy snow will come that will effectively cover the food supply. This will be followed by some thaw or a rain that will put a glazed surface on the snow. Now the birds are helpless. Day after day they forage in vain. The weather becomes colder. Their vitality decreases. They begin to suffer from the cold. At last, huddled in a corner, they will perish—from cold that, because of their starved condition, they cannot resist. Repeatedly coveys have thus been found when the snow thaws. A few quarts of screenings or chicken feed or of small grain of any kind would have saved them. From such a fate the quail's larger relative, the ruffed grouse, is free; for the grouse feeds on buds when the ground is covered with snow, and in bitter weather he sleeps under the snow. Occasionally, indeed, quail will feed upon buds, but rarely only. In narrow valleys which are overhung by mountains, quail often gather in the late autumn in immense flocks, aggregating more than a hundred individuals, and these resort to the mountain glens for the winter. They undoubtedly become budders. But the birds of the flat lands, of the typical farming landscapes, need vitally the help of the landowners in the winter.

They need food. The favorite kinds have already been mentioned. A mixed pigeon food is ideal. If, however, the birds take the feed immediately upon its being spread for them (as, for example, when they have been caught and are being wintered indoors, or when they come up to the barn like tame things to feed with the chickens), the grain should be soaked in water. If this is not done it will bring on crop trouble. Many wintered quail have died from their crops bursting from swelled grain. In feeding quail it is better to scatter the food over a considerable area, and to feed sparingly. It is better, too, to stick to natural, well-tested foods rather than to experiment. It is dangerous to feed moldy wheat or corn; and a very little corn at a time should be fed. It is best cracked. Bobwhite likes corn, but he prefers the small grains. Often in the autumn he will leave the wheat stubble to feed on the piles of nubbin corn in the comparatively bare cornfield adjoining the land where the wheat was grown. So much for the feed. Now as to the best way to distribute it.

The man who has quail on his place knows where they stay. Their range will become more and more limited as the winter sets in. If all the cover fields are plowed up and all the briared fences are cleared out, the quail will move off to a farm where these requisites are to be had. But if the cover and the shelter remain, the quail will also. If the food-supply is plowed down, it may be supplied, and if the shelter is cut off, a few shocks of corn fodder, leaned against the northern side of the fence near which the quail resort, will make excellent protection for them. In place of this, a few shocks of fodder can be left standing, some provision being made to keep them firmly in place; and an entrance being made into the sheltered side. Even a pile of brush will do; in fact it is excellent, especially if it be evergreen, or if it has been cut with the foliage on. About such shelters quail will live through the winter. Such water as they need they can procure. They will keep warm enough if they have sufficient food. They can eat, rest, and roost in safety and comfort if they have the proper shelter; and such protection guarantees, too, that they will not be snowed under while on the roost.

But probably the most important use of the shelter is to protect bobwhite from those grim and solitary marauders of winter, the red-shouldered and the Cooper's hawks. They are deadly enemies of quail; and when snow is on the ground, bobwhite fall easy prey to these sagacious harriers. A big hawk will locate his covey; and if the birds do not have a refuge, he will take one or even two each day. He will not let up on this until the whole covey has been destroyed. If such hawks have been seen on your farm during the previous winter, and if your quail have had no shelter, there will be no need to expect to hear bobwhite calling when the spring begins. He is in the "maw of a kite." And you are largely responsible for his untimely fate.

The best way to deal with these big hawks, which are too shrewd to be readily approached, is to pick them off at a distance with a good rifle. If a peep sight is used, the feat is not a difficult one at 150 yards; and there is an element of sport about it that is enjoyable.

Many a good farmer protects his quail religiously from hunters; but as the hunting season closes and winter sets in, he is too liable to let the coveys shift for themselves. What is necessary for their safety is assuredly simple enough. A shelter can be constructed in a few minutes. The food is needed only when the ground is covered through a considerable period with snow. Then, simple food supplied twice a week, proportioned in such a manner that the birds can get at least some each day, will winter the quail comfortably. Don't imagine that because they are wary and wise and wild (as they assuredly are) that they can fight blizzards and big hawks. And the cleaner a farm is, the more the owner owes it to his birds to build shelters; for in becoming an up-to-date agriculturist, he has done away with the natural homes of the birds. In building up his own place he has torn down theirs.

Of all the great family of game birds the bobwhite is really the only one that loves civilization; it thrives best near the habitations of man. Let us give him the best possible chance to survive. Let us help him to see the winter through. It is his time of peril; and we are his only allies.

Quail of the Kalmias

Here again we have a Rutledge story set in Pennsylvania. After all, the southern portion of the state was home to him for all but a few weeks of each year for the thirty-three years he taught at Mercersburg Academy, and Old Flintlock was the sort of man who firmly believed in finding sport wherever fate might place him. He had no use for Pennsylvania traditions such as hunting deer with rifles. But give him his trusty Parker double-barrel and a few idle hours, and he would take to the fields and woods to good effect. It was an escape from the demands of the classroom, a chance to search his soul in solitude, and always, more grist for his storytelling mill. This selection originally appeared in *Field & Stream,* November 1933, and later in *Heart of the South* and *Fireworks in the Peafield Corner.*

———

Just as I had found a splendid flight of Wilson snipe where I least expected them, so, too, I have found quail where many good hunters would never dream of looking for them. These birds are said never to migrate; but unquestionably they move considerable distances as the frosts come on and as their autumn cover gets thin. Repeatedly at twilight on an October day I have seen large coveys rise of their own accord, attain unusual height, and head off in a southerly direction; and every quail hunter has had the experience of finding coveys in places where, a short time before, none were known to be.

Wherever bobwhite is found, he will have a regular feeding ground and a regular sanctuary. Immediate shelter from danger is as essential to him as food; one preserves his life as essentially as the other. In the Deep South quail will take refuge from peril in swamps, along briared ditch banks, in marshes, and even across rivers. In Maryland and Virginia they usually take to friendly patches of woods, to wild ravines, and even to dense smothers of wild honeysuckle.

In southern Pennsylvania, about which I am writing—a region that represents, in the East, the northern limit of this fine bird in natural abundance—one of his favorite retreats is into the mountains, where he finds admirable shelter in the great laurel thickets that clothe with eternal greenery the lonely glades of these wild hills. As this type of quail shooting has something different about it and is exceedingly sporty, I believe that my fellow huntsmen may like to hear some account of my experiences with this beloved and wily bird as he is found close to the bases of the picturesque Tuscaroras.

I think it is true that quail develop habits in keeping with their environment. While, in a sense, like people, they are always the same, nevertheless their manner of behavior differs in separate localities. They all have the same heritage, but they vary in character somewhat with their surroundings. In the South, for example, the birds of the cultivated lands have different ways from those of the pine barrens. So these quail, which are bred close to the mountains, vary from the birds of the lowlands and the wide valleys. They are true highlanders, and they have preserved an intensely wild and romantic spirit. Big and strong, they have managed to take on some of the superb speed of the ruffed grouse.

In this part of southern Pennsylvania the Tuscarora Range is only about 800 feet high, but the hills are rugged and slope rather sharply to the pleasant farmlands of the Cumberland Valley, which of old was a happy hunting ground for the Indians who ranged between the Susquehanna and the Potomac. Now, the whole valley is cultivated, up to the very edges of the mountain slopes. Within the shadow of these lie long wheat fields, separated from one another by ancient stone walls and briared fencerows. Tiny rivulets trickle down the gullies along the fences from springs high in the hills.

Here, then, we have ideal quail conditions: water, food, good loafing places, and a nearby sanctuary in the mountain itself. And here in these stubble fields and in the adjoining thickets I have, for a matter of thirty years, enjoyed as sporty quail shooting as can be had, I think, anywhere in America. These birds are big, they are wise, they fly almost like grouse, and they know more tricks about getting away than a debutante knows about getting her man. Sometimes they lie unbelievably close. They light in trees. They run long distances. And occasionally they take a flight that looks as if it were intended for a world tour. But some real memories of my adventures with them will do more to convince you than general statements.

Except under unusual circumstances, these birds always roost in the fields. I remember going out one misty November morning at daybreak with my old Llewellyn setter, Bell. She was at that time old and slow, but she was infallible. She was then seven. From the time she was five years old, I do not recall ever having to tell her what to do. I would just get out of the car in bird country and follow her. A good dog knows the habits of quail and where they are likely to be at certain times of the day.

Almost as soon as we were in the stubble field Bell began to trail. About two hundred yards from the fringes of the mountain, right in the valley end of the wheat field, she came to a stand. Experience had taught me that these birds would fly straight for the mountain, regardless of where they were flushed in the field. If I walked ahead into them, I would have a right-hand or a left-hand shot at the covey streaming by, or perhaps they would go straight over my head, which makes the chance an awkward one. If I wanted a straightaway shot, I would have to go round them, so that they would rise between me and the heavy cover which they would surely seek.

When Bell drew to her point in the brown stubble, I thought it would be sporty to walk right in, compelling myself to take the birds at a quartering shot as they passed me to escape into their mountain haunts. What they did always seemed to me about as adroit a maneuver as this crafty little aristocrat ever executes. They arose in two small groups, one led by the old cock and the other by the old hen. There was a difference in intelligence, though not in the size of two birds. Separated by only a few yards, the two groups came hurtling by on either side of me, in strong, low, level height.

Of course, the thing I did was a foolish one; for when a dog draws to a point on quail, the first thing for a hunter to do is to scrutinize the adjacent country to discover where the flushed birds are likely to go. Depend upon it; they have a sanctuary in mind before they are flushed. It may be a patch of woods, a creek bank, a briared fencerow, a laurel thicket. Since the direction of your approach will not make them change their minds as to where they are going, the sensible maneuver is to work around behind the covey until the probable refuge lies dead ahead. Then and only then can the hunter be sure of a normal chance at straight-aways.

Perhaps one reason why the amateur or the careless quail hunter does not really make good at this exacting game is that he takes too little into account certain standard habits of these fine birds. So many hunters blindly fight their game. But hunting is essentially a matching of wits instead of a physical con-test. All the effort and all the endurance in the world will not count if there is a lack of wary intelligence.

With my right I made one of those perfect misses—perhaps the most ordinary of all shots. My second barrel brought a bird down. In a minute the fine covey had crossed the field, topped the fence, risen high above the first fringing thickets of the mountain, and had been lost to sight among a growth of pine and hemlocks.

Whether I follow a covey into such a place depends entirely on how ambitious I am feeling. As the day was young, and as I had not as yet distinguished myself, and as Bell would have it no other way, we entered this difficult fastness. Here are jungles of sassafras and birch, rising out of a low sea of kalmias; here are evergreens and massive oaks and stretches of young locust; here are patches of wild raspberries, wild grape, and honeysuckle. And in a place like this, hunting quail is likely to be a romp of some kind, merry or otherwise.

I had marked the birds down by a towering dead chestnut, but it was nearly a hundred yards farther on that Bell began to get interested. She fell into a stealthy walk, now pausing, then stepping forward like a ghost trailing a ghost. These quail of the kalmias never seem to stay put. They keep moving ahead of dog and man, and they usually move as a covey. After their long fly from the field, they alight almost together, and then proceed to take a swift sneak. If they are followed, they keep on going. And sometimes they flush out of gunshot. In these thickets, with their dense undergrowth of thick evergreens, and the birds as big and as wild as they are, I think the shooting every whit as difficult as that on grouse, perhaps more so, because the hurtling targets are so much smaller.

On the far edge of a little rise the laurels temporarily end. And it is in this green fringe that Bell finally comes to a halt. A man never quite gets used to a big covey's explosion in his face; and under the conditions described, if he can get in both barrels, he is lucky. As I walk forward, making a noise that cannot be helped, the birds run again, chittering; then they are off. And how! This time their flight is eerie and enigmatic. Some slip off on almost noiseless wings, in a low, terrifically fast but unerring flight. Some rocket upward to the treetops and drop on set wings toward some far sanctuary.

One bird spiraled upward, making almost as much noise as a grouse. This one I managed to get. But before I could put my gun on a second, they were all out of range. Up the mountain they had gone, into one of my favorite grouse haunts. Here, then, would be a double chance. They would fly, I knew, on the average of about two hundred yards. They don't go so far in the woods as they will from the field into their mountain fastness. As every hunter knows, a covey will have its natural place of safety; and when once in it, will be loath to leave. I have seen a quail rise in a little thicket, spin round a corner, and drop again into the cover, not over thirty yards from the rise.

The birds were now scattered, and if old Bell's nose was anything better than a decoration, she would find some of them. In such cover, while the bevy will be exceedingly restless and light-footed, single birds, even in the bare woods upon the dead leaves, will lie exceedingly close—in fact, uncomfortably so. There is a psychological distance at which a quail should rise; and anything short of this is likely to be as unfortunate for the hunter as if the quail got away out of range.

These woods have a strange picturesqueness of their own. While they are almost primeval in their wildness, the reminder of a grim calamity, with which man had nothing to do, is constantly evident. All the chestnut trees are dead from the blight—the only disease, so foresters tell me, which ever destroyed a whole species in wide reaches of its range.

By the base of one of these dead patriarchs Bell suddenly hesitated, and then froze. I have often wondered how frequently a bird-dog sees the game it is pointing, and whether sight of it makes for staunchness or otherwise. There seems to be a strange light in the eyes of a standing dog, as if it were in a trance.

In this case Bell was "sleeping" on her point. She was as certain that she had game as if she saw it. I was at the time in an old animal trail that wound easily up the wooded slope. As the leaves were damp, I could step forward almost without sound. The bird must be behind the big chestnut. Before edging nearer, I took a look for the chances for a shot, for in the woods one of these preliminary surveys is often mighty helpful. Directly in the probable line of flight were two big hemlocks, between the dusky intertwining arms of which was a lane of light. The dark trees were only thirty yards off.

"If it were a grouse," I thought, "I know just where he would go." Hardly had the thought crossed my mind when I heard a slight rustle in the leaves behind a tree, and in an instant a lordly cock grouse was up and away. Straight as a rocket for that aperture between the hemlocks he headed, and instinctively I aimed at the right place. So great was his speed that he fell fully ten yards beyond the point at which he started to fall. Here was luck indeed! And the quail were still ahead of me.

Retrieving my princely bird, I followed Bell into a dogwood thicket, in which, her instinct declared, our birds were. She was right. In ten minutes she had made six points and I had shot three more quail. To be an honest man, I must not forget the detail of missing four, including a double. But if we could kill every one we shot at, where would be the sport, and how many birds would be left at the end of a season?

My old dog and I returned to the stubble fields, which lie parallel to one another below the slope of the mountain and stretch for some three or four miles. In each field there is sure to be one covey; sometimes I have found four in one field. And all these birds act just alike. The minute they are flushed, they head for their home in the hills, and following them there is as I have described.

About noon, when I had almost my limit, I found an old spring in an abandoned orchard, and there Bell and I had a humble lunch together, share and share alike. It had turned out to be a mellow autumn day, with the woods as fragrant as Winesap apples, with tawny leaves drifting lazily down, with a golden haze over the world. Far behind me in the mountain I could hear the scattered coveys calling together. These mountain birds use their wings a good deal more than the birds of the open valleys, and fly together at the gathering call. Occasionally, in this way, two coveys get together—which leads me to tell of a remarkable experience I had in the laurels near the top of these same Tuscaroras one winter day.

I had taken out some ears of corn to spike on short bushes for the wild turkeys. There was a little snow on the ground, and in it I noticed a good many quail tracks. As they were fresh, I followed them out of the grapevine-hung dogwood thicket into the kalmias. After a while I saw the birds running on the snow ahead of me. Then what I supposed to be the covey got up. But the getting-up business would not stop. After at least thirty had gone out on the laurel, I began to count; and by the time the flushing ceased, eighty-seven quail had been counted. How is that for a covey?

"Now let me tell one," you say. But this thing is true, and it serves to disclose a habit of these dwellers in the kalmias that is worth recording. In the dead of winter these coveys from the valley climb the mountain to the shelter of the laurel, and there they naturally come together. Old lumbermen of this region have told me that the birds always congregate in the winter. Moreover, in blizzard weather they seek out an overhanging rock shelter, where they remain dry and warm until the storm has passed—in this way imitating perfectly what the ancient Indians used to do. Under the same rock shelter on the shoulders of these wild Tuscarora hills I have found modern quail roosts and old-time Indian arrowheads!

This congregating of the birds does not take place until after the hunting season has closed; but even if it did, I do not think that the gunner could do much with these birds in a place like that. Immense boulders are brimly strewn, there are many pines and hemlocks, the footing is precarious; and the birds, when they rise, spread out in an immense fan all over the least accessible places. Besides, these birds of the hills develop both a speed of flight and finesse of dodging that are superior to anything the field birds can show. Hunting such quail in such a place is worse than following the Astor markhor or the Nubian ibex.

As soon as spring comes, these wary mountaineers troop once more into the smiling valley, pair off, and raise their coveys of little patrician hillbillies—if you'll admit the paradox. And after them, when the season opens once again, will come an old quail hunter, with his aging setter Bell, to try to make life a somewhat lively affair for the brown birds.

You may remember that my hunt broke off when Bell and I were drowsing in the old orchard. We did better than drowse. When I woke up, it was nearly three o'clock, and Bell was whining over my prostrate form.

"Old girl," I said, "we have a grouse and eight quail—enough for one day. Going home, I might kill a rabbit for you on the fly, if you don't chase him too hard. But no more birds—until tomorrow."

Part Four

A MIXED BAG

Rutledge spent a life devoted to nature, and no matter where he was or what he was doing, communion with the wild world was never far from his thoughts. In this final section, we get a true mixed bag of stories, including a sport that Rutledge had little chance to enjoy, pheasant hunting, and the thought-provoking "The Philosopher Among Dogs." One may argue with Rutledge's excursion into anthropomorphism, although I don't, but it is difficult to deny just how well he knew and understood the canine tribe. The closing selection is one of the most powerful and meaningful Rutledge ever wrote. "What Sportsmen Bring Home" is an eloquent expression of the broader meanings of sport. It deserves to be widely read and should rank right alongside words from the likes of Ortega y Gasset and Aldo Leopold any time the hunter endeavors to share with others the spirit of the sporting experience. Hunting does not need justification, for it is deeply rooted in humanity's innermost being, but when we try to convey in words what we feel in our souls, it can be difficult. Rutledge overcomes those difficulties in a fashion that is an ideal way to conclude the book.

Ringnecks in the Stubble

For the most part, pheasants lay outside the geographical purview of Rutledge's hunting experiences. Ringnecks cannot survive and reproduce naturally in the Carolinas (except for a small portion of North Carolina's Outer Banks), but as one moves closer to the Mason-Dixon Line, that changes. Many readers will remember Robert Ruark's story, one of the finest of his "Old Man and the Boy" tales, when he joined his grandfather on a pheasant hunt with one of the latter's affluent acquaintances in Maryland. The youthful Ruark got a taste of terrapin stew, sampled the heady nectar which would eventually destroy him, and likened the first ringneck he saw to a feathered Zeppelin. Here Rutledge indulges in more common literary fare, but he does so in his standard enchanting fashion. This piece first appeared in the January 1921 issue of *Field & Stream*. It is also included in *Days Off in Dixie*.

––––––––––

It is one thing to hunt in a strange country and to find strange game; it is a different matter to hunt in familiar territory and run across something in the way of game that you never saw there before—there or anywhere else outside of an aviary. The feeling it gives one is a thriller—making a man feel as he probably would if, when following reedies in the Hackensack marshes, he should flush a wild gobbler. I experienced the emotion last autumn, and there was a mighty cheerful kick to it.

Our State Game Department had been, for some years, liberating some ringneck pheasants in those counties supposed to offer the most congenial conditions for their survival and increase. My own county, Franklin, in the extreme southern part of the State, got some of them. The first of November of last year opened the first season on these birds, but as very few had been reported in our vicinity, I had small hope of being allowed the privilege of saluting any of them. It was a misty afternoon, and the only wind was an occasional fitful and rainy swish that shook all the raindrops on the trees down on a man's head. But all day long I had been thinking how my dog would work in the stubble. Quail are likely to be restless on such a day, and a good dog can follow them to perfection. But it was two o'clock in the afternoon before I could jump the traces of work and take to the open. I was alone, preferring that kind of hunting to any other—except when an old, tried comrade can be with me. A run of three miles back into a valley that withdrew from the farmlands, famous in this part of the county because of their richness, brought me to a stretch of hunting land that looked very inviting. As it was viewed from the road it showed an old pasture thickly grown in blackberry canes, then a briared gully with a small stream in it, then an immense field of wheat stubble, golden against the blue mountains to the west. Clumps of woods rose here and there. It looked birdy to me. Water, stubble, woods, briar patches, dusting places in the gully—what more would quail want? And I was after quail. I just happened on the ringnecks.

Leaving the car along the road, my dog and I started up the briared gully. Evidently no one had been hunting there that season, for five cottontails compelled me to hail them. They were strangers and I took them in. I hung them on a rail at the head of a gully and forthwith entered the big stubble field.

Now, I do not want to describe this little hunt as if I were the original finder of ringnecks, for I realize that there are scores of good hunters to whom the experience must be rather familiar. But perhaps I can tell the thing in a new way, and mayhap some of the details will be different; for hunting is like a game of chess; you can play it a million times, yet never play any two games all the way through in exactly the same way.

When about two hundred yards into the golden brown stubble, my dog, a wide-ranging pointer, began to behave in the way that makes a hunter feel that the joy bells are going to ring for him very soon. But clearly the dog was puzzled. I thought, of course, that he was on the track of a covey of quail. But on a damp afternoon, with just the right wind moving, he should have gone straight to the target. Quail do not run much in the stubble, but evidently these birds were different. We followed the track more swiftly than I care to follow any game trail, and ere long reached the crest of the great hill whose sides were clothed in the stubble. As far as I could see, there was not a farmhouse visible. Oh, what a grand and glorious feeling, when hunting in a civilized community, to feel that no one is after you with a pitchfork!

My dog worked on; he drew to a point a hundred yards from me. I moved down. So did he. Then my eyes were opened and a great light dawned upon me—I think that's the way to say it. For out of the short stubble ahead of the dog there arose an old cock ringneck. He made a lot of noise with his wings and with his voice, and his manner of going would make Immelmann and Guynemer and those other great flyers envious. I watched him until my eyes got tired. Off that hill and down across innumerable other fields he fled. He was smart at this fledding business, or sledding, or whatever you care to call it. I did not see him come to ground. He simply faded away in the distance. And I did not follow; for one of the fields over which he had planed on those mighty wings of his was ploughed. Kind reader, take it from me that one of the simplest ways of losing your religion is to try to cross a half mile of newly ploughed, nice sticky clay in the juicy month of November. But though I did not follow, I thought hard—which is often what a hunter does when a great chance escapes him. I thought this: that cock pheasant is no solitary bird. I called to my dog and we began a long circle of the field.

Perhaps three hundred yards from where this pheasant flushed, my dog drew to a sure point. I approached, thinking that another cottontail would compel me to 'phone him. But no cottontail crouched in the stubble could I see. Yet my dog claimed earnestly that something was there. I looked and then I looked some more. At the end of the some-more gaze, I saw the object of the pointer's attention. It was another cock pheasant—and not six feet away from me. The rest is easily told. I can only say that such a bird is almost too big to shoot in open country. If a hunter is close on him before he flushes, he has not one chance in a thousand; and I think that all game should have a show at getting away. However, I first shot the bird and then, having bagged him, I considered what a poor chance he had had. Hunters are human and they like to take home something. I have always thought that there's something pretty guileful about these fellows who say, "Oh, it doesn't matter what we get. It's getting out in the open that we like." For my part, I haven't climbed into that sublimated class as yet, being just a plain hunter who does not care about telling hard-luck stories and looking like a four-flushing piker when his family greets him on his return from the woods and fields.

Considering the behavior of these two pheasants in the wheat stubble, I am certain that the first one had run a half-mile ahead of the dog, whereas the second one had not run at all. Each had chosen his way of eluding danger, and one had to guess wrong.

Another half hour in the stubble gave me one more bird and two rabbits. The expected quail were found on the edge of a thicket, and seven were secured; also, some shot at were not secured. It is not easy when the birds are big, when the light is foggy, and when the game goes whirring at cubist and futurist angles over the high briars and scrub locusts. It was now nearly dark, and I turned toward the car, collecting my cottontails from the rail fence en route.

Passing down the briared gully, I came to a haw tree red with its autumn fruit. It seemed a good place to cross the water. As I stooped under the first fringe of thorny boughs, there was a mighty whirr from the other side of the tree, and another big cock ringneck went rocketing off over my head. Had the bird been a ruffed grouse, I do not believe I could have stopped him. But my left barrel, having a good reach, brought him down. Perhaps the dampness of the atmosphere prevented his getting all his cylinders to working; I have frequently observed that quail fly less swiftly and with a kind of muffled flight on such days as this one which I have described.

It was about dark when my pointer snuggled down beside me in the car, and all the lights of the village were shining mistily when we drove into town.

The Philosopher among Dogs

Here we have a lengthy sampling of Rutledge's writing on dogs. He knew canines of all sorts intimately, and in this, as was ever the case in his work, his words come from long familiarity and careful reflection. There were always dogs in abundance wherever Rutledge resided, and among them there were invariably hounds aplenty. They are the heroes of this tale. It isn't a hunting story, per se, but it is a tale exceptionally well told with which any hard hunter, any lover of dogs, will identify. Dogs are the only creatures on earth privileged to see their god in person, and in this story we get a feel for the uncanny devotion underlying that worship through not one but several dogs. It originally appeared in *Bolio and Other Dogs* and later in *Children of Swamp and Wood*. A portion of the rather lengthy piece subsequently appeared separately as "Sarsaparilla" in *Wildlife of the South* and in *The World Around Hampton*.

There is a certain type of man who, if you ask him to meet you at a definite place, will be sure not to be there. It was so with Steve. I had told the Negro not to fail to have a rendezvous with me at the plantation house that afternoon, as I was bringing up a hound puppy that I wanted him to keep for me. A Negro always likes to have a hound handy, so that when his wife heaves the frying pan at him, he can chuck something at the dog.

The puppy and I arrived duly, but apparently we made up the whole party. I had driven ten miles in a rickety buggy over a wilderness road, and it was late in the afternoon. I had to return that night. It seemed wise for me to make the little hound comfortable under the big plantation porch, leaving him there until the next day, when I should return. By that time, Steve might come too. For a plantation Negro to be a day or so late in an appointment is to him a trivial detail.

There was, under the porch, a huge drag log with a ring and staple in its end; we used it to keep a dog from straying. To this I now tied the black pup—a big-eared, wavy-tailed, liquid-eyed youngster, five months old. His mother had been killed in an accident before this little one's eyes were open. I had raised him on a bottle. He cared a good deal for me, as I did for him. Already, true to form, on a trial run in a thicket, he had begun to yowl amazing music—strangely discordant in the house or yard, but entrancing in the wild woods.

Now I gave him a little feed. I arranged a pine straw bed for him. Then, leaving him alone, his big eyes gazing after me with wonder and regret, I started on my long drive homeward.

I know not exactly why, but I worried a good deal about the pup. He looked so little and human, so lonely and appealing as I left him; and there shone in his eyes that strange, beautiful, patient light of utter fidelity and persistent affection. I thought of him throughout the homeward drive; and when I woke after a restless night, he was first in my thoughts. And well he might have been! For when I went out into the yard, there he lay at the gate—a pathetic, heartbreaking urchin, cringing lest I should punish him.

Honestly, I could have wept like a child. I suppose that as soon as I had left him on the plantation he had started his Odyssey. Ulysses may have had his Scylla and Charybdis, his Sirens to forego, his Circean isles to pass. But at least he was a strong man, with hardy comrades, the master of a great ship. My little adventurer was chained to a dastardly log that wouldn't even drag straight (I read the whole story that day when I retraced his marvelous journey), chained by the neck to a ponderous log! He had a dark and unknown road of ten miles through mysterious woods; he had never traveled it before, save with me in the buggy that afternoon. There were long waterslashes through which he had to wade and swim; there were dreary stretches of deep sand; there were wayside stumps and bushes that caught at the drag, which trailed at a crazy angle. Yet through it all the little black hound came, a heroic spirit, not satisfied until, at dawn, when the morning star rode dying in the sky, he lay prostrated at his master's gate. A man did not have to be sentimental and imaginative to discover in that youngster's behavior proof of what love can and will do.

Possibly the very smartest thing I ever saw a hound do—as the story just told illustrates the most touching and affecting—happened late one afternoon while I was in a small outbuilding in the plantation yard that we called "the Castle." It had been a big smokehouse; but we put windows in, built benches along its sides, and transformed it into a place where Negroes who came to see us could wait comfortably. A plantation Negro does not mind a half-day's wait if he can sit by the fire, especially if he has company. In many ways he has solved the problem of life as an Oriental; and with amazing equanimity he accepts the changes and chances of existence.

I was waiting for a Negro who had promised to give me the exact street address of a flock of thirty-four wild turkeys that rumor had reported his seeing. Beside me lay a black and tan hound pup of which I was very fond. He was drowsing contentedly, but his head was toward the open door, and I noticed that he roused himself several times to look out. I shifted my seat so as to get his vision. Full in the doorway, regally framed by the sunset, stood a sagacious old hound named Ringwood, a black beauty with great down hanging ears, heavy dewlaps, and with a grand, melancholy face. It may really be a shame to say so, but this hound's countenance, in its serene majesty and in its profoundly erudite expression, always strongly reminded me of highly romantic pictures of Dante and Tennyson! Apologies are, I presume, due; and such as are necessary are proffered.

But Old Ringwood would bear watching. He had a way of going skylarking at night all by himself. Sometimes, when there was no reason apparently for him to feel guilty, he would give me casual sidelong glances. Also I heard rumors that sheep, miles from the plantation, had been slaughtered by a monstrous black hound. I had no proof of Ringwood's implication in such sinister business, but I was kept uneasy. Yet the dog was so superb after deer, and his career had been so long and splendid, that I hated to suspect him. Of one thing, however, I was determined: he should not ruin the pup. Dogs are laughably like people; one may go straight, but two will jump the traces and splurge all over the landscape. I have often noticed that when two dogs take a shine to each other, frolic much together, execute little secret expeditions, form a soulmateship, it is high time to look for trouble. This is especially true if the older dog has questionable motives. Is it not the same with us?

I had noticed a decided intimacy springing up between Ringwood and the pup; and while I counted on the old dog to train the youngster legitimately, I didn't want any special courses in sheep killing given. The pup was just like a schoolboy—innocent, and ready for any fun. I could tell now that he wanted to join the old hound, and would have done so but for my admonishing him to lie still. Yet the thing went on. Ringwood kept coming to the door, luscious invitation glowing in his eyes; once, too, he whined enticingly. At last I told him shortly to get out. Crestfallen and thoughtful, he turned away. Within a few minutes, however, he had come back and had stalked into the little room, where he stood by the fire, gazing into its depths. He did not lie down. Infected by his mood, I began the same kind of silent gazing into the flames, when I was roused from my reverie by a slight scuffle beside me. The two dogs were already halfway to the door.

Ringwood had the puppy by the scruff of the neck, and was gently and guilefully dragging him off for a frolic! The big dog's demeanor was so clumsily surreptitious that I couldn't be angry, and his maneuver was so crafty that my admiration was greater than my annoyance. Ringwood had figured out the whole thing in that massive head of his; and his way out of the difficulty was as clever a one as a man could have devised. He wanted the pup; the pup wouldn't come. What then remained but to wade right in and steal the comrade for whom he was lonely? I went out into the yard with them, the world aglow with sunset, and there let them have their fun together; but I saw to it that they did not get out of my sight.

Whether considering dogs or men, thinking on their character and their destiny, I always wonder what it is they really want in life? Is it wealth? Sympathy? Power? Understanding? The strong desire for fame inherent in us may be just a passionate yearning to have others recognize our own aspirations. A man, perhaps, bears the same relation to a dog as God does to a man. A dog is certainly happiest when he can please his master. With all reverence I can say that if I would only trust God as my dog trusts me, there would be no trouble for me henceforth, even in this difficult world.

About four miles from home there is a strange, wild region known as "the Big Ocean." It is a singular stretch of inviolate country. I have been deep into its mysterious heart; but there are parts of it that no human eye has ever seen. It is a famous sanctuary for deer; and I used to love to haunt its fringes late in the afternoon in order to see the deer come trooping from their daytime fastness, to roam the starlighted pinelands.

One afternoon I went through a wild thicket on the edge of this place, emerged on an airy ridge grown to huckleberries, and here waited for what might come for me to see. Two fox squirrels, a wild gobbler, a covey of quail, and a doe rewarded my wait. I stayed later than I had planned to, and it was dusk ere I roused myself to turn homeward. A fog had set in; and in getting up from my seat on an old log, I turned—and in that instant lost my sense of direction. In fog, in the forest, at twilight, that is a perilously easy thing to do.

Disconcerted, I stood looking all around at the beautiful, sinister place, fading, lonely, mist-wreathed, full of wonder, hinting of eternal things. To be truthful, I was lost; not because I did not know where I was, but because I did not know which way to go. While thus standing in doubt, I heard a solitary hound, deep in the fathomless swamp. He was holding a lone trail, a deer's, I thought. Perhaps he might get me out of my plight.

In that part of the country we have a signal in deer hunting. Three long blasts on a horn mean, "It is all over; come to me." It is really meant for fellow hunters, but smart dogs quickly become aware of the significance of the signal. I decided to try it now. I blew my hunting horn three times, the sound carrying far through the damp, still woods. Almost immediately the hound stopped trailing. After one or two desultory yelps he was silent. I continued to sound the signal. Within five minutes, out of the dripping bushes came the hound. He was a stranger to me, but I took him in. We made friends; but to bind our friendship fast I ran a buck hide string through his collar.

"Old fellow," I said, "the hunt's over for today. Let's go home."

The hound whined. I let the string lie slack on his neck, giving him the lead. The string tightened. He started, leading me out of the swamp, far through the dim green night of the forest. I felt that he was going in the wrong direction; but it pays to trust a dog. A hound will seldom go home directly through the woods. He prefers to make for the nearest road, down which he can make better time. My rescuer led me through wild thickets, across water, over some log bridges that he clung to easily enough, but off which I slipped with equal ease. At last he came to a dead halt. It was not quite dark. In a moment I realized that we were on a big road; in another moment I recognized which road it was, and my sense of direction was restored. Home for me lay to the northward; but my guide wanted me to turn toward the south. I loosed him, and into the misty darkness he vanished. He had hardly saved my life, for I had been in no real peril; but he had helped me vitally when I was helpless. I often think of that mysterious and opportune stranger; but his identity I never discovered.

Of all the dogs that I have ever known, Sarsaparilla, an alleged hound, was the least promising in appearance. He was owned by one of the Negroes on our South Carolina place; and he was named back in those old days when patent medicines and soft drinks were first making their way into the remote hinterlands of the plantations, and when Negroes got a social kick out of naming their dogs, their children, and their mules Neuralgia, Asthma, Sarsaparilla, Ambrosia, and Dandruff.

This beast, Sarsaparilla, had other faults besides his effervescing name: he had apparently no sense at all, he was too tall, his head had no particular shape, his gait was an absurd walk. He gave one the impression of traveling on stilts. His color was a discord of mangy yellowish white. His facial expression was notably vacant. Sarsaparilla was simply ludicrous; he just wouldn't do. So, for a long time, I thought. But there came a day when I was to learn a mighty lesson about not judging by appearances. I was to learn that courage, like wealth, is solely a matter of the heart; and it took a yellow dog to teach me.

When great floods swept down the Santee River, they dislodged from the gloomy and impenetrable swamps above us a good deal more than mere sedge and drifting logs. Live things were in the flotsam. Deer came to our very back yard, shy wild turkeys, roving cattle, wild hogs of huge size and savage temper.

One morning when I went down to the stable yard, I was greeted by shrill complaining from the hogs that were penned in the ample enclosure. Something was badly disconcerting them. When I came up I found that they had a visitor, a rangy wild boar from the swamps, a shaggy hyena-like creature, with gleaming tusks, alarming bristles, and a most truculent mien. I at once saw that he had jumped a low panel in the fence, and that, by setting two rails there, I could effect his capture. The thing was managed. But when I came to open the gate, he charged me, mouth wide, bristles high, tail erect. I got the gate shut not a second too soon. He checked his speed, champed his great jaws at me sullenly, and then turned back to torment the other dwellers in the yard.

Not wishing to shoot the boar, I decided to catch him with dogs. I therefore repaired to the nearby Negro settlement, where I gathered in seven dogs and as many Negroes, all of whom read between the lines of my story the glad tidings of Christmas bacon to be had for the catching. We had a motley pack: a bulldog, two hounds, an alleged collie, two plain curs of the most obscure antecedents, and Sarsaparilla. I remonstrated with Sarsaparilla's owner about bringing this soft drink to the slaughter. He laughed in a shamefaced way, as if he thought his dog was being taken along to be the clown of the fray. I recalled the boar's size and mien, looked at this burlesque on rickety stilts, and pity filled my heart.

Reaching the barnyard, we decided that an assault *en masse* was the proper maneuver. The dogs were to be the shock troops, and we were to follow up the advantage that they had obtained over the common enemy. We had sundry cudgels and ropes with which to belabor the victim.

The seven dogs went through the gate in a body; and the wild boar accommodated them by not permitting them to hesitate for a moment as to which hog they were after. Incontinently he rushed them. With great valor we watched the fray from the farther side of the fence, waiting until our chance seemed secure enough to enable us to cross the obstruction that protected us. Suddenly, hurled high over the fence, the bulldog rejoined us; all the zest seemed gone out of him. Then the two hounds fled across the yard and skulked into the stable; their attitude indicated that they carried no tornado insurance. The collie stood off and barked with hollow ferocity. The two plain dogs went manfully to work, as if the matter of laying in a supply of Christmas bacon interested them personally. But one dog was trampled by the boar. The other seized the monster's ear and hung on grimly. Yet the beast would rip him open, I knew.

Just then, Sarsaparilla, who had calmly and aloofly watched the proceedings, stepped niftily in. He approached rather fastidiously, not from dismay but from a certain curious regard for finesse. Stationed behind the hog, he looked thoughtfully at the shaggy brute; then he quietly bowed his lunatic, dolesome head, mouthed the boar's upper haunch until he had a deliberate hold, sunk his teeth, set his legs, and began grimly to shake his head.

The boar, I think, got one glimpse of what had him; he probably imagined it a saber-toothed tiger. Savagely shaking off the dog from his head, he squealed shrilly and turned to run.

Sarsaparilla said quite firmly, "Not so fast."

The bewildered boar could not get loose. The other dogs came back. We jumped the fence, and soon we had the old marauder from the swamps securely roped. Sarsaparilla then stalked sedately off; he had condescended to help us; but he was not going to join in any of our puerile excitement.

"What kind of dog is that?" I asked his owner.

"God in he'ben knows," replied he, meaning no irreverence; "but he got all de sense. Sometime I gwine change his name to Solomon."

Many people of enlightened minds often gravely argue the question, do animals reason? Is their apparent mental power but instinct? For my part, I think many animals do not have to reason: they are too smart. I have a great reverence for instinct. It is like tact, taking one where all the logic and all the knowledge of the world cannot gain admittance. Infallibly certain and direct, it reaches its goal before reason has decided whether or not to leave the mark. I wonder whether we have not been rating instinct too low? Women, we say, have a sixth sense, knowing clairvoyantly baseness or nobility in men. Is it not instinct? The wild creatures of my acquaintance and the dogs of high and low degree—they may not reason, they simply know. What is the use of traveling in the ox cart of reason if you have the racing car of instinct at your disposal? Dogs do not reason, because they who have the exquisite gift of instinct do not have to go through laborious and bourgeois mental processes!

I used to have a big foxhound named Blue; and I found him capable of carrying a trail almost as old as one that a bloodhound will take. He would follow deer, fox, or turkey. One day I was greatly amused over his bafflement. He had a wild gobbler trail on damp leaves and wet sand. As the scent was heavy and fresh, he was absolutely sure of himself. Suddenly the trail ended. Blue cast wildly about in little circles, then in wider ones, snuffing feverishly, gulping avidly. Ravenously he sought, and he knew that I was watching him.

Aware of his own ability and of my faith in him, his loss of the trail hurt him cruelly. Of course I knew that the turkey had simply taken wing. But I let Blue work on for a while. At last he gave up, came to me humbly, sat down beside me and whined uneasily, saying as plainly as could be, "It must have been a ghost. I never was so swindled in my life. But try me on something else."

That same week I tested his nose in a rather interesting way. I used often to take him in the buggy with me, and when I came to an interesting track, would let him try its savor. Coming through a small thicket of pines, I saw a peg horn buck launch himself lithely over the road. That was just four o'clock of a winter's afternoon. Blue was in the buggy with me then; but I did not set him on the trail. The next morning, driving over the same road, sixteen hours later, I alighted from the buggy with Blue, just to see if the trail meant any-thing to him. He took it eagerly. I followed; and it was not hard to keep up with him, for when he gave tongue he had a habit of turning partly 'round, throwing his head back and sinking on his haunches while his wild music rang out. Some three hundred yards from the road, we started the buck that I had seen the afternoon before. I have heard many tales of hounds following cold trails, but I have never actually known one to find and to follow one older than that.

Then there was a hound named Whistling Buoy, a great black and white beauty from the mountains of western North Carolina. He gave me cause to christen him as he was named. The very morning after his arrival I took him on a leash with me into the home woods, walking down some of the old sandy roads, just to see whether he would take urgent notice of some of the fresh deer tracks that crossed the old trails. About a mile from the house, the hound, which until then had been very intelligent and friendly, suddenly developed a stubborn streak. He pulled back, he whined, he looked at me with the narrowed, glittering eye of strange misgiving. He appeared badly frightened; he might be sick, I thought. I tried to lead him forward, but vain was my coaxing. When I stroked his massive head, he threw it back and gave a wild melancholy howl. It had all the weird eeriness and warning heard in the deep mysterious tone of a whistling buoy. Hence, I christened my min-strel. Again he howled. Then I remembered.

Full five months before this, there had been killed, some fifteen feet from where the hound had stopped, a monster diamondback rattler, a veritable chimera. Nearly eight feet it had measured. Its body had for a long time been hung on a little persimmon tree. Nearly a half-year later my new hound caught the dread scent with which the ground had been impregnated, knew what it was, halted on what he knew was the brink of death, and warned me to imitate his wariness.

A hound has a genuine and profound distrust of the general scheme of things in this life. Melancholy of an ancient and appealing sort is his. What makes his pessimism worthy of regard is the fact that it has its source in remarkably sagacity. His honest and steadfast refusal to be optimistic not only lends to his character a noble severity but also gives to his philosophy the serene charm of truth. He invariably seems to me to belong to an older and a wiser generation, which regards the behavior of all other living things as an exceedingly juvenile performance. A hound is the only dog that can make me self-conscious of my own ridiculousness. Fixed by his appraising eye, I shrink into my true stature.

Along with most people, I have always noticed that Negroes have a peculiar and amiable deftness in controlling animals; and the more intractable the animal, the greater the Negro's skill. He employs tones that we cannot imitate; he cajoles irresistibly. Goats and mules, houn' dogs, and oxen with a fearful placid stubbornness yield to the Negro's persuasion. There's some subtle mutual understanding. Nor can the white man imitate it; its source is deep, racial, almost occult. The white man can never be so close to the hound as the Negro is. I confess, with more pride in the Negro's achievement than shame in my own shortcoming, that whenever I can do nothing at all with a hound I turn him over to the good Negro, Prince Alston, with whom I have roamed the woods since boyhood. I hand over to Prince what apparently is but worthless, perhaps dangerous, stuff; the magic of his alchemy will transfer the base material into gold.

Yet I never saw him whip a hound. He does the thing by looks, by tones in his voice; occasionally by fearful imprecations, which the hound appears perfectly to understand. I shall never forget the sudden and obedient and conciliatory look that came on the face of a certain brash hound, when Prince, from the back of his mule, yelled to the careless dog, "If you don't come yuh, I'll douse yo' head in a bar'l o' kerosene, and set fire to yo' tail."

The hound heard and heeded the warning. When Prince speaks, hounds listen; and when a hound listens it is because he has caught a tone that penetrates to the place where he lives. There is never a hound, it has seemed to me, but Prince has his wave length.

I remember how Prince explained to me, one day, the matter of a hound's behavior. I had wounded a buck, and the trail was hot. I had one old hound following, a big black and tan dog that resembled a bloodhound. He was about a hundred yards ahead of me, and from the news he was broadcasting, I thought he would catch the buck at any minute.

When he suddenly fell quiet, I thought it was all over. But then he gave a peculiar squeal; and to my astonishment back he came through the woods on a dead run, his tail between his legs, his ears mashed against his head, his back arched by the strong ignominy of arrant fear. Close on his heels rushed a frightful shape—a huge razorback sow, a thing all snout and ribs and bristles and menace. After the hog came about nine little pigs, ludicrous imitations of her, both in contour and in mien. Every little pig, without apparently knowing exactly what it was all about, was valiantly trying not only to keep up with the savage old mother, bent upon the destruction of the hound, but was striving to assume her ferocity of aspect and her earnestness of purpose.

The mad troop headed for me. The hound took refuge behind me. The old sow stopped abruptly, and every little pig executed comically the same maneuver. Then the old marauder, her bristles still high, turned and went grumbling off through the forest.

"All right," I said to the hound; "that's over. Now let's find the buck."

But the big hound, his grave and beautiful face full of profoundest thought, appeared not to hear me. I coaxed. I scolded. He maintained his quiet but determined demeanor. Not one step would he go. At last I had to abandon the chase. Telling Prince about it that night, I asked him why it was that, when any ordinary dog would have relished going after either the deer or the sow the hound had shown the white feather. Prince listened in his quiet, amused, understanding way.

"He wasn't jes' scared," he finally told me; "he hab as much sense as people. A houn' is jes' like a sensible man; he done know when the chance to die is jes' a little too good."

There it was. Prince fathomed the dog's mind. I did not.

I recall with what delight I used to watch a Negro named Henry Washington feed a pack of a dozen ravenous hounds. He had on the ground a long cypress board, and this was apparently divided into spaces, one of which was apportioned to each hound. Bringing out the pot of steaming food, he would line up his famished army, addressing them thus: "How come you ain't find yo' place, Music? Ain't you know you have a place at table 'tween Buck and Doe? Don't you cross dat line, Check; I don't care how hungry you is. Gambler, you ain't gwine git a t'ing if you edge up on me. Bugle, if I bat you with this spoon, yo' jaw will ache till New Year's Day."

During this admonitory address Henry would be ladling the food on the big board, a portion for each dog; and he had them so trained that, until the banquet was properly spread, not a dog would care to begin, though certain lean, melancholy faces would loll forward languishingly. Had a white man attempted so delicate a feat as this, the result would have been a complete failure.

The character of the hound appears to undergo no change as the generations pass; he will be as he has been and as he is. His character has much to suggest to the human heart. A sensitive and reflective soul, his spirit has a savor of astute meditation. A hound always seems to have something on his mind.

I once had a pair named Fife and Drum; of these, Fife had a quality of cogency that often astonished me. It paid me to watch him. He spent much of his time sleeping in the sun; but if ever he became uneasy, his unrest meant that he had something heavy on that discriminating mind of his. I remember watching him rise restlessly, one day, out of a perfectly good straw bed in the sunshine, look wisely and benevolently about, start off across the yard, and look back at me with sapient bright eyes, as if to communicate to me that he knew something worth knowing. I got my gun and followed him.

Across an old field he went, and into the woods; almost at once we came upon the track of a buck that had apparently just swum the river. This deer we followed slowly, and with ultimate success.

When the deer was swimming the river, Fife had been sleeping. How had the dog detected his nearness? Was it purely the matter of the wafting of a hot scent his way, or did he have an intimation that game was in his neighborhood? Is there a wireless, a radio, by which dogs get messages in their way as we do in ours? I do not affirm it; but to explain some phenomena in this world, we have to admit the possibility of things not yet understood.

A hound is the only dog I know which cannot be said to bark; he sings. He is a music-maker; and if he is well-bred, he takes his art seriously. I love to blow a hunting horn just to get the hounds' lyric reaction to it: bass, alto, tenor, soprano—the mournful sweet yowling begins. Some hounds take the matter of their music so religiously that often, even on a hot trail, they will stop to go through the performance, and what they render will be real music. I have seen an old, proud hound with a superb alto, of which he was inordinately vain, fall considerably behind a running pack just because he would pause to give tongue, going through his burst of songs as if he were a priest performing a religious rite.

Sometimes a hound will do a good deal more singing than the occasion appears to call for. I once asked a Negro why it was that a hound just revels in yowling rapturously, upon even the slightest, and sometimes upon no, provocation.

"When I go to church," the Negro said, "I sing; and sometimes when I is working turpentine I sing and whoop. I do that to ease my soul. A hound, he will ease his soul in the same way."

I love a hound because he appears to me to be a dog of some spiritual significance. His sagacity begins where that of most dogs ends; where his ends, I know not. He has a perception poignant and true. He has taught me much about life. My obligation to him is that unpayable debt that we owe to one who has given us an insight into the meaning of existence; whose spiritual genius has led us to understand that life has about it a great deal more magic and mystery than people with dismally literal minds would have us believe; whose prescient hand has set ajar for us casements of the soul, through which are far gleams of what may be, for all I know, the gorgeous frontiers of Eternity.

What Sportsmen Bring Home

As anyone who has read Rutledge's wonderful evocation of the meaning and ethical underpinning of hunting, "Why I Taught My Boys to Be Hunters," surely realizes, he had an exceptional knack for expressing in words what every hunter feels in his heart. Here, in a guest editorial he wrote for the October 1936 issue of *Field & Stream,* is a powerful statement of just what it means to hunt. While it would abysmally fail any test of that dread phrase, "political correctness," it should be required reading for every sportsman. Better still, one could wish that some day, some way, anti-hunting zealots (Rutledge called them "sentimentalists") would bring themselves to read these words.

Should they do so with anything approaching an open mind, they would pause and ponder, full of wonder. For Rutledge makes an eloquent, compelling case for hunting. If you hunt or have ever hunted, his closing thought will ring true: "Yes, a sportsman brings home infinitely more than the game he may have taken; he brings home a saner, finer, and stronger self." Those are fitting words with which to end, as this essay is a fitting conclusion for this anthology.

———

There are a lot of sentimentalists who think of the sportsman merely as a killer, and their erring imaginations picture him as going forth to slaughter and returning home lugging with him dead animals and birds and fish. They regard his activities with aversion, and they condemn him, sometimes in speech and in writing, sometimes by scornful silence. I have sometimes found myself in company where my interest in field sports has been regarded as sin and shame and crime are ordinarily regarded. For these critics I feel more pity than resentment, for if they could only know what a true sportsman really brings home they might come to a just appraisal of the littleness and the sterility of their own souls.

And what are these things that we bring home? Sometimes we bring trophies of our prowess with the rod and gun; and no reasonable human being can deny that these are natural and legitimate fruits of our efforts. We teach our children to read stories of Daniel Boone and Davy Crockett, and we regard them as American pioneer heroes; but somehow, when we of this generation seek to imitate their feats, we are regarded in some quarters as barbarians. For my part, I love to enter a home where there is a deer head hanging; it makes me feel that a real man is around.

We bring home our game—when we are fortunate; and if that were all we brought, I should still be proud of a race that produces hunters and fishermen, and I could never experience any feeling of guilt in considering their achievements. But we bring home much more, and only true sportsmen know what those things are.

A sportsman brings home more than dinner for his family and trophies for his den; he brings home a body toughened by hardy exercise and disciplined by following the rules of an ancient and exacting game. He returns to the world of work and of care a better man physically. He has renewed his youth. It may be that he has added years to his life and to his effectiveness as a toiler among men. He has recaptured in the wilds something of the spirit and the strength of his boyhood. He goes into the woods with two strikes on him, and he comes out ready to knock a liner clear over the center field fence for a home run.

Oh, I know that the sentimentalists say that these same beneficent effects can be had by hiking. I would not say anything against hiking, but it is as much like hunting or fishing as a mother-in-law's kiss is like a bride's. You simply cannot classify them together.

In hiking, you go out and you come back. When you hie yourself into the wilderness with your rod or your old blunderbuss, you are playing a game; and in this game your antagonist is not the wild creature you are after. He is the prize. You have many antagonists to overcome before you win that prize: your own weakness of will, your inclination to give up, adverse conditions of weather and of terrain, a run of bad luck, the acute disappointment over those near chances that never really become chances. In brief, your two main opponents are wild nature and yourself.

And when you come back from a hunt or from a fishing trip, you feel more of a man, not necessarily because of what you have killed or caught, but because you have put yourself to the test against those forces against which only real men will enter the lists. Your confidence in yourself is restored. You can take it. And the appetite you bring home makes your wife wonder whether she has not, after all, married the caveman of her secret dreams.

But you bring home more than a better body. You bring back a mind from which the cobwebs have been swept; a mind keen, alert, hale, and wholesome; a mind that refuses to accept sofa lounging and tap dancing as forms of manly endeavor; a mind reconciled to the daily grind, and ready to tackle the next problem with courage and confidence. You bring back a better husband and father; or, if you haven't gone so far as that, you bring back a better lover. Show me the girl who loves a sportsman, and I'll take my hat off to her. She knows more than some of her elders, and her natural devotion is deepened by an ancestral preference for a mate who has some hardihood in him. Every community is better for the sportsman in it; every woman is better for having married a sportsman; and every child is fortunate who has a sportsman for its father.

The true sportsman also brings home what never can be taken from him: he brings home memories that make all life different, even to the very end. He thinks of the true comrades he has made, friends who could have come to him nowhere but in the woods, on the plains and by the streams. He brings home the recollection of those modern pioneers whose homes are in the wilderness—people whose hospitality he has shared. The memory of them serves to redeem humanity for him. He brings back a knowledge of the creatures of the wild—a knowledge that the hunter alone can gain. He remembers their resourcefulness, their courage, their sagacity and their obedience to the great laws of nature. He brings home with him the beauty of the elder world: the fragrance of primeval forests; the laughing light on crystal streams; the tattered gold of autumn leaves.

These things enter his spirit and abide there. Because, far back at the eternal source of things, he has heard a voice saying that all is well, he gives less heed to calamitous voices of civilization. In the unsullied silence of the deep woods he has heard the true and steady heartbeat of life, unwearied since creation. He is reassured by finding no change in the order of the universe. He comes home with a sense that the beauty which God created is going to stay created. He has found for himself that at the fountain of life the waters are still flowing. He has learned what he could learn in the wilds alone: that he is no stranger on the earth, but a legitimate son who is privileged to share a great inheritance.

Yes, a sportsman brings home infinitely more than the game he may have taken; he brings home a saner, finer, and stronger self.

BIBLIOGRAPHICAL ESSAY

Bibliographical details have been provided for each of the selections, but for those interested in fuller information, some additional comments are in order. A prolific writer for virtually all of his adult life, Rutledge was motivated by the dual drives of the muse and materialism. He needed every dollar he could scrape together, for always in the forefront of his mind was a desire to resurrect the former splendor of his beloved Hampton Plantation home. His salary as a teacher was anything but munificent, he had a wife and three sons to support, and his "Santee Paradise" stood in desperate need of repairs to the home and improvements to the grounds.

Accordingly, Rutledge appeared in print from the era of World War I (when he was in his thirties) until shortly before his death in 1973. He wrote a great deal of poetry as well as prose, although it is primarily for the latter that he is remembered today. Virtually every story he ever wrote was intended for multiple usages—all of his books except *My Colonel and His Lady* and a few shorter inspirational titles are anthologies. The majority of his books utilized material which had, for the most part, first appeared in magazine form. In all likelihood this approach was a conscious one, for it allowed him to garner a bit of extra income from sale of onetime rights to a magazine before bringing various tales together in a book.

Indeed, most if not all of the pieces contained in this book, even though I have been unable to ascertain this in several cases, probably first saw the light of day in magazines. Where this information is known to the editor, it is included, but one of the frustrations of dealing with sporting literature is that cumulative indexes do not exist for the popular sporting magazines of yesteryear. Likewise, most were not included in standard reference sources such as *The Reader's Guide to Periodical Literature*. What that means, given that few on-line indexes are retrospective, is that the only way to locate the original place of publication for articles by individuals such as Rutledge is through tedious, issue-by-issue, year-by-year perusal of back issues of magazines to which he likely contributed. Lengthy runs of many of these are almost impossible to find, although for popular publications such as *Field & Stream* (to which Rutledge contributed scores of articles), locating complete sets is a bit easier.

All of this is to suggest that the bibliographical citations for articles given below are unquestionably incomplete. Certainly the editor would welcome information on any such pieces. Readers may contact him through his website, www.jimcasadaoutdoors.com.

As for Rutledge's books, you can get all sorts of arguments about exactly how many he wrote. This is in part because he contributed to the confusion through citing various figures in his later years. There are a number of "ghost titles," many of them listed on the dust jackets of his published books, which can send the assiduous bibliophile down frustrating dead-end trails. Bibliographical vagaries aside, all of his books (and I'm confident the listing of fifty-seven titles covers all of them), along with articles on dogs and upland game hunting, are listed at the conclusion of this note.

Information on Rutledge himself is surprisingly sparse. There is no full or carefully researched biography. The only biography is Idella Bodie's *The Story of Archibald Rutledge: A Hunt for Life's Extras.* It was written for a youthful audience and is, while interesting and well crafted, lacking in depth. Quite different and delightful, although highly personal and quite brief, is Irvine Rutledge's little memoir of his father, *We Called Him Flintlock.* It pays richly deserved tribute to the man who wrote that enduring piece, "Why I Taught My Boys to Be Hunters," and surely the senior Rutledge would have been pleased with the warm and winsome words of his protégé.

There are, in addition, several shorter biographical pieces. Among these are Virginia Ravenel, "South Carolina's Poet Laureate," *Sandlapper Magazine* (October 1968): 47–51; Benton Young, "The Squire of Hampton," *South Carolina Wildlife* (September–October 1983): 16–21; and Rob Wegner, "Flintlock: A Dixie Deer-slayer," *Deer & Deer Hunting* (June 1990): 23–44. Wegner's excellent article also appears in his seminal work, *Deer & Deer Hunting: Book III* (1990). George Bird Evans has short but insightful sketches of Rutledge in two of his books, *Men Who Shot* (1983) and *George Bird Evans Introduces* (1990).

Building on my researches connected with this anthology and four others, together with numerous magazine articles on Old Flintlock, a chapter on him in my book, *Remembering the Greats: Profiles of Turkey Hunting's Old Masters* (2012), and sundry other writings on the man, I am currently working on a full-scale Rutledge biography.

He was close to completion or likely had completed an autobiography when he died, but that manuscript mysteriously disappeared in the immediate aftermath of his demise. It is likely gone forever, as are other relics of his life. Just how and where they dispersed (and he had more than a modicum of the packrat mentality when alive) is difficult to determine. I have heard all sorts of stories, none of them fully substantiated, of folks making off with bits and pieces of memorabilia, and even my conversations with his son, Irvine, did relatively little to clarify such matters.

Although the previous anthologies I have compiled on Rutledge for the University of South Carolina Press remain in print, as do a few original works by him, most of his contributions to the field of sporting literature are now long out of print. Some of his best-known works, such as *An American Hunter* and *Hunter's Choice,* show up regularly in booksellers' catalogs, but they bring premium prices. More obscure books—*Bolio and Other Dogs, Tom and I on the Old Plantation,* and *Old Plantation Days*—are virtually impossible to find. If you are a bibliophile, a few details on the various editions and values of these and other works are available in a couple of the book columns I have written for *Sporting Classics* magazine (January–February 1992): 84–86 and (March–April 1992): 86–87, 91. His rarest books are all works of poetry, but many of his collections of tales fetch high three-figure or four-figure prices. Several of Rutledge's works were published in special or deluxe editions. Obviously they demand fancy prices, and you will pay a premium for books signed or inscribed by Rutledge, an indication of his enduring popularity. At a guess, it would probably take twenty thousand dollars to form a near-complete collection of first editions of his books (one or two early items were published in extremely low numbers for family friends and are in essence impossible to find), although you could probably skimp a bit through a lot of digging and even more patience.

The list that follows includes all of Rutledge's books. It is followed by a selective bibliography of his magazine stories relating to the subject matter of this anthology which I have been able to locate. Obviously his books of poetry are of lesser significance here, but it should be noted that a goodly number of his poems dealt, in one way or another, with hunting and dogs.

BOOKS

An American Hunter. New York: Frederick A. Stokes Co., 1937. 461 pages.

The Angel Standing; Or Faith Alone Gives Poise. New York: Fleming H. Revell Co., 1948. 48 pages.

The Ballad of the Howling Hound and Other Poems. Richmond, Va.: Dietz Press, 1965. xi, 89 pages.

The Banners of the Coast. Columbia, S.C.: The State Co., 1908. 47 pages.

Beauty in the Heart (Including "Meet Archibald Rutledge" by Frank S. Means, 9–20). Westwood, N.J.: Fleming H. Revell Co., 1953. 63 pages.

The Beauty of the Night. New York: Fleming H. Revell Co., 1947. 43 pages.

Bolio and Other Dogs. New York: Frederick A. Stokes Co., 1930. 249 pages.

Bright Angel and Other Poems. Columbia, S.C.: R. L. Bryan Co., 1955. x, 59 pages.

Brimming Chalice. New York: Henry Harrison, 1936. 95 pages.

Brimming Tide and Other Poems. Westwood, N.J.: Fleming H. Revell Co., 1954. 160 pages.

Children of Swamp and Wood. Garden City, N.Y.: Doubleday, Page & Co., 1927. xii, 280 pages.

Christ Is God. New York: Fleming H. Revell Co., 1941. 47 pages.

Collected Poems. Columbia, S.C.: The State Co., 1925. xiv, 302 pages.

Days Off in Dixie. Garden City, N.Y.: Doubleday, Page and Co., 1924. xiv, 298 pages.

Deep River: The Complete Poems of Archibald Rutledge. Columbia, S.C.: R. L. Bryan, 1960. xxiv, 635 pages.

The Everlasting Light and Other Poems. Athens: University of Georgia Press, 1949. xii, 115.

The Flower of Hope. New York: Fleming H. Revell Co., 1930. 30 pages.

From the Hills to the Sea: Fact and Legend of the Carolinas. Indianapolis, Ind.: Bobbs-Merrill Co., 1958. 201 pages.

God's Children: My Negro Friends at Hampton. Indianapolis, Ind.: Bobbs-Merrill Co., 1947.

Heart of the South. Columbia, S.C.: The State Co., 1924. viii, 391 pages.

The Heart's Citadel and Other Poems. Richmond, Va.: Dietz Press, 1953. 176 pages.

The Heart's Quest. No place, publisher, or date given. 164 pages.

Home By the River: The Story of Hampton Plantation. Indianapolis, Ind.: Bobbs-Merrill Co., 1941. 167 pages plus 28 pages of photographs and map endpapers.

How Wild Was My Village. Columbia, S.C.: Wing Publications, 1969. 153 pages.

Hunter's Choice. West Hartford, Vt.: Countryman Press, 1946. viii, 210 pages.

I Hear America Singing. Columbia, S.C.: R. L. Bryan Co., 1970. x, 60 pages.

In After Years. Listed on a pamphlet Rutledge evidently had put together in the 1930s and in various other places such as *Brimming Chalice.* I have seen the date given as 1907, but it was more likely 1906 (a clipping in the Rutledge file at Union College gives that date). Confirmation that the book was published comes in a February 10, 1940, letter from Rutledge to C. L. Rasor in which the former mentions he is searching for his copy of the book. Confirmation of the book's existence was provided by Don Rutledge, Old Flintlock's grandson, who has a complete collection of his books. This work likely was done in a very limited printing for friends and family. I have never seen a copy.

It Will Be Daybreak Soon. New York: Fleming H. Revell Co., 1938. 129 pages.

Life's Extras. New York: Fleming H. Revell Co., 1928. 64 pages.

Lincoln: A Southern View. Chapel Hill, N.C.: Leonidas Polk Chapter of the United Daughters of the Confederacy, 1925. 16 pages.

Love's Meaning. New York: Fleming H. Revell, 1943. 42 pages.

A Monarch of the Sky. New York: Purdey Press, 1926. 12 pages.

My Colonel and His Lady. New York: Bobbs-Merrill Co., 1937. 189 pages.

New Poems. No place or publisher given, 1915, but a list of Rutledge's books in *Brimming Chalice* indicates it was published by The State Co. 72 pages.

Old Plantation Days. Cumberland, Md.: Eddy Press, likely 1913. A single illustration by Charles Livingston Bull. 160 pages.

Old Plantation Days. New York: Frederick A. Stokes, 1921. vi, 344 pages.

Peace in the Heart. Garden City, N.Y.: Doubleday, Doran & Co., 1930. xvi, 316 pages.

Plantation Game Trails. Boston: Houghton Mifflin Co., 1921. xiv, 300 pages.

Plantation Song. No place or publisher, 1908. 16 pages. Illustrated with tipped-in photographs. I have never seen this rare Rutledge item, but bookseller David Cupka said he "obtained this book from a woman whose grandmother was a close friend of Rutledge, and there is some indication that he did a very limited printing and gave them to close friends as a Christmas present." Poetry.

Poems in Honor of South Carolina Tricentennial. Columbia, S.C.: R. L. Bryan Co., 1970. viii, 18 pages.

Rain on the Marsh. Columbia, S.C.: Bostick & Thornley, Inc., 1940. 236 pages.

Santee Paradise: The Beautiful Wilderness Around Hampton Plantation. Indianapolis, Ind.: Bobbs-Merrill Co., 1956. 232 pages.

Songs from a Valley. Chambersburg, Pa.: Public Opinion Print, 1919. 62 pages.

The Sonnets of Archibald Rutledge. Spartanburg, S.C.: Williams Printing Co. (privately printed for the author), 1938. 39 pages.

South of Richmond. Chambersburg, Pa.: J. R. Kerr & Bro., 1923. 123 pages.

The Spirit of Mercersburg. Harrisburg, Pa.: McFarland Publicity Service, 1909. This booklet was bound using blue cord and apparently intended for promotional use. Prose.

Those Were The Days. Richmond, Va.: Dietz Press, 1955. xiv, 426 pages.

Tom and I on the Old Plantation. New York: Frederick A. Stokes, 1918. x, 214 pages.

Under the Pines and Other Poems. Winchester, Va.: Eddy Press, 1906. 44 pages.

Veiled Eros. New York: Henry Harrison, 1933. 95 pages.

Voices of Long Ago: Bible Stories Retold. Columbia, S.C.: R. L. Bryan Co., 1973. viii, 96 pages.

When Boys Go Off to School. New York: Fleming H. Revell Co., 1935. 124 pages.

Wild Life of the South. New York: Frederick A. Stokes Co., 1935. x, 253 pages.

A Wildwood Tale: A Drama of the Open. New York: Fleming H. Revell Co., 1950. 48 pages.

Willie Was a Lady. Columbia, S.C.: Wing Publications, 1966. 123 pages.

The Woods and Wild Things I Remember. Columbia, S.C.: R. L. Bryan Co., 1970. xii, 260 pages.

The World Around Hampton. Indianapolis, Ind.: Bobbs-Merrill Co., 1960. 192 pages.

ARTICLES

These articles deal primarily with upland game or dogs. They are but a sampling of Rutledge pieces which touch on the subjects, since scores of his stories ranged widely in terms of their content. Still, they provide a solid indication of the fact that bird hunting and dogs, working and otherwise, figured prominently in his literary endeavors and in his life.

"Archibald Rutledge on Hunting Dogs." *Progressive Farmer* (January 1940): 10.

"The Baby Toddles." *Field & Stream* (August 1922): 433–34.

"Bird Dogs I Have Known." *Progressive Farmer* (November 1935). Not seen.

"Bobwhite—Farm Asset." *Country Gentleman,* March 28, 1914: 653.

"Boll-Weevil Bores In." *Outdoor Life* (October 1928): 20–21, 83.

"Bonniest of the Game Birds." *Outdoor World and Recreation* (December 1913). Not seen.

"Chance Shots." *Field & Stream* (January 1927): 34–35, 67.

"The Deer and the Hound." *Outer's Recreation* (February 1919): 752.

"Dogs That Awe Me." *Reader's Digest* (July 1935): 67–69.

"The Enemies of Quail." *Sports Afield* (July 1959): 50–53, 56, 100.

"The Friend of Man." *Forest & Stream* (October 1923): 552–53, 590–93.

"Grouse of the Cloudlands." *Field & Stream* (March 1933): 30–32, 66–67.

"Grouse of the Little Hills." *Field & Stream* (November 1929): 29, 30, 76.

"The Hound Is the Philosopher Among Dogs." *American Magazine* (November 1926): 14–15.

"How I Train My Puppies." *Progressive Farmer* (September 1935): 24.

"Hunting Dogs." *Progressive Farmer* (January 1940). Not seen.

"It's the Scotch in Them." *Field & Stream* (February 1939): 22–23, 48, 51.

"My Last Grouse Hunt." *Outdoor Life* (March 1941): 18–20.

"O Ringing Bells!" *American Boy* (December 1919): 26–27.

"The Odyssey of Bolio." *Outdoor America,* Part 1 (September 1925): 5–7, 69; Part 2 (October 1925): 25–27, 59.

"Patsy and the Princes." *Field & Stream* (September 1935): 26–27, 62–63.

"Poinsettia and Sparkplug." *Field & Stream* (October 1922): 652, 700–701.

"Prince of the Swamplands." *Field & Stream* (July 1930): 32–33.

"Quail of the Kalmias." *Field & Stream* (November 1933): 26–27, 74.

"Ringnecks in the Stubble." *Field & Stream* (January 1921): 841.

"Rodney's Bolio." *Classmate,* February 3, 1923, 3.

"The Secret Killer." *Youth's Companion,* January 2, 1919, 3.

"Shooting Bucks Over a Bird Dog." *Outdoor Life* (August 1929): 22.

"Snipe of the Pinelands." *Field & Stream* (February 1931): 22–23, 84.

"Some Startling Dogs." *Outdoor Life* (August 1932): 12–13, 53.

"The Sorcery of the Trailing Hound." *Harper's Monthly Magazine* (February 1924): 325–33.

"Start 'Em Early Arch." *Field & Stream* (October 1919): 565–66.

"A Unique Quail Hunt." *Field & Stream* (August 1920): 395.

"A Walt Whitman Grouse." *Recreation* (October 1916). Not seen.

"Wild Bird Dogs I Have Known." *Hunter-Trapper-Trader* (December 1916). Not seen.

"Wintering Bobwhite." *Field & Stream* (November 1919): 677.

Printed and bound by CPI Group (UK) Ltd, Croydon, CR0 4YY

01/06/2026

14891045-0001